This thoroughly revised edition of *Funding Your Ministry* by Scott Morton provides even more helpful, hopeful guidance for those in ministry fundraising. Expanded in cross-cultural, universal application while deeply rooted in timeless biblical truth, Scott's book provides encouragement and hands-on practical application for those just starting out as well as for the long-termers who may have become weary and disillusioned.

BETTY BARNETT
Author of *Friend Raising: Building a Missionary Support Team That Lasts*

Scott Morton has produced one of the most practical and needful books that I have ever seen for self-supported foreign missionaries. This is a must-read book for an itinerant missionary. I highly recommend it.

DR. HOWARD FOLTZ
Professor emeritus at Regent University

If you raise support, then *Funding Your Ministry* is a must-read. Scott Morton's biblical and practical insights hit the bull's-eye on the issues that Christian workers and missionaries wrestle with in raising up financial partners.

ELLIS GOLDSTEIN
Director of ministry partner development for Cru

Whether seeking personal or institutional funding, principles such as face-to-face solicitation and the importance of writing a plan are totally interchangeable. Morton has done all of us in resource development a favor by writing this book. Crafted in a light, airy way, it takes the mystery out of fundraising without taking out the teeth. I intend to refer to it repeatedly in presentations. It has great crossover appeal and application.

CHRIS WITHERS
President of D. Chris Withers, Inc.

This is more than a book on fundraising. It's a book on biblical thinking about money and ministry, and it's filled with intensely practical guidelines on how to involve people in your ministry through giving and praying. I'm impressed with this guide. It works and has been tested in the fire of experience with hundreds of our Navigator staff. This is the best resource I have seen—a must for those who raise financial support.

JERRY E. WHITE, PHD
International president emeritus of The Navigators

Scott Morton is one of the best nonprofit development professionals I have ever been associated with. He has trained more faith-based nonprofit individuals in personal fundraising than anyone.

LAUREN LIBBY
President and CEO of TWR International

Funding Your Ministry

A Field Guide for Raising Personal Support

Third Edition

SCOTT MORTON

A NavPress resource published in alliance
with Tyndale House Publishers, Inc.

NavPress is the publishing ministry of The Navigators, an international Christian organization and leader in personal spiritual development. NavPress is committed to helping people grow spiritually and enjoy lives of meaning and hope through personal and group resources that are biblically rooted, culturally relevant, and highly practical.

For more information, visit www.NavPress.com.

Funding Your Ministry: A Field Guide for Raising Personal Support

Third edition copyright © 2017 by Scott Morton. All rights reserved.

Revised and updated edition © 2007 by Scott Morton. All rights reserved.

First edition © 1999 by Scott Morton. All rights reserved.

A NavPress resource published in alliance with Tyndale House Publishers, Inc.

NAVPRESS and the NAVPRESS logo are registered trademarks of NavPress, The Navigators, Colorado Springs, CO. *TYNDALE* is a registered trademark of Tyndale House Publishers, Inc. Absence of ® in connection with marks of NavPress or other parties does not indicate an absence of registration of those marks.

The Team:
Don Pape, Publisher
David Zimmerman, Acquisitions Editor
Mark Anthony Lane II, Designer

Cover illustration of tree copyright © R. Hilch/Depositphotos.com. All rights reserved.

Author photo by Katherine Moum, copyright © 2014. All rights reserved.

"The Wheel" is a registered trademark of The Navigators in the United States. Used by permission of The Navigators. All rights reserved.

Unless otherwise indicated, all Scripture quotations are taken from the New American Standard Bible,® copyright © 1960, 1962, 1963, 1968, 1971, 1972, 1973, 1975, 1977, 1995 by The Lockman Foundation. Used by permission.

Scripture quotations marked AMP are taken from the Amplified Bible,® copyright © 2015 by The Lockman Foundation. Used by permission. www.lockman.org.

Scripture quotations marked MSG are taken from *THE MESSAGE*, copyright © 1993, 1994, 1995, 1996, 2000, 2001, 2002 by Eugene H. Peterson. Used by permission of NavPress. All rights reserved. Represented by Tyndale House Publishers, Inc.

Scripture quotations marked NIV are taken from the Holy Bible, *New International Version,® NIV.®* Copyright © 1973, 1978, 1984, 2011 by Biblica, Inc.® Used by permission. All rights reserved worldwide.

Scripture quotations marked KJV are taken from the *Holy Bible*, King James Version.

Some of the anecdotal illustrations in this book are true to life and are included with the permission of the persons involved. All other illustrations are composites of real situations, and any resemblance to people living or dead is purely coincidental.

For information about special discounts for bulk purchases, please contact Tyndale House Publishers at csresponse@tyndale.com or call 1-800-323-9400.

Cataloging-in-Publication Data is available.

ISBN 978-1-63146-684-7

Printed in the United States of America

23 22 21 20 19 18 17
7   6   5   4   3   2   1

To Alma, my wife and partner in ministry, who in our first year of ministry asked the question that launched me into biblical fundraising: "Are you going to support this family or not?" Thank you. You've made me a better husband, a better father, a better servant of God.

Contents

Section Five—Especially for You

Section Six—Biblical Financial Management for Gospel-Workers

Acknowledgments

THIS BOOK DID NOT arise out of a vacuum. I'd like to thank especially the gospel-workers from many ministries who had the courage to try my stuff in the early days, then passed it on to others. And . . .

Rod Sargent (1927–1987), Navigator pioneer, who encouraged me to put my teaching on video.

Ray Hoo, who suggested that if I was going to teach funding, I should be at 100 percent of budget—not 92 percent.

Noel Owuor, who came to my office from Kenya to say, "This book doesn't work!" And for his partnership and friendship to bring success to Africa.

The international staff of The Navigators, who took a risk to invite me to help slay the "Goliath of fundraising."

Finally, I'd like to thank my parents, John and Mildred, who taught me to say thank you.

Introduction

IF YOU ARE in Christian ministry anywhere in the solar system, this book is for you.

Whether you raise personal support, lead a ministry, or pastor a church, you understand the pressure of poor funding. And you know the challenge of staying fully funded month by month, year by year. You also understand the importance of *biblical* fundraising as opposed to secular best practices. You've come to the right place.

Why a new edition of *Funding Your Ministry*? Because in ten years the world has changed—and I have changed! The first two editions were written for a mostly American audience, but in the last ten years I have focused on international ministry. I learned a ton that needs to be passed on to you.

International leaders tell me, "Scott, this stuff won't work in our culture!" Beginning with Noel Owuor from Kenya, who showed up unannounced in my office eleven years ago. This stranger asked if I was the author of *Funding Your Ministry*.

"Yes," I said confidently.

Then he held up a copy of my precious book, looked me in the eye, and said pointedly, "It doesn't work!"

I was taken aback, but I had the good sense to say, "What about it doesn't work?" And so Noel and I went to a flip chart. He drew a map of Africa, and for two hours we discussed why personal-support fundraising "doesn't work" in Africa. That was the start of a great friendship.

Soon, Noel and I were traveling to other countries to work with local leaders to put biblical cross-cultural funding principles into practice. After Bible study, prayer, animated discussions, disagreements, and scary on-the-job training, God showed up. Biblical fundraising does work—but it must be customized to each situation. The

Bible has answers for funding the work of His Kingdom—in every culture. Let us not doubt that for a moment!

In this new edition I bring you important, fresh insights on tested fundraising guidelines, plus insights from non-American gospel-workers. And I have added new teaching on

- social media and email fundraising,
- helping supervisors and mission leaders overcome fundraising blind spots,
- cultural views of money versus a biblical view,
- new funding insights for gospel-workers of color in America, and
- four money-words gospel-workers must know well.

The practical worksheets in previous editions are revised and simplified and, rather than tightly packed into the back of the book, offered online at scottmorton.net for your convenience. Feel free to download and print them for your personal use. The website is created with you in mind and features continually updated articles, videos, and Q and As.

It is my prayer that this book will bring you hope! You may be

- a new missionary, not knowing where to begin;
- a veteran missionary with much to offer, but frustrated financially;
- experienced in raising support but somehow not consistently funded;
- a missionary's friend who winces when you see God's servants underfunded;
- a pastor who is asked for fundraising advice and needs a resource to offer;
- a missions committee member who wants to help missionaries succeed;
- a missionary spouse who feels trapped; or
- a mission-agency executive whose staff are underfunded.

This book is for you if you've ever struggled with questions such as the following:

- Is it biblical to *ask*?
- Why do I feel so worldly when I raise funds?
- Why can't I just "pray it in" like the famous British orphanage director George Mueller?
- Where will we get the money to make our house a warm, loving home?
- Will we ever be able to save or invest? Own a home? Send our kids to college?
- What can I do—besides give—to help my missionary friends be fully funded?

- What do I say when I'm asked for fundraising advice?
- What is the role of social media in my fundraising?

I welcome you on this wonderful, scary journey. You can count on three things:

1. The Scriptures will be our guide. I long for your fundraising to be anchored in the Bible rather than worldly best practices.
2. The direction in this book shows concern for the spiritual growth of your giving partners. I won't advise you to use tactics that abuse your friends just to get a financial transaction.
3. I will be genuine with you. I'll admit my own fears and mistakes.

What does this book seek to accomplish? I pray that *Funding Your Ministry* will do the following:

- Enable you to reach full funding—110 percent of your approved budget— in less time than you imagine. You will break through the glass ceiling of "get-by" missionary funding.
- Guide you in preparing a fundraising plan that recruits giving partners who enthusiastically share your vision. You are not merely "finding money" but building and blessing a team of people who care about you and your vision.
- Protect you from discouragement. Fundraising can be lonely and defeating.
- Move you toward joyfully embracing biblical fundraising as a ministry rather than an unfortunate "have-to." Gone are the days of resenting fundraising!
- Empower you to successfully manage the funding you raise so you can accomplish your God-given life dreams.

Let's get started!

As You Begin

Chapters 1–4 are about you—*your* opinions, *your* obstacles, *your* conscience, and *your* attitudes about fundraising. We cannot dive into what you will *do* in funding until we review who you *are* in funding. Just as a smooth-looking automobile is going nowhere without a well-built engine, so a smooth-looking fundraising plan is going nowhere without a gospel-worker whom God has touched in the inner person on the topic of money. Please surrender your financial biases and opinions to the One who has called you to ministry as you begin.

1
HALF-TRUTHS I BELIEVED

My Total Fundraising Makeover

MY FUNDRAISING ADVENTURE BEGAN the day I took my boss to lunch at Lum's Restaurant. I confidently told Carl I would soon quit my well-paying job at the newspaper to go into full-time Christian service. How I looked forward to it! No more hassles with the accounting department. No more criticism from penny-pinching shopkeepers. No more office politics.

Carl didn't seem impressed. "How are you going to support yourself?" he asked.

"Not to worry," I said. "The Lord will provide!" I knew that was the "right" answer, but little did I know how much I would be tested about it.

Pause. Long pause.

A skeptic, I mused. *I'll show him*. Nothing could deter me. After all, the old adage "Where He guides, He provides" was surely true, wasn't it?

Two weeks later, the office gang sponsored a going-away party and presented me with a huge penny in the shape of a plaque. The inscription read, "In God we trust. All others strictly cash."

And so it began.

My first fundraising appointment was at the home of two elderly, blue-haired ladies from the church my wife and I attended during our university days. As I knocked on the door, I noticed the dilapidated front porch and wondered whether I had the right house.

After a few pleasantries, I asked whether I could tell them about our ministry. They eagerly rearranged the chairs so they could see the pictures in my presentation notebook. They were beaming. Expectations were high. But as I turned the pages, I couldn't help noticing the worn furniture and the bare spots in the carpet.

My mind raced ahead to the financial appeal on the last page. I couldn't concentrate. I couldn't remember whether I had mentioned finances when I phoned to make the appointment. A voice inside me said: *Scott, you can't ask these ladies for money. Look at that worn carpet. Look at that old sofa. Look at this dilapidated house! You're better off than they are.*

I retorted: *No, I've quit my job. I'm in God's work now. These ladies are glad I've come. Go ahead, turn to the money page.*

Back and forth the mind game raged as I flipped pages and answered questions, smiling on the outside but sweating on the inside. Should I ask or not?

Just as I arrived at the money page, a Scripture came to mind: Jesus saying to the Pharisees, "You devour widows' houses" (Matthew 23:14). There was my answer! Scripture memory saved the day.

I quickly closed the book without mentioning financial support. I asked the ladies to pray for our ministry. They asked me if I wanted cookies. And I drove home wondering if I should try to get my job back at the newspaper. What would Carl say now?

I repeated this "no-ask" scene several times. I wanted to ask for financial support, but I felt guilty doing it. Sometimes I hinted, but nobody took the bait.

Nevertheless, I had confidence that someday, somehow, people would generously give.

A couple of friends volunteered support out of sympathy, but that was it. The months were slipping by. The mailbox was empty.

During this time I received suggestions. One missionary told me, "Money follows ministry." The people to whom we were ministering should support us. He quoted Galatians 6:6: "The one who is taught the word is to share all good things with the one who teaches." But our ministry was start-up evangelism. I couldn't make financial appeals to a few new believers and nonbelievers.

What about friends from Bible studies I had been part of in the past? I assumed they were supporting other missionaries. I felt guilty asking them.

A pastor in Cedar Rapids, Iowa, said, "Scott, don't ask people to give; just ask them to pray. They will catch on." The osmosis method. That didn't work either.

Another adviser said, "Bible study materials. Sell materials to supplement your income." Another suggested, "Christian businesspeople, they've got money." Fine, except the businesspeople from my newspaper days didn't seem interested. And I was scared to ask them anyway. A business friend at church promised to give from the sale of an apartment building, but it didn't sell.

Some people said they'd support us but never did. And sometimes large gifts came from strangers. But we were always well under budget. It made no sense.

In the back of my mind, I was counting on our mailing list. I sent a letter to 150 friends asking them to pray about our finances. Nothing came in. Not one response. Maybe they did pray—that's what I asked them to do!

Most of the time I felt secular trying to raise money. I criticized myself, wondering why I couldn't be like those great missionaries of the 1800s—George Mueller or Hudson Taylor—who saw money pour in by telling only God in prayer. But for me, "Where He guides, He provides" wasn't working. What was I missing?

In the midst of this frustration, God was abundantly blessing our ministry. Nonbelievers were coming to Christ and growing in discipleship. This was the "real" ministry. Fundraising was a necessary evil—ministry's icky-tasting medicine. I gladly gravitated toward discipling and away from money matters.

Once a month, I decided to do something about our funding—the day we got our below-budget paycheck. But my motivation faded as I got busy again with ministry.

I had told Carl at the newspaper that the Lord would provide. Did He? Yes. We didn't starve. We had a roof over our heads. My wife, Alma, heroically stretched our meager funds for food and kids' clothing. But I overdrew our ministry account a little each month, thinking, *Next month the money will come in . . . next month.* We were in deficit to our mission agency, with little hope of repaying.

I was in denial. Alma paid the bills and handled our finances. She was good at it, but she felt most of the pressure. I felt little. I hated bills arriving in the mail. When donors skipped a month, I criticized their spirituality.

Giving? We gave some, but not consistently. In filing our income taxes, we had only seven receipts from a mission to which we pledged monthly. We should have had twelve.

Finally, out of desperation, I turned to my Bible concordance and searched for the word *fundraising.* Nothing. I was on my own! But I was confident the Bible would help me. Soon I stumbled upon Philippians 4. That day was the turning point. Over several months, one verse led to another as I searched the Scriptures.

I had hoped to find a quick and painless technique for funding, but through my Bible study I discovered that my original opinions about fundraising needed a total makeover. The funding aspect of ministry forced me to look deep within myself, and

I didn't like what I saw. God pointed out deeper issues—such as my sour attitude. I finally understood that I was unbiblical in my view of money. The Word of God clearly pointed out my errors, and the Word of God enabled me to do something about it.

I come to you as a fellow traveler in the adventure of raising personal support. Through the Scriptures, God has brought me from resenting fundraising to enjoying it.

Since those early days, I find I still need makeovers. I've experienced frustration, and I'm still learning. I still get butterflies when I pick up the phone to make an appointment—just as I get butterflies before an evangelistic Bible study. But I've come to see fundraising as a ministry rather than a burden.

And I have also seen that when the biblical guidelines are conscientiously applied, full funding can be achieved—for anyone, of any background, in any part of the world. Resist the temptation to say, "It won't work!"

Let's get started! The first step? Identify the icebergs in your shipping lanes—your personal obstacles to raising support.

2

OBSTACLES

Know What's Holding You Back

BEFORE YOU LAUNCH your fundraising efforts—stop! Answer this question: What specific obstacles keep you from reaching 100 percent of your approved budget? Not taking time to identify what could cripple your fundraising efforts is like spraying white paint over a dark wall. The old paint shows through. Your obstacles will come back to haunt you.

At first, I thought I was the only missionary in the solar system who faced the issues below, but I've discovered that missionaries of all cultures deal with these roadblocks. Your obstacles might be attitudinal. Or they might be a couple skills you need to develop. Address your obstacles with humility and honesty, and you will find freedom as you execute your funding plan.

The obstacles presented below will be dealt with directly and indirectly throughout the book. Which are yours?

1. No potential givers

"I've run out of people to talk to." This is common for Christian workers who do not come from an evangelical background or for those who purposely limit their mailing lists. Some also say, "My people have no money."

At the start of fundraising, many gospel-workers ask the question, "Whom do I know who will give me money?" Wrong question! The right question is, "Who needs to hear my story?" God has providentially put you in the midst of people (or will soon put you in the midst of people) whom He will call to join you as giving partners. The mystery of fundraising is to find out who they are. (More on finding potential partners in chapters 8 and 11.)

2. Fear

In teaching biblical fundraising around the world, I find that the obstacle of fear ranks first in every culture, in every organization—fear of failure, fear of rejection, fear of ruining relationships. It is not easy to admit we are fearful because "ministry workers" are supposed to have life all together. Fears? Naah! Not me.

Sometimes gospel-workers mask their fears with "theological reasons" or philosophical reasons for not inviting partners to join them. But great freedom comes when we admit our fears. Psalm 56:3 says, "When I am afraid, I will put my trust in You." The psalmist doesn't say *if* he is afraid, but *when*. He admitted his fears. It is not a sin to have fears, but it is a sin to live in constant fear.

If you're fearful, call it that. It's okay. And identify the specific people whom you fear. See what God will do.

3. Lack of diligence

Most missionaries are hard workers—except in fundraising and donor ministry. As I prepare to phone for appointments, my mind is flooded with other things I must do—good things! Bible study. Preparing seminars. Washing the car. Going to the dentist. Checking the fridge for a much-needed snack. And no one criticizes missionaries for doing these good things instead of fundraising.

But there's no other word for it—it's laziness! You know it, and God knows it.

4. "Get-by" mentality

I once picked up an inebriated hitchhiker in rural Wisconsin. I like to ask hitchhikers the question "What is your major life goal?" My liquor-smelling seatmate announced resolutely, "My goal is to get by!"

He and I launched into a lively discussion about knowing Christ. But the next day his phrase "get by" haunted me. My hitchhiker friend helped me realize I had a financial get-by mentality. I never planned on raising 100 percent of my official approved budget. I drifted month by month, hoping that enough money would come in without my having to invite donors. As long as we squeezed by each month, I was satisfied.

But *getting by* wears thin, especially with a family. Missionaries who live day to day with no financial margin are tempted to overuse credit cards, borrow from family, or ask the national office for an advance. And some quit. Savings? A far-off dream.

5. Lack of fundraising skills

Christians who have been trained with evangelism skills usually lead more people to Christ than those without training. The same is true in funding.

In West Africa I insisted that my fundraising students role-play their phone calls not once, not twice, but three times. They rolled their eyes—enough! But when they started phoning to set appointments, they brimmed with confidence and enjoyed the calls. They were able to concentrate on the person they phoned rather than worrying about what they were going to say. They admitted that the role-playing was worth it. Skills breed confidence!

6. Lack of time

"I don't have time to raise funds. My schedule is packed!"

Of course, we *make time* for what is important. When someone tells you they don't have time to read the Bible, you understand their real issue is setting priorities, not a lack of time.

Many missionaries fill their year with ministry activities, then try to do fundraising during their holiday. Sadly, they neglect themselves and their families.

Ask yourself two questions:

1. Why do I not take more time to actively raise support?
2. What will I cut out of my schedule to make time for raising support?

7. "In-house" mentality

One gospel-worker couldn't bring herself to expand her mailing list beyond fifty to sixty friends. Finally, out of frustration she confessed, "I don't know any more people who understand my mission!"

I responded, "They don't need to understand your mission *now*! But they will understand it as you send them your newsletters." With that comment something clicked. Within twenty-four hours she "found" one hundred additional friends and acquaintances.

An African friend of mine says, "If you never leave home, you will think your mother is the best cook in all Africa!" Similarly, some gospel-workers never "leave home" in fundraising. They limit their appeals to "in-house" support from Bible study members, peers in ministry, or family.

If you hope to be fully funded by the people who already understand your ministry, you'll be disappointed. But if you expand your support horizons beyond personal friendships, you will be surprised at whom God will send your way.

8. Lack of accountability

What will happen if you're not up to 100 percent of budget? Will your supervisor stop you from getting on an airplane or going to campus? Not if he is below budget too! I once asked a missionary, "Do you think your directors would tell you to stop your ministry to work on your support?" He glanced furtively around the room and then said, "No, I don't think they have the guts!"

Some mission organizations have a rule that you may not launch your ministry until you are 100 percent underwritten. That rule is easy to apply if you are going to another country—you can't board an airplane until your budget is met. But it is often ignored when your assignment is across town. Although some mission agencies have a "100 percent policy," they seldom enforce it.

Certainly situations occur where gospel-workers will minister at less than 100 percent of budget, but that ought to be the exception rather than the norm. Here are two examples of what can happen.

I once taught a funding school in Illinois for missionaries to the college campus. On the second day, at precisely 11:00 a.m., the Illinois director announced that no staff would be allowed to resume their campus ministries until they were fully funded—100 percent! During the lunch break, pent-up emotions broke loose. "He can't do that!" the missionaries clamored. "Our ministries will be devastated!" But the director stuck with his decision. Nine Illinois missionaries had only four days to set their campus ministries in order before they pulled back to devote themselves to face-to-face funding appeals.

To their surprise, within three months they reached full funding and were back on campus. Was the ministry devastated while they were gone? "Regrettably, no!" one staff friend humorously replied. His student leaders had risen to the challenge.

By contrast, a director in another district did not insist on his missionaries leaving campus to do full-time fundraising. His staff tried to do both at once—raise support and minister on campus. After six months, they were nowhere near full funding.

Who will hold you accountable in fundraising? If not your supervisor, who? A friend? A donor? Choose someone who does *not* have the gift of mercy!

9. Cultural barriers

For many cultures around the world, including some communities of color in America, sending monthly support to a far-off mission headquarters sounds odd. If your culture does not have a history of designated missionary support, you will face resistance. But don't give up. You can creatively and sensitively teach your culture new methods of giving to advance the Kingdom.

For perspective, consider this: Passing a basket at church services is now accepted around the world as a means of collecting an offering. But 120 years ago it was a revolutionary new method of fundraising—especially in the West, where the accepted norm was "pew rent."

10. Emergency-only strategy

Many gospel-workers wait until they have an urgent need before they do fundraising. In some cultures that is acceptable, and their friends and family (usually) bail them out. But is this biblically wise?

Other missionaries go through fifty-one weeks of good intentions before engaging in one week of fourteen-hour days sending desperate emails pleading for help.

Panic fundraising may produce results once or twice, but your giving partners will tire of it.

11. Fuzzy vision

If you're not sure of your ministry calling, or if you no longer believe passionately in your ministry, you'll hesitate to invite support. Fuzzy vision is a major reason missionaries lapse in sending newsletters to their financial partners for twelve or twenty-four or even thirty-six months. They wonder, *What will I say?*

If you are not sure of your next step in ministry, you are in good company. In 1 Corinthians 16:6, Paul says, "And *perhaps* I shall stay with you, or even spend the winter, so that you may send me on my way *wherever* I may go" (emphasis added). Even the seemingly confident apostle Paul wasn't sure of his next step in ministry, but that didn't prevent him from appealing to the Corinthians for financial support. Like Paul, you may not know the specific details of your ministry future. That's okay! Tell people what you *do* know, and ask them to help you accomplish that.

In the meantime, use these times of uncertainty to clarify what God has called you to do. Is it time to start a new chapter in life? If you are struggling with a career or "calling," don't bravely soldier on. Stop. Spend extended time alone with God; take aptitude tests; consult with your mission leaders, your church, and your friends. Review the booklet *The Sacred-Secular Mistake* (available at scottmorton.net), which contains a practical Bible study on "the mystery of calling."

12. Indirect culture

Most cultures of the world are indirect. But each *person* in your culture is an individual. Not all react the same. Some (especially younger generations) prefer you to be more direct. By the grace of God, creatively bring each potential donor to the place of seriously praying about your support—making a stewardship decision. Use a unique strategy for each one. Building mutually trusting relationships helps to carry the weight of sensitive issues in any culture.

13. Long-haul pessimism

A missionary who worked hard to get up to budget came to me in tears. "I succeeded for one year, but when I think of raising support for the next five years, I want to quit."

Let me encourage you to put aside this overwhelming thought until you've finished the assignments in this book. You will then be able to view your funding challenge with a more objective perspective. You cannot confront the uncertainties of the future with today's grace. I find God gives me grace only for today's challenges. I cannot experience tomorrow's grace today. But "grace to help in time of need" will be there in abundance when tomorrow arrives (Hebrews 4:16).

14. Believing core lies

A Japanese gospel-worker languished in funding for years. Even though he participated in funding seminars, his income barely improved. Finally, at a funding school last January he had a breakthrough. He confessed with tears to the entire class, "I think I know why I have struggled in funding. When I was a kid and into adulthood my father told me over and over, 'You will be a financial failure like I am.' I have believed that lie for years. It has imprisoned me, but today I choose to be free of it!"

With that, his missionary peers gathered around him and his wife and prayed for deliverance from this core lie he had believed all his life. Today he is boldly and successfully making face-to-face appeals, and giving partners are wonderfully responding.

What core lies affect mission-workers? Here are some common ones from around the world:

- I'll never be fully funded.
- I don't deserve to be fully funded.
- No one wants to support me.
- If God wants me funded, He will do it (without my doing much).

Take a moment to identify your two biggest obstacles from the list in this chapter. Name them! Be honest enough to say, "My main obstacle is fear—particularly of my peers." The first step to overcome obstacles is to admit they exist. Educator Booker T. Washington said, "Success is to be measured, not so much by the position that one has reached in life, as by the obstacles which he has overcome."[1]

. . .

Review these fourteen obstacles in your daily devotional times over the next few days. If you're married, share them with your spouse. Pasting wallpaper over your obstacles won't resolve them, and you will miss out on deep character changes that God will bring.

With your obstacles identified, you are ready to examine your attitudes toward raising support.

3
QUESTIONS OF CONSCIENCE
Understanding the Biblical Basis for Raising Support

I TEACH BIBLICAL fundraising to gospel-workers from many cultures. They appreciate the workshops on communication skills and developing strategies. But the highlight is always the Bible study. The Scriptures satisfy the soul.

Investing many hours learning what the Bible says about fundraising is more important than anything else I can tell you. Merely grabbing fundraising best practices without developing biblical convictions is like receiving an empty Valentine's box.

It is only because of the Bible that I write this book. Early in our ministry, I tried several approaches in funding—but failed. Out of desperation I picked up my Bible and stumbled across Philippians 4. From that small beginning I gained fundraising freedom—and you can too.

Here are twelve conscience issues related to fundraising, with insights from my studies of the Bible. How do they compare with your understanding of Scripture?

1. What right do I have to be supported by others?

Sooner or later every missionary in the world is asked, "When are you going to get a *real* job?" Family and friends often equate fundraising with begging.

Missionaries fall into this thinking as well. One clueless missions writer unwittingly said, "Lois and I almost did not come to the mission field. We couldn't bring ourselves to *beg* for support." Another said, "Our lifestyle was a peculiar mixture of prayer, faith, action, communication, and *begging*."

A "begging" mentality is a tip-off that a missionary doesn't feel he or she has a right to receive support. As a result, some seek outside employment or quit the field—not because they want to but because they can't stomach raising support. Do they understand they have a biblical *right* to be supported by the church?

The Bible strongly shows that missionaries called to full-time service have the right to be supported. We find evidence of this right in the following:

- the example of the Levites
- the example of Jesus
- the teaching of Jesus
- the example of Paul
- the teaching of Paul

The example of the Levites

"For the tithe of the sons of Israel, which they offer as an offering to the LORD, I have given to the Levites for an inheritance" (Numbers 18:24). Eleven of Jacob's twelve sons received an allotment of real estate, but if you check the map of Canaan in the back of your Bible, you'll not find Levi's name. Instead of land, Levi received the promise of the tithe.

As Christians today, redeemed by Christ's once-for-all sacrifice, we do not require Levi's descendants to administer sacrifices on our behalf. However, the model—one tribe supported by others to advance God's Kingdom full-time—is still valid. Or is it?

The apostle Paul says yes. In 1 Corinthians 9:13 he defends being supported by the gospel: "Do you not know that those . . . who attend regularly to the altar have their share from the altar?" Paul used the Levite example to show the Corinthians that he had the right to receive support. (Don't take the Levitical example too far, however. The Levites were to retire at age fifty!)

Are you a modern-day Levite? New Testament theology says the sacrificial system is over. But if God has called you to "full-time" ministry, then yes! Like the Levites, you are a called-out worker in His Kingdom. As God provided for His Old Testament full-time workers, He will provide for you.

Actually, God already has provided for you. When God selected the Levites for special service, He had their funding provision (the tithe) in mind. Similarly, your funding partners have already been "called" by the same God who called the Levites. Through biblical fundraising, you will discover them!

The example of Jesus

Jesus did not work a "real job" after He began His ministry. He chose to depend on a support team of ordinary people. "Mary who was called Magdalene, from whom seven demons had gone out, and Joanna the wife of Chuza, Herod's steward, and Susanna, and *many others* . . . were contributing to their support out of their *private means*" (Luke 8:2-3, emphasis added). Three women are named, but "many others" contributed to Jesus' ministry. If it were wrong to be supported by personal gifts, Jesus would not have allowed it.

An African friend said, "Scott, you misunderstand. The women supporters did not give money, they *served* by cooking food and such."

How would you answer? Looking more closely, the word for "private means," *huperchonte*, is also used in Luke 12:15: "For not even when one has an abundance does his life consist of his possessions [*huperchonte*]." The women gave that which they owned, not simply service. A Singaporean woman discovered this verse and spouted, "They gave their personal spending money!"

Furthermore, this giving was not one-off, but repeated. In Matthew 27:55 we read that during the Crucifixion, "many women were there looking on from a distance, who had followed Jesus from Galilee while ministering [*huperchonte*] to Him." Again—"many women" traveled sixty miles south from Galilee to Judea, supporting Jesus until the bitter end. These women were touched by Jesus' ministry, and they participated as giving partners for up to three years—and even into the new church! After Jesus' ascension into heaven, 120 disciples awaited the Holy Spirit "along with the women" (Acts 1:14).

Jesus did not need to be supported by donors. Could not the One who turned water into wine support Himself? Could not the One who multiplied fish and loaves support Himself? If anyone could have been self-supporting, it was Jesus Christ. Yet He purposely chose to live by the gifts of "many others"—a dedicated support team. And who were the first ones to see Jesus in His resurrected body? The donors! What high value God places on giving partners—and women!

Recently I was told that the "raising personal support" model of fundraising is no longer needed—it is an old paradigm. My reply? Yes, it is an old paradigm: two thousand years old, a biblical paradigm that is reproducible in all cultures.

It is humbling to be dependent on others. But if the One who didn't need to be dependent on others freely chose to, then you and I must be willing too. This model of funding is not to be resented. It is Jesus' model—celebrate it!

The teaching of Jesus

Here is a third reason you have a right to be supported. Jesus said, "Do not acquire gold, or silver, or copper for your money belts . . . for the worker is worthy of his support. And whatever city or village you enter, inquire who is worthy in it, and stay at his house" (Matthew 10:9-11). When He sent out His disciples to minister, Jesus did not give them weekend spending money the way my baseball coach did with us ballplayers on a road trip. Jesus commanded the Twelve to seek out "worthy" hosts for lodging. Although Jewish culture advocated hospitality for travelers, seeking a worthy host was still an "ask."

Is the sending of the Twelve a one-off nonrepeatable event—not helpful for today? Jesus makes donor support a timeless principle by saying, "The worker is worthy of his support." He repeats it in Luke 10:7 when He sends out the seventy. Paul paraphrases it in 1 Corinthians 9:14 and quotes it directly in 1 Timothy 5:18. You, too, are worthy of your support! Timeless.

The example of Paul

"When Silas and Timothy came down from Macedonia, Paul *began* devoting himself completely to the word" (Acts 18:4-5, emphasis added). Did Paul suddenly become more dedicated? No, scholars agree that Silas and Timothy brought money or worked jobs so that Paul could stop making tents and preach full-time.

In Philippians 4:16, Paul affirms the Philippians for having supported his ministry "more than once." If it were wrong to be supported, Paul would not have allowed others to participate. Instead, he warmly endorsed their gifts.

The teaching of Paul

Who paid for Paul's food and drink? Scholars say that when Paul asked, "Do we not have a right to eat and drink?" (1 Corinthians 9:4), his audience understood him to mean the *expense* of eating and drinking. The Amplified version of the Bible adds the phrase "at the expense of the churches." In verse 6 (AMP) Paul asks bluntly, "Or is it only Barnabas and I who have no right to stop doing manual labor [in order to support our ministry]?" Paul is asserting that other apostles were indeed supported by the church without controversy.

Paul's question is the same question we are addressing: Do you have a right to refrain from manual labor to do the work of ministry? It is a two-thousand-year-old issue.

In 1 Corinthians 9:7-18, Paul gives a lawyerlike answer in five "Ls."

- *Logic* (verse 7). Does a soldier serve at his own expense? Does a farmer plant a vineyard and not eat the fruit? Of course not! Common logic teaches that.
- *Law* (verses 8-10). Paul quotes Deuteronomy 25:4: "You shall not muzzle the ox while he is threshing." Even the ox is allowed to dip his head and munch while treading out the grain. But Paul goes further by suggesting that Deuteronomy 25:4 was written for our sake. "Yes, for our sake it was written." Deuteronomy is for us—not oxen. Or as Martin Luther wryly commented, "Can oxen read?"
- *Leading spiritually* (verse 11). Paul states a principle: "If we sowed spiritual things in you, is it too much if we reap material things from you?" Repeating this in Galatians 6:6 and Romans 15:27, Paul teaches that believers ought to support their spiritual leaders.

Paul's final two "Ls" are arguments we reviewed earlier:

- *Levites* (verse 13). Those who attend the altar share the food of the altar.
- *Lord* (verse 14). To cap his argument, Paul paraphrases Jesus' principle in Matthew 10 and Luke 10: "So also the Lord directed those who proclaim the gospel to get their living from the gospel."

But notice Paul's warning in verses 12 (reiterated in 15-18): "We did not use this right . . . so that we will cause no hindrance to the gospel of Christ." Do you have a right to receive support to minister the gospel? Paul answers with a resounding "Yes!" But he also sternly warns: "Don't demand your right, or you may hinder the gospel."

A former missionary said, "Asking for money is like asking for a handout. I don't think it's a matter of pride but of old-fashioned *inner feelings*." Of course it is inner feelings! But who says your inner feelings get to make your financial decisions? Inner feelings told me to take a third serving of chocolate cake at the office party. You don't allow your feelings to dictate your walk with Christ, so why let them dictate your fundraising? *Acknowledge* your inner feelings, but don't give them decision-making power.

2. Is it okay to ask? It feels like begging.

One missionary told me, "I know I have a right to receive support; I just don't want to ask for it." Asking, we think, puts us in the same camp as slick-haired TV evangelists or panhandlers at busy Nairobi intersections. We prefer to distance ourselves from these embarrassing *beggars*.

One frustrated missionary was given this guideline: "Full disclosure but *no appeal*." She was allowed to tell donors how much she needed but could not ask them to help. On the verge of tears, she never knew how much to say. Plus, the donors were puzzled, not knowing how much to pray about. The policy attempted to be altruistic, but it was wrong-headed.

What does the Bible say about Kingdom-workers asking? Do any Scriptures prohibit it? None I know of. Although we have no record of Jesus asking for support, that is an argument from silence. We also have no record of Jesus blowing His nose or piercing His ears. However, He did ask for an upper room, a donkey, Peter's fishing boat, lunch at Zacchaeus's house, and for John to care for His mother!

> Don't simply adopt my convictions— start with the joy of your personal discovery by studying what the Bible says about personal fundraising. The *International Fundraising Bible Study* can be found at scottmorton.net. Not enough time? Two suggestions:
>
> *Daily devotions.* Meditate on one or two verses daily.
>
> *Professional development.* "Go to class" for fifty minutes a day on Monday, Wednesday, and Friday.

The Bible gives specific examples of appeals, but we might not notice unless we understand the hospitality culture of the Middle East. In Jesus' day, custom dictated that you should receive a traveling rabbi for up to three days and then supply him for his journey. A traveling teacher showing up at your door is a not-so-indirect appeal for lodging and provision. No words are necessary.

This helps us understand Matthew 10:11, where Jesus sent out the Twelve, saying, "Whatever city or village you enter, inquire who is worthy in it, and stay at his house until you leave." That was an "ask." Similarly in Romans 15:24, after Paul announced his vision to reach Spain, he says, "I hope . . . to be *helped* [*propempo*—practical assistance] on my way there by you" (emphasis added). Another example of solicitation occurs in 1 Kings 17, where God tells Elijah to seek provision from a widow in Sidon.

I never ask people to "give to me." That is horizontal—merely charity. You are not asking for yourself, but for the work of the Kingdom. Appealing for the Kingdom takes the "me-ness" out of asking—even though I eventually receive the money. I remind donors that they are giving to God according to Philippians 4:18—"an acceptable sacrifice, well-pleasing to God."

Finally, let's be practical: If asking is wrong, what about churches passing the offering basket? We acquiesce that churches may ask—that's okay. Why not other Kingdom groups?

Some gospel-workers follow the famous missionary George Mueller's method of "telling only God" about their ministry need. That concept lives today in statements such as "Don't ask; just pray." Though Mueller is one of my heroes, history is helpful.

Mueller lived in Bristol, England, in the late 1800s. He funded his orphanage work by "relying on God alone." Why did Mueller hold this view? Before he was converted, Mueller was materialistic and manipulative. As a child in Germany, he habitually stole money from his father's desk. His father had to lay an elaborate trap to catch young Georgie.[1]

As a young man, Mueller checked into hotels wearing expensive clothes to give the impression of wealth, but he ducked out without paying.

Later, after becoming a believer in Christ, he moved to England and became a pastor. In Mueller's day, churches were financed by renting or selling pews to parishioners, the higher-priced ones near the front and free ones in the rear. Mueller believed this violated the partiality teaching in James 2, so he placed a chest at the rear of his church for free-will gifts and told his congregation he would say nothing about support. It worked, and he carried his "pray but don't ask" conviction into his orphanage work.

But there's another side. Although Mueller never made appeals, he and his followers shared answers to prayers in public speeches. These stories informed listeners about how they could give. Mueller also sent annual reports of orphanage finances. He didn't ask, but needs were revealed.

To this day, Mueller's "no-ask" legacy has a huge influence on mission agencies around the world. The Navigators founder Dawson Trotman intended to follow Mueller's "no-ask" example in the 1940s. Harvey Oslund, a contemporary of Trotman, told me that staff members were instructed to "change the subject if finances came up." But Mueller's practice is only one method of fundraising.

I suspect many missionaries are attracted to the Mueller method because they won't suffer the risk of asking. Maybe it "feels more spiritual." But the Bible's teaching on funding is broad—broader than one man's personal practice.

3. I find it easier to raise money for others than for myself.

Third-party fundraising is often heralded as an ideal way of funding. Many gospel-workers say early on that they'd rather raise support for anyone but themselves. But eventually most leave this emotional view behind.

Recruiting support for others is certainly biblical. Paul raised support from the Corinthian and Macedonian churches for the saints at Jerusalem. John, the apostle, encouraged Gaius to send traveling missionaries "on their way in a manner worthy of God" (3 John 1:6).

How can you come to the point of being just as confident about raising funds for yourself as for others?

First, remember that biblical fundraising is vertical—people give to God, not to you (Philippians 4:18). You are raising money for the Kingdom, not for your *needs*. My Kenyan friend Noel Owuor said it this way: "We are fundraising not to pay for school fees or to buy chewing gum. We fundraise for the Kingdom."

Second, do you believe your ministry is significant? Some gospel-workers prefer to raise funds for others because they don't think their own work is impactful enough to warrant support.

For example, years ago my colleagues at a missionary retreat gave glowing reports of changed lives and booming Bible studies. By contrast, in my ministry only eight to ten people attended my Bible studies in small dormitory rooms—with empty seats! Was my small ministry worthy of support? Was *I* worthy of support? I didn't think so.

But if God has truly called you, then your ministry is significant—whether you lead student Bible studies in Kisumu, Kenya; teach power lunch seminars in New York; or serve behind the scenes as an office assistant in Colorado Springs. Your ministry is significant not because you're talented or successful but because it is God's calling *for you*. There are no little people; there are no little places in God's vineyard.

Remember 1 Corinthians 12:21: "The eye cannot say to the hand, 'I have no need of you.'" Get excited about the important work God has called you to, and stop comparing yourself with others.

Does third-party fundraising have a downside? Yes. Look at it from the donor's perspective: By whom does the donor prefer to be asked? Even in indirect cultures such as Asia and Africa, mission-workers are learning that many donors (especially those from younger generations) appreciate being asked by the missionary directly—rather than by a proxy. Their money ultimately goes to you; they should hear from you.

Furthermore, no one else has a heart for your ministry as you do. No one can bring the passion like you. Donors need to feel *your* passion.

Here is the biggest downside: Most third-party friends will ask on your behalf a few times or send a letter on your behalf, but they will not make dozens of appeals. They don't have time. In the best example I know, an Asian third-party asker recruited eight to ten donors for the national gospel-worker—helpful, but not nearly enough.

Finally, when you send a third party to ask on your behalf, the bonding deepens between the donor and the third party—not with you! Their giving will continue longer if they bond with you directly.

I once asked for monthly support on behalf of a missionary friend. One of his lapsed donors asked, "Why won't Joe come see me?"

Caught off guard, I stammered, "He's pretty busy."

Silence. Then it registered—too busy for the donor. If you don't have time for your donors, they sense it.

Penny Thomas, a former colleague of mine, was calling people to raise monthly support for a missionary named Bob. She was asked, "Why are you phoning on Bob's behalf? Why won't Bob phone me?"

Penny, known for her no-nonsense demeanor, didn't hesitate: "Cuz Bob's a chicken."

"He is, isn't he!" said the donor. "Give me his phone number, Penny. I'm going to call him and talk about this right now!"

Penny told the truth. Are we sending third-party proxies because we're "chicken"?

There are exceptions. In some cultures with some potential donors, third-party solicitations are effective. My Asian missionary friends tell me that some Asians are conditioned to say yes to any appeal since a no would cause the asker to lose face. But consider your appeals person by person. One size does not fit all.

In summary, we see biblical evidence for sending third-party emissaries, but it should not be the major part of your funding strategy. And don't ask others to do your fundraising just because you're chicken!

4. Isn't tent making the primary New Testament model?

Paul modeled tent making as a means of funding his ministry—but only three times that we know of. The first was in Thessalonica, at a young church hastily founded and including Greek converts (Acts 17). Obviously, a Jew wouldn't ask new Gentile believers for support. Later, the Thessalonian believers stopped working, waiting around in excited idleness for the Lord to return. Paul chose to work at tent making "in order to offer ourselves as a model" (2 Thessalonians 3:9).

Second, Paul took no money from the Corinthians *while in Corinth*. Why not?

Even a casual reading of 1–2 Corinthians reveals a church with a party spirit, sexual controversy, divisions over what to eat, and a movement to discredit Paul, the church's founder! Corinth had big problems!

But in 2 Corinthians 12:13, Paul says, "For in what respect were you treated as inferior to the rest of the churches, except that I myself did not become a burden to you?" Paul may be speaking sarcastically; he would have preferred to receive support from Corinth, but because of their many problems, he would not take it. Because of this example, I do not appeal to emotionally distraught people.

The third place Paul made tents was at the church in Ephesus—neither a young church nor a problem church. Acts 20:33-34 reads, "I have coveted no one's silver or gold or clothes. . . . These hands ministered to my own needs and to the men who were with me." Why not receive money from Ephesus? Pagan religion at Ephesus was centered on Diana, goddess of the Ephesians. Silversmiths and other craftsmen made their living selling idols of Diana. But as Ephesians converted to Christ, they stopped buying. If Paul had received gift-income, he might have been accused of using the gospel for profit—putting the silversmiths out of business and putting himself in business.

In summary, tent making was not Paul's main model of funding. He both made tents and received support, *depending on how it would affect the progress of the gospel.* And that's a position you and I can take. We must be willing to do either, depending on how it will affect the gospel. This implies that your emotional comfort or "preference" in funding is not the decision-maker. Your funding method must be governed by this question: How will it affect the progress of the gospel? (See 1 Corinthians 9:23.)

5. Is it okay to appeal to nonbelievers?

The question of appealing to nonbelievers presupposes that we can distinguish between believers and nonbelievers. If we may only appeal to believers, then we have the impossible role of inquisitor. Because you are not the judge of the universe, you will unknowingly appeal to nonbelievers, particularly in mailings.

Do churches pass the offering basket only to believers, forcing ushers to whisper, "Excuse me, please bypass the gentleman with the rock-band tattoo—he looks unsaved." Really! Appealing to nonbelievers is impossible to avoid. Wheat and weeds look alike until harvest.

The Scriptures give examples of nonbelievers receiving appeals from God's servants. Elijah appealed to a non-Jewish widow in Sidon, an area outside Jewish territory where pagan deities were on display (1 Kings 17:9). Nehemiah appealed to a pagan Persian king, Artaxerxes Longimanus, for timber to rebuild the gates of Jerusalem.

Prohibiting a nonbeliever from giving might inhibit his or her pursuit of God. In Acts 10:4, Cornelius, a seeker of truth, gave alms that "ascended as a memorial before God." His alms demonstrated his search for God. Like Cornelius, nonbelievers seeking God frequently include their pocketbooks in their search. Some seekers may give to try to buy God's favor, but you can use their giving as an opportunity to explain the gospel.

Funding appeals to non-Christians should be springboards for evangelism. I do two simple exercises with donors who I suspect do not know the Lord:

- In my funding presentation I *always* share my spiritual journey, and I ask potential donors to share theirs. Any lack of assurance of salvation is invariably revealed. Recently on a funding appointment with "George and Anne," my wife Alma and I each shared our testimonies. After Anne explained hers, it was George's turn. He hesitated but finally nodded to Anne and said, "I don't have a faith story like hers."

  "But honey," she said, "you prayed the prayer!"

  "Yes," he replied sarcastically, "*I prayed the prayer!*"

  The atmosphere suddenly became tense. I nervously took a sip of water and said, "George, I appreciate your honesty. Maybe you and I could meet to discuss the life of Jesus. I need to grow in Christ too." Alma and I did not pursue our funding appeal, and soon George and I were meeting biweekly to read through the Gospels. We became good friends, and he seems to be in the Kingdom now. He and Anne even started giving—without being asked.
- When I report on ministry progress with giving partners in person, I say, "May I show you a diagram we use in our ministry?" Then I draw out the Gospel Bridge illustration, a Navigator tool for evangelism. Their response to the illustration is an indicator of where they stand with Christ.

The most specific passage on receiving funding from nonbelievers is 3 John 1:7-8: "For they went out for the sake of the Name, accepting nothing from the Gentiles. Therefore we ought to support such men." Don't *depend* on unbelievers to fund your Kingdom work. But go ahead and appeal to *known* non-Christians if you believe their giving might nudge them toward Christ. Help them understand that their money will not get them to heaven, but do explain the secret of getting to heaven.

The story is told that William Booth, founder of the Salvation Army, was asked whether he would accept gifts from nonbelievers—"tainted money," it was called. His legendary reply, lost to history: "'Taint theirs and 'taint mine! And 'tis God's! I will accept any kind of money—even the Devil's. I'll wash it in the blood of Christ and use it for the glory of God."

6. What about appeals to family members?

Mark 6:4 says, "A prophet is not without honor except in his hometown." You may be the prophet Elijah on Mount Carmel in your discipling ministry, but to Aunt Gladys back home, you'll always be the little kid who put Fluffy the cat in the washing machine.

The guideline: Don't treat family like everyone else.

An American missionary mailed a tactfully written cash-project letter to his extended family. Family members received the same preprinted form letter as everyone else, including a pledge card. Sadly, they reacted poorly. Ten years later, he's still overcoming barriers erected by that letter. He erred by treating his family the same way he treated everyone else.

If your relatives are warm to the things of God, give them an opportunity to support you, but don't merely send a mass appeal. Contact them individually to ask whether you can tell them about your ministry face-to-face.

If your family members are not believers, add many of them to your mailing list. They are curious to know what you're up to, and your well-written, jargon-free letters (see chapter 16) may be their only link with the gospel. But be wary of mailing them financial appeals. If you offend them, you will be the topic of conversation at family gatherings. On the other hand, inviting them for support in a personal manner can be a wonderful springboard for the gospel.

When your family sees that you have adequate finances as a servant of Christ—what a testimony! My African friends emphasize that mission-workers must generously help family members *or their ministry is discounted.*

7. May I appeal to people to whom I have never ministered or don't know well?

Believers should give where they receive help—whether from their church, a Christian radio station, or a missionary. Those to whom you have ministered should support you according to Galatians 6:6: "The one who is taught the word is to share all good things with the one who teaches him." But this context describes a mature fellowship with established pastors. It is not prescriptive for all ministry situations, especially start-ups.

Some overly conscientious gospel-workers mistakenly assume they can receive support *only* from those who receive their teaching or friends who know them well. They say, "Money follows ministry." But what about the admonition to support traveling missionary *strangers* in 3 John 1:5? Similarly, in Matthew 10, had the disciples previously ministered to their worthy hosts? Had Elijah previously ministered to the widow?

Many gospel-workers say, "I don't feel comfortable appealing to someone I barely know or haven't talked to in a long time." But do givers feel this "pressure"? Alma and I recently made a support appeal to a couple we barely knew. They didn't say, "Wait a minute! You've never ministered to us! We don't know you well." They pledged, and we're ministering to them now through newsletters, occasional visits, and prayer. Ministry follows money!

If giving is a privilege, why prohibit anyone—even strangers—from participating? Don't disqualify them by implying, "Sorry, folks, I've never ministered to you. I don't know you well. I'm not going to give you an opportunity to invest in this exciting ministry." Don't take Galatians 6:6 too far.

To an old but absent friend I say, "Bob, we haven't seen each other in years, but I hope we can get together. I want to tell you all about my ministry with students and ask for your help. But besides that, I want to catch up on the last few years and find out what you have been up to." I mention my "business" item first, and the catching up second. That takes the manipulation out of it.

What about Christ's laborers who serve behind the scenes? God calls assistants, accountants, and techies to fulfill nonteaching, often invisible, but highly important ministry niches. Are these uniquely gifted servants not allowed to recruit support teams? Hogwash! They are as worthy of support as any pastor or missionary. "The eye cannot say to the hand, 'I have no need of you'" (1 Corinthians 12:21).

You don't need a long list of satisfied ministry pupils or a gazillion close friends in order to raise support. I'm not advocating phone-book fundraising, but to reach 100 percent you must go beyond your comfort zone of friends. This may be a stretching, fearful experience, but God will mold you through these encounters. And you will be a blessing to your new friends.

8. What about appealing to those who already are giving heavily?

Before I became a missionary, I worked for the *Ankeny Press Citizen* newspaper selling advertising. One bright Monday morning, I drove to Ralph's Grocery—my biggest account. I was hoping for a warm response from Ralph, but as I got out of the car, I heard a voice in my head saying, *Ralph doesn't want to see you today. You're an interruption. He can't afford advertising anyway. In fact, Scott, Ralph doesn't like you very much. Did you notice that he frowned the last time you were in?*

I got back into the car and drove to the hardware store. The voice in my head was back: *Scott, the hardware man doesn't want to see you. He can't afford it. He doesn't like you anyway.*

What was happening? I was making the store managers' decisions for them. I wasn't giving them a chance to say no!

We do the same thing in raising support. A voice inside says, *They already give. They can't afford it. They don't like me anyway.* Giving in to this voice robs the potential supporter of the privilege of deciding. Second Corinthians 9:7 says, "Each one must do just as he has purposed in his heart"—not as *you* purpose for him! It is the giver's decision whether to give.

Furthermore, how do we know whether people are giving heavily? Or if they give at all? Are you their accountant? Do you believe God blesses sacrificial givers? In Luke 21:1-4, Jesus commends the widow for sacrificial giving. Why didn't He stop her?

Some Christians give heavily or even sacrificially. But that is no reason to withhold your appeal to them. However, most believers do not qualify for the category of "sacrificial giving." American Christians give on average 2.43 percent of their gross income to Christian causes. (Evangelicals give at a slightly higher rate of 4 percent.)[2] My African friends tell me that even though most sub-Saharan African Christians say they tithe (10 percent), everyone knows it is not true.

Let the donor decide. Years ago I was sitting at our kitchen table reviewing our mailing list, and I saw Joe's name. Joe and I had briefly served together on a church board. As a doctor and leader in the church, Joe was the target of many funding appeals. He also likely contributed heavily to the church. I considered asking him.

What's the use? I thought. *He's probably giving all he can.*

Nevertheless, I decided not to decide for him. I phoned Joe and asked whether we could meet for lunch so I could tell about my ministry. Anticipating my appeal, Joe said, "We can meet, but I can't promise anything financially."

The appointment was cordial, though Joe was noncommittal. I assumed his answer was no. But two weeks after our meeting, his pledge card showed up with a generous monthly commitment and a warm note of appreciation.

Don't edit potential donors off your list because they are "already giving." Let the donor decide.

What about "disclaimers?" For example, someone tells you, "Our church started a building program" or "My sister is widowed and needs school fees for her three kids." Disclaimers are a potential donor's way of telling us she has other financial responsibilities. Does hearing a disclaimer mean it is time to put away your pledge card and go home? Is a disclaimer a no?

To a disclaimer I say, "It sounds like you have many giving opportunities these days. Isn't it wonderful there's so much going on for God!" Then I ask, "How do you feel about receiving so many appeals?" Let them respond.

When you receive a disclaimer, empathize. Tell them you realize they are the target of many giving appeals from missions or family, and that it is impossible to give to every project. Donors appreciate that you are aware of their dilemma.

Then I add, "I hesitate to invite you to join my support team because I thought maybe you are overwhelmed by appeals. But I felt led by the Lord to invite you even if the answer is no. That's OK. No matter what your decision, our friendship is not on the line." They seem to appreciate that. But I still go ahead and make my appeal. Then I review 2 Corinthians 9:7 as I close. "Each one *must* do just as he has purposed in his heart, not grudgingly or under compulsion, for God loves a cheerful giver."

Be sensitive to disclaimers, but remember it is the heavy givers who most likely have discovered the joy of generosity. And they most likely are more sensitive to the Lord. Don't shy away simply because they are giving already.

9. What if the person I'm asking is poorer than I am?

Confession time! Years ago I scanned giving prospects' clothing, cell phone, car, house, job, spouse's job, neighborhood, and jewelry. Then I made a judgment about whether they could afford to give based on these external things. I chickened out if they "looked poor." Sound familiar?

What does the Bible say? "*Every* man shall give *as he is able*, according to the blessing of the LORD your God which He has given you" (Deuteronomy 16:17, emphasis added). Note the word *every*. If someone has an income, he or she has the responsibility and privilege of giving. No exceptions. I like the way Navigator mission pioneer Jim Petersen put it: "People need to give much worse than I need to receive."

Of course, not everyone can give in the range you suggest. Note the phrase "as he is able." People are to give in proportion to how God has blessed them. Someone earning $30,000 per year won't be able to give as much as a person with a $100,000-per-year income—nor should they!

A classic story shows how giving brings dignity:

I was the minister of a small Baptist congregation in a railroad town just outside of Lynchburg, Virginia. My deacon sent for me one day. "We have in our congregation," he said, "a widow with six children. . . . She is putting into the treasury of the church each month $4—a tithe of her income. Of course, she is unable to do this. We want you to go and talk to her and let her know that she needs to feel no obligation whatsoever, and free her from the responsibility."

I am not wise now; I was less wise then. I went and told the widow of the concern of the deacons. I told her as graciously and as supportively as I knew that she was relieved of the responsibility of giving. As I talked, tears came into her eyes. "I want to tell you," she said, "that you are taking away the last thing that gives my life dignity and meaning."[3]

These deacons failed to see that giving to God bestows honor and dignity—especially to someone with limited means. Jesus said in John 7:24, "Do not judge according to appearance, but judge with righteous judgment." Don't deny God's people the honor of giving.

10. At what level should gospel-workers set their lifestyle? How nice is "too nice"?

It's an unfortunate worldwide axiom that if you're in Christian ministry, you are expected to be poor. Potential gospel-workers from younger generations hesitate to enter full-time ministry because they don't want to be poor! But this pattern is not new.

- Francis Asbury, Methodist leader in America in the 1700s (for whom Asbury College is named) wanted his circuit-riding preachers to be poor; he thought it helped them trust God more.
- A Child Evangelism Fellowship staff worker bought a nice new kitchen appliance. The pastor of their church noticed it and recommended that the church cut support.
- Deacons at a Midwestern church voted to lower the new pastor's salary by $2,000 to keep it below the salary of the lowest-paid deacon.
- A pastor at a start-up church told me he had a parishioner call his $29,000 part-time salary "way too high." But this *part-time* work requires fifty hours per week. Hmmm . . .

Does the Bible teach that gospel-workers must be poor? Was Jesus an itinerant beggar living off scraps of food? How do we understand Luke 9:58: "The Son of Man has nowhere to lay His head"? By contrast:

- Jesus and the Twelve had a money box out of which they bought supplies and gave to the poor—they had cash flow (John 12:6; 13:29). In John 4:8 the disciples went into town to *buy* food—not beg for food!
- At the Crucifixion the soldiers did not tear Jesus' robe because it was seamless and high quality.
- Jesus was often hosted by generous friends such as Mary and Martha, Zacchaeus, and Peter's mother-in-law.

Though not wealthy, Jesus did not live in poverty.

Other Scriptures contradict the assumption that God's workers should be poor. The Old Testament tithe represented the *best* of the grain, the *best* of the flock. In Malachi 1:8, the people were upbraided for offering blind or lame lambs to the Lord and keeping the best for themselves. But the Lord commanded that *the best* be given to the Levites—not exactly a stingy God.

Referring to traveling missionaries, 3 John 1:6 says, "Send them on their way in a manner worthy of God." How do you support workers in a manner worthy of God?

See 1 Timothy 5:17: "The elders who rule well are to be considered worthy of *double honor*, especially those who work hard at preaching and teaching." Double honor? The Greek word used here for "honor" is *timao*, literally meaning "the sale price or to fix a value upon." (*Timao* is used in Matthew 27:6, where Judas returned the thirty pieces of silver—"the price [*timao*] of blood.")

But "double" what? Possibly double the amount used to assist widows in the church who are "put on the list" (1 Timothy 5:9). Some say Paul cannot possibly mean financial remuneration, but the context supports the financial meaning. Verse 18 says, "'YOU SHALL NOT MUZZLE THE OX WHILE HE IS THRESHING,' and 'The laborer is worthy of his wages.'" We don't know whether Timothy paid the elders double, but Paul thought they were worth it.

Does "double honor" mean presenting a nice plaque or a gift certificate at the Christmas Eve service? No. Paul knew what the Iowa farmers I grew up with used to say about money—cold cash warms the heart.

In the 1800s a small country church wanted to hire a pastor, but the salary they were prepared to pay was very small. Charles Spurgeon contacted the church: "The only individual I know, who could exist on such a stipend, is the angel Gabriel. He would need neither cash nor clothes; and he could come down from heaven every Sunday morning, and go back at night, so I advise you to invite him."[4]

I'm not advocating exorbitant salaries; I dwell on 1 Timothy 5:17-18 because of how resistant religious leaders are to paying pastors and missionaries generously. Paul had no such hang-up.

What about living the same lifestyle as the people you're ministering to? Famed China missionary Hudson Taylor adopted the level of living of the villagers he ministered among. That is wise in some cross-cultural situations, but it may not be appropriate in others.

Practically, at what level should we set ministry budgets? Three Scriptures are helpful:

1. "Give me neither poverty nor riches; feed me with the food that is my portion, that I may not be full and deny You and say, 'Who is the LORD?' or that I not be in want and steal, and profane the name of my God" (Proverbs 30:8-9). Simply put, avoid extremes. In my experience, extreme wealth and poverty subject us to greater temptation. Health-and-wealth ministries claim that financial success is a sign of God's blessing. But such teaching spawns what appear to be financial abuses—such as the pastor who personally owns two jet planes. Ministry leaders who live extravagantly, making excessive profits through the gospel, have a history of eventually failing. The newspapers gleefully report about them.

2. "For John came neither eating nor drinking, and they say, 'He has a demon!' The Son of Man came eating and drinking, and they say, 'Behold, a gluttonous man and a drunkard, a friend of tax collectors and sinners!'" (Matthew 11:18-19). John the Baptist lived meagerly—unless you consider insects and wild honey to be gourmet food. I have eaten locusts in Uganda—tasty if grilled and salted, but as a steady diet like John's? No thanks. Of his subsistence lifestyle in the desert, critics said, "He's got a demon." Jesus, on the other hand, circulated among tax-gatherers and sinners. And He was criticized as a glutton and a winebibber. No matter how you live, someone will criticize your lifestyle. What you consider reasonable may appear to others as luxurious. You can't please everybody.

3. "But we endure all things so that we will cause no hindrance to the gospel of Christ" (1 Corinthians 9:12). Make sure your lifestyle does not hinder the gospel. For example, a student confided to me, "I am ashamed to bring people to the campus minister's home. It's sloppy, and he dresses

sloppy too. It hinders some of the new Christians." Later I discovered that staff worker was receiving US government food stamps because of his low income. Just last summer, a funding coach from a respected ministry told me of his aim to help his fellow staff raise enough donor income so they could get off government food stamps. Certainly we must be frugal. That's good stewardship, like Jesus collecting leftover fragments of bread (John 6:12). But extreme asceticism, even though it might save money, hinders effective ministry. There is nothing innately spiritual about living in poverty. Being in poverty does not make you immune to temptations toward greed.

What about minimalism? Perhaps as a reaction to rampant materialism, some younger gospel-workers espouse spending as little as possible, living simply, and doing without. This is a refreshing change from materialism, but extreme minimalism can hinder the gospel. Speaking at a gospel-worker conference, the late Howard Hendricks of Dallas Theological Seminary told of a missionary who prided himself on frugality. The missionary's newsletter described how he spent three days paddling upriver in a canoe, preached one full day, and paddled back in a canoe for three days—six days paddling, one day preaching. Hendricks suggested this instead: Hire Mission Aviation Fellowship to fly him into the jungle in one hour so he could preach six days and then fly back in one hour. It would cost more, but he would accomplish more. Is the chief goal to live super frugally or to effectively advance the gospel?

Where should you set your lifestyle? How about this: Order your lifestyle such that you are at maximum fruitfulness in life, marriage (if you're married), and ministry. It takes money to provide a warm, friendly home to visitors—that's a ministry! It's not a sign of weak faith to have a generous grocery budget to feed a locust-horde of hungry students.

What kind of lifestyle will help you be most effective? Don't live so frugally that you cannot buy a new believer a Coca-Cola. And don't live so extravagantly that people whisper about how rich you are. The balance is 2 Corinthians 8:21: "We have regard for what is honorable, not only in the sight of the Lord, but also in the sight of men." Don't let your liberty to live frugally become a stumbling block for the gospel. And don't let your liberty to live well become a stumbling block for the gospel.

In summary, I'm not suggesting that you be rich or poor. Simply this: Figure out what income will help you minister most effectively. Bring that figure before the Lord daily (Matthew 6:11).

11. How can I ask others for support when I have significant savings?

Investments per se are not wrong, but you must identify godly purposes for your savings and investments. If you don't know why you are saving, you may be guilty of hoarding—like the rich young ruler whose assets were his idol (Luke 18:22-23).

It's easy to identify "ungodly" purposes for saving—things that are purely for self-gratification, illegal or immoral activities, or to "keep up with the Joneses." Godly purposes are those things that enable you to accomplish what God has purposed just for you—unselfish things such as saving for your own education, old age, children's education, taking care of aged parents, starting a God-ordained business, saving for a house or vehicle—anything that God has led you to do in the future that requires more than your monthly cash flow. Of course, every dollar or shilling or rupiah that a believer has accumulated must be available for the Lord to use as He directs. Since all resources are owned by God, He might lead you to give away "His" savings. (Many Christians reject that—give it away? Really!)

But you need not feel guilty keeping your savings intact so you can accomplish future God-ordained purposes. If you use all your savings for the mission field and return home penniless, how will you launch the next chapter of life?

12. If I have the means, should I support myself?

Self-supported ministry is more of a calling question than a funding question. Both self-supported and gift-income gospel-workers are needed. Scripture contains examples of both. There is no formula to discover the answer. If you are considering funding yourself merely to avoid the challenge of fundraising, please consider the following facts:

- Jesus did not support Himself.
- The apostle Paul did not support himself—except for three times we know of.

Self-funding your ministry has some disadvantages:

- You are robbed of prayer partners. Friends will pray more fervently when they give. "For where your treasure is, there your heart will be also" (Matthew 6:21).
- You rob people of the blessing of giving. Each missionary has a unique web of relationships. No one else knows these people quite the way you do, and they

might not give to any other cause but yours. You are helping them learn the joy of giving.

- You rob your friends of growth in world vision. When your giving partners hear your wonderful ministry stories, they are stretched to think beyond their local lives.
- You rob yourself of the character-building, faith-deepening experience of raising support.

Now it's time to ask yourself which of these questions of conscience grabbed your attention. You needn't have them fully answered before you dive into fundraising, but do not ignore your conscience. Let the Lord speak to you. Will you surrender that issue in prayer before you begin the next chapter?

4
TEN CRUCIAL ATTITUDES YOU MUST NOT NEGLECT

WHEN YOU DIVE INTO biblical fundraising, your core values will be exposed, and you might not like what you see! Before I started fundraising, I *thought* I was the following:

- Confident! But I stammered and perspired as I answered questions from donors.
- Fearless! Until I chickened out of making appeals.
- Not manipulative! So why did I make a "holy hint" appeal to a rich stranger?

When you signed up for ministry, no one told you that fundraising pushes you to the limits of your character. Fundraising helps you apply the admonition to all believers of 2 Corinthians 3:18—to be "transformed into his image" (NIV). That is a good thing!

Before you meet with one more person or send one more email, compare your attitudes with these ten. Which ones do you need to shore up?

1. God—not our donors or hard work—is the source.

The Levites understood that God was the true source of their support. Notice the pronoun *I* in Numbers 18:24: "For the tithe of the sons of Israel, which they offer as an offering to the LORD, I have given to the Levites." The lamb or grain was given to the Levites but was "an offering to the LORD"—not a *horizontal* gift from Israelite to Levite, but a *vertical* gift to God. Donors give to God. Levites receive from God. Both are vertical.

Paul understood this. In Philippians 4:18, he called the Philippians' gift a "fragrant aroma, an acceptable sacrifice, well-pleasing to God." From the Philippians to God to Paul. All vertical.

When I put my giving envelope in an offering plate at a church service, I imagine an usher commenting on the fresh burn marks on the edges (like reentry tiles on a space shuttle). He says, "This envelope's warm, and it smells like charcoal!" Of course! It's been to heaven and back.

By contrast, if you view people, not God, as your source of funding, you have a horizontal view. Depending on the day, you may feel deserving or undeserving of their gifts.

One particular month in my first year as a campus minister, I was lackadaisical. Instead of studying the Scriptures, I watched *Sesame Street* with my kids. I learned to count to ten in Spanish! When I finally would go to campus, instead of talking with students, I watched daytime TV in the dormitory lounge.

At month-end our donor income arrived. It was the most we'd ever received! I was humbled. People were investing money so I could watch *The Price Is Right*. Hoping for sympathy, I told my wife, Alma, "I don't know why *anyone* would want to give to a sloth like me."

She surprised me by saying, "I don't either. I think they give to God."

Her comment was humbling. Donor income is not earned.

On another occasion, I felt deserving. Because I'd done extensive fundraising the month before, I was confident new donors would appear on our income report. But the report was disappointing. Many who had pledged to give had not! I'd worked hard! Disappointment turned to resentment toward those who had not given. My resentment showed that I was looking to people—not God.

We sometimes look not to other people but to *ourselves* as the source of funding—our hard work, our vibrant personalities, even our technology. But getting a ton of "likes" on Facebook will not get you up to budget! Having a sharp ministry video will not get you up to budget. Being outgoing and friendly will not get you up to budget. Even having a successful ministry will not get you up to budget. Sorry.

Certainly we must communicate well. But let's look to God—not our donors, our skills, or hard work—as the Source. A young missionary candidate asked me for advice. "Scott, our pastor has made terrible mistakes, and I'm an elder. I've got to confront him."

"What's stopping you?" I asked.

He hesitated. "Well, the church is thinking about sponsoring me for $200 to $500 a month when I join the mission next year. If I confront the pastor, well . . ." My friend stopped to clear his throat. "Well, there's a chance I could lose that support," he said, staring at the ground.

A week later, he confessed that he had been looking at people as his financial source instead of God. He said, "I worry about minding my Ps and Qs around the church so I won't offend them, so I will get a lot of money."

Look to God, not to people.

2. Prayer demonstrates our dependence on God.

Nehemiah modeled an attitude of dependence on God. Seconds before he fearfully asked King Artaxerxes for timber to rebuild the Jerusalem wall, he "prayed to the God of heaven" (Nehemiah 2:4).

In my second year as a campus minister, I was grumbling about our support to Duane Bundt, a friend who had helped me grow spiritually when I was a new believer. I appreciated his down-to-earth Iowa pragmatism. But I was stuck.

Duane asked, "Scott, do you pray about it? Do you pray about it every day?"

I said, "Well, I pray about it, but I don't pray about it every day."

"Well, you should pray about it—*every day*."

So I prayed—every day—and our income went up. I was accidentally following Jesus' model prayer, "Give us this day our daily bread" (Matthew 6:11).

May I ask you the question Duane asked me? Do you pray about your financial support *every day*? Do you name your budget and ask the Lord specifically to supply 100 percent of it? Do you name people one by one before the Lord, asking Him to lay it on their hearts to join your support team?

On page 1 of my daily prayer journal I have written the words "Daily Bread" and my exact monthly budget beside it. On page 2 I record the next six to ten friends who, I am praying, will support us. Beside their names I include the specific amount or range I intend to ask each one to consider. Then I pray for each person.

Within a few weeks, I phone to make appointments with each one. Frequently they say, "It's interesting that you called. We had just been talking about you." I've heard that statement too often for it to be coincidence.

Years ago, Alma and I prayed specifically that four couples would begin supporting us monthly for $50 each (a sizable amount in those days). Because we were in a discipling relationship with them, we didn't want a financial appeal to cloud our relationship. So I put their names down in my journal and began to pray daily. We agreed not to hint to them about our finances.

A month later, one of the couples phoned to ask how to give to our support. About that same time, the second fellow, an older man, stuck a check in my pocket and, rather embarrassed, said, "Send that in for us." His $50 gift continued monthly.

The third couple pledged at our all-city conference. We were not the offering project, but they started $50 monthly support.

The fourth couple didn't give. In my annual prayer review (I do it on New Year's Day, instead of watching perky young Hollywood stars host football parades), I thanked the Lord for these three new monthly partners—but I wondered about the fourth!

The next month, our report revealed a gift from the fourth couple for $600. Divided by twelve, that equals $50 per month! God answers prayer!

May I suggest two action steps? As you've read these pages, perhaps the faces of potential donors have come to mind. Jot their names down in your prayer journal. You might aim for ten.

Second, start a "by prayer alone" short list. Jot down names of people who you hope will support you but whom you don't feel led by God to ask. (Make sure fear doesn't influence your decision! If you're fearful, you probably *should* ask them.) Can you think of two names for your "by-prayer-alone" list? Take a moment right now.

3. Understand your job versus God's job.

Lorne Sanny, former international director of The Navigators, once told of going through a frustrating phase of ministry leadership. He was feeling overwhelmed, lonely, and discouraged. But then he humorously (but pointedly) said, "Everything changed when I officially resigned from being president of the universe." It seems obvious, but we bring ourselves frustration when we slide into roles God intended only for Himself. It's true in evangelism, in leadership, and especially in fundraising. As I look back on my frustration in funding, it has often been because I confused my role and God's role.

It is clear throughout Scripture that God is our provider. Psalm 104:14 says, "He causes the grass to grow for the cattle, and vegetation for the labor of man, so that he may bring forth food from the earth." Men and women do their part to "bring forth food," but it is food that God has provided. As a beginning model of this principle, Adam and Eve in the Garden were expected to cultivate their food—they had a responsibility to do their part (Genesis 1:29-30). Work was and is honorable.

But some gospel-workers misunderstand. They think God's provision means that they need not take action to garner what God has provided. God may provide for the birds (Matthew 6:26), but they still spend hours each day searching for food! And so must gospel-workers.

God's Job
Calling me to special ministry

God's Job
Surrounding me providentially with friends and family, and bringing acquaintances across my path

My Job
Inviting friends, family, and acquaintances to join me financially in ministry

God's Job
Providentially guiding friends, family, and acquaintances to make a stewardship decision to support me

My Job
Thanking, informing, and ministering to financial partners

You have two jobs in funding your ministry. God has three—and His are harder! Yours are the following:

- Invite friends, family, and acquaintances to join your support team.
- Thank, inform, and minister to your giving partners.

God's three jobs are more complicated:

- Calling you to ministry.
- Surrounding you with potential partners.
- Leading them to make stewardship decisions.

When you try to do God's job in fundraising—for example, pressuring people to give—you are out of His will. Limit yourself to doing your two jobs with all the grace He gives. He will do His part.

Of course, God could fund you without your lifting a finger—and that would be a miracle. But He will also do miracles as you faithfully do your part. When

God gives you the grace to phone or text to set an appointment with someone who intimidates you, isn't that miraculous?

Remember, you can't do God's job. And He *won't* do yours!

4. The Bible is the standard—not secular best practices nor personal opinions nor cultural traditions.

Growing up on a farm, with a frugal background, I secretly prided myself on my good financial sense. Even though Alma and I sometimes disagreed about the exact meaning of *frugality*, I was sure I was right. But my opinions about finance management changed one sunny Saturday morning on the shores of Lake Mendota in Wisconsin as I studied every passage in Proverbs dealing with money and possessions. Until that day, I was a prisoner to my cultural "common sense." The Bible revealed to me that I was *too* frugal! The Bible!

I am not alone in having strong opinions about money and fundraising. Gospel-workers from around the world struggle to let the Bible lead them in money matters. Here is what I tell gospel-workers from every culture who are complacent about their funding: Your personal opinions about funding are sincere and contain much common sense. And that has brought you to this point:

- You are far short of your funding goal.
- You have almost nothing in savings.
- You will have to scramble to appeal to your friends if you have an emergency.

"It is not enough," George Mueller once said, "to obtain means [funding] for the work of God. . . . These means should be obtained in God's way."[1] Our task is not simply to raise support but to do it in a biblical, God-honoring manner. The late Rod Sargent, my mentor and the former director of development for The Navigators, used to say that "just because a fundraising tactic works doesn't make it right."

Nonetheless, abusive fundraising exists today among Christian ministries. I received a letter from a television evangelist describing the Luke 17 story, in which Jesus directs Peter to take a coin out of a fish's mouth to pay a tax. The fundraising letter contained two coins—a big one for me to keep and a smaller one with the following instruction: "Wrap your largest bill around this smaller coin and send it to God's work."

This two-coin hocus-pocus is a spiritualized version of the secular two-penny gimmick: "You keep one penny, but return the other one to me because it doesn't belong to you." The writer promises health and wealth if you merely "plant a seed"—which is code for "give money to the man of God."

I also have a letter containing two packets of mustard seeds from the Mount of Olives gathered by an evangelist's children. I am to keep one packet, but I must return the other along with a $33 love gift and prepare to receive a blessing.

Gospel-workers have the right to ask (see 1 Corinthians 9:1-14), but promises of wealth and health go too far.

In 2 Corinthians 4:2, Paul used the phrase "not walking in craftiness" to describe his ministry among the unpredictable Corinthians. Though he was not offering fundraising advice, gospel-workers must heed his words well. Are we tempted to be "crafty" to reach full funding?

How about you? You will probably never send mustard seeds, but when funds are low, mission-workers are tempted to manipulate the truth. For example, a missionary wouldn't tell his donors he was fully funded for fear they'd stop. And what about the P. S. in missionary letters—"Please pray for our financial support"? I call that a disguised appeal: "holy hinting"! Many godly missionaries have never done a Bible study on money or fundraising, yet they have strong opinions about it. Are their opinions biblical?

Beyond personal opinions about fundraising are cultural traditions. My rural culture in the Midwest frowned on talking about money or religion. I have been told by gospel-workers in other cultures that "direct asking will never work in our culture." It is "too pushy" or "too American." But as I probe these statements, I find that these gospel-workers do not want to challenge cultural traditions about money. It is dangerous.

Yet gospel-workers challenge their cultures in other issues, such as evangelism and discipling. Will you allow your personal common sense or cultural traditions to continue to dictate your financial practices? Or will you choose the Bible's wisdom for your fundraising practices?

Don't spout your personal opinions until you've spent at least twenty hours in personal Bible study on money and fundraising. Start with the Bible study in the online appendix at scottmorton.net.

5. Biblical fundraising is a spiritual ministry, not a worldly effort.

Gospel-workers around the world tend to separate life into spiritual and nonspiritual categories. Spiritual activities include discipleship, evangelism, and prayer meetings. Money matters are nonspiritual.

A missionary once told me, "I could never choose money over the souls of men and women." He saw fundraising as a plague, not a privilege; a curse, not a call; a menace, not a ministry. He did not joyfully embrace fundraising; he was trying to get out of it.

A few years ago, the director of an international sending agency wrote in *Christianity Today* that raising personal support is a "demeaning method." This nationally known leader fed the bias that fundraising is shameful. Is that the Bible's view?

Zambian Navigator director Nelson Musipa offered me a refreshing view:

What made me take fundraising more seriously? God's marching orders when He called me! The day I realized that my marching orders included fundraising was the day I realized that it was no longer a matter of debate but obedience.

In Exodus 25:2, God told Moses to "raise a contribution" for the tabernacle tent. Did Moses consider it "demeaning?" Or did he consider it an unpleasant duty? Did he embrace it reluctantly? Can you imagine him saying, "Lord, are You asking me to do fundraising? Anything but that! I'll teach the Ten Commandments. I'll eat manna. But don't ask me to do fundraising! And especially for a capital project! It's going to burn anyway!"

Quite the opposite! Moses carefully received God's detailed instructions for the tabernacle; then he invited the Israelites to give. And give they did! Everyone "whose heart stirred him" (Exodus 35:21) brought contributions.

Did Paul consider fundraising demeaning? Three times he called the collection for the saints in Jerusalem a "gracious work" (2 Corinthians 8:6-7, 19). He even postponed his ministry to Spain to personally deliver an offering to Jerusalem (Romans 15:28).

Similarly, today pastors say, "Let us *worship* God through the giving of our tithes and offerings." They do not apologetically announce, "We now come to that part of our service where we must do something secular. I hate it, but the bills must be paid. Ushers, please come forward, and let's get this nasty business over with."

The late author Henri Nouwen originally considered fundraising "a necessary but unpleasant activity to support spiritual things." But later in life he realized that "fundraising is as spiritual as giving a sermon, entering a time of prayer, visiting the sick, or feeding the hungry."[2]

He goes on to say, "Fundraising is precisely the opposite of begging. When we seek to raise funds we are not saying, 'Please, could you help us out because lately it's been hard.'" Instead, Nouwen defines fundraising as "proclaiming what we believe in such a way that we offer other people an opportunity to participate with us in our vision and mission." Exactly! We are not asking people to give their hard-earned funds so we can put groceries on the table or buy socks. Rather, we are asking them to join us in advancing the Kingdom. Nouwen concludes, "We must not let ourselves be tricked into thinking that fundraising is only a secular activity."[3]

If giving is biblical, then can't the appeal also be biblical? Worldly people make fundraising worldly, just as worldly people make evangelism worldly.

Furthermore, we don't *do* fundraising merely so we can *do* ministry. Biblical fundraising itself is ministry. Why? It helps people lay up treasure in heaven. It challenges them to dismiss the idol of mammon and live Matthew 6:33, seeking first the Kingdom.

Philippians 4:10 gives a simple formula for fundraising: "You were *concerned* before, but you lacked *opportunity*" (emphasis added). People need *concern* for the Lord's work and an *opportunity* to show their concern. This simple equation from Philippians 4:10 helps me:

$$S = C + O$$
Support = Concern + Opportunity

Without realizing it, churches utilize the S = C + O formula every Sunday by passing the offering basket. The basket is simply an *opportunity* for parishioners to show their *concern*.

In the same way, your financial appeal gives your friends an opportunity to demonstrate their concern. If through your newsletters you raise concern for your ministry but never provide a meaningful stewardship opportunity, your friends will likely not give. If, on the other hand, you constantly present giving opportunities but neglect to elevate your people's concern, they will view you as money-hungry.

Notice I said "meaningful stewardship opportunity." A missionary told me he gave the four hundred people on his mailing list an "opportunity" to support him monthly, but 399 said no. "How do you know they said no?" I asked. "They didn't respond to the letter!" he replied.

However, relying on mass letter, text, or email appeals for support (especially monthly support) does not give readers enough of a meaningful stewardship opportunity. It's like driving an ice cream truck through a neighborhood at forty-five miles per hour—it doesn't meaningfully engage with customers. Similarly, a mass email blast asking for monthly support does not meaningfully engage potential donors. There is a proper place for appeal letters, but often gospel-workers send "hinting letters" as a substitute for meaningfully inviting giving partners one by one. "High-altitude letter-bombing," I call it.

Besides recruiting support, giving people stewardship opportunities also opens doors to further ministry. Presenting your ministry in person takes ten to twenty minutes, but it also gives you entrance to your listeners' lives.

What about you? Do you see fundraising as "a necessary but unpleasant activity to support spiritual things" (Nouwen)? Or have you journeyed to wholehearted acceptance of fundraising as a spiritual ministry?

Review the fundraising acceptance barometer below. Where would you place yourself today?

- Trying to get out of it? (You creatively seek ways to avoid fundraising.)
- A sense of resignation or duty? (You fundraise only when the situation is desperate.)
- Embrace fundraising reluctantly? (You do funding dutifully and mechanically but without joy.)
- Embrace fundraising joyfully? (Though it is still a risk, you accept fundraising as part of your calling and delight in doing it.)

What can you do to move toward joyful acceptance of your fundraising ministry?

6. Receiving support does not entitle you to be demanding.

Paul writes in 1 Corinthians 9:14, "So also the Lord directed those who proclaim the gospel to get their living from the gospel." He was paraphrasing Jesus, who said in Matthew 10:10, "For the worker is worthy of his support."

Clearly, we have a right to be supported by the gospel. But Paul says earlier in verse 12, "We did not use this right . . . that we will cause no hindrance to the gospel."

Because we are comfortable being in charge, Christian leaders can be demanding without realizing it. In making financial appeals, missionaries often say, "I want you to pray about giving toward my ministry." Intended as a question, the statement is actually a command—not an appeal. Let's be careful to make *appeals* for support rather than giving commands.

I like the way Bill Hybels, pastor of Willow Creek Community Church, says it over a lunch table:

> God has led me to challenge you with something today, but please know from the outset that we'll be okay whether you accept this challenge or not. . . . It won't affect our friendship or my respect for you because this is not between you and me as much as it is between you and God. Are we on the same page here?[4]

I'm afraid some missionaries who attend fundraising seminars come away with the impression that they have the right to force pledge cards into the hands of reluctant listeners. Not true. You have the right to be supported, but you don't have the right to be demanding, discourteous, or pushy—thereby causing hindrance to the gospel.

7. Expect to raise 100 percent of your approved budget.

Does going into ministry include taking a vow of poverty? Are gospel-workers supposed to be poor? Is it okay for Christian teachers, Christian farmers, and Christian businesspeople to have adequate funds or even to be rich, but missionaries must be poor?

In my experience, many missionaries do not expect to receive 100 percent of support they need. Around the world and in many different ministries, I find gospel-workers who believe 100 percent is an unreachable, far-off "ideal"—not a serious goal. A mission administrator once referred to his staff's budgets as "wish lists." One said, "My budget might as well be $1,000,000 because I will never reach it anyway."

Isn't 60 or 80 percent of budget enough?

No.

Gospel-worker Margaret thought she was ready to launch a new ministry at a state university with only partial funding. But it was tough. No one seemed interested in hearing about Christ. Finally, one skeptical student agreed to meet Margaret to talk about the Bible and Jesus. Margaret was ecstatic. This might be a spiritual breakthrough. The appointment was set.

But when Margaret was to go to campus, she discovered she didn't have four dollars to buy her new friend a Coca-Cola. Rather than be embarrassed, Margaret postponed the meeting, not telling her new friend the real reason. Because of a measly four dollars, the gospel was lost that day.

I once helped a missionary write a funding letter for his daughter's first year of university. He confessed that he disdained fundraising and tried to "get by" year after year below his approved budget. He ignored saving for legitimate needs such as old age, resettlement, housing, and his kids' college. He hoped that a dynamite appeal to his mailing list would cover his daughter's schooling. It didn't. It wasn't even close. His living at 80 percent for twenty years had caught up to him.

Besides not having enough cash flow, low funding threatens marital happiness. A friend in funding development was discussing 100 percent funding with a European missionary husband and wife over a pleasant lunch. Soon the missionary began sermonizing that raising full support was merely an American idea. As he pontificated, tears formed in his wife's eyes. Choking back tears, she finally said, "It's great to live by faith, but I'm the one who has to buy the bread and cheese." Her husband did not realize she was under such pressure.

At 80 percent you can "get by" for the short term—until your car needs repair, until you need to fly home for a parent's illness, until your kids want to go to university, or until you want to buy a Coca-Cola for a skeptical friend.

Why do we excuse ourselves from full funding? It is not simply a private matter between you and God. Skeptical but hungry God-seekers are waiting! Full funding is a gospel issue—it is not about your preference! God has enough resources in His big world to fully supply your "prayed-over-organization-approved" budget!

(Singles, be particularly careful here. Just because you have fewer expenses than married people with children, you might think you can "get by" on less. Your present circumstances don't mean you should settle for a lower budget.)

Ask yourself these questions: If you were at 100 percent of budget for the next twelve months:

- What would you do in ministry that you can't do now?
- If married, how would your marriage be different?
- What are some things you'd like to do for your spouse? For your family?
- What would you personally do differently?

If nothing would change, then you are thinking too small. Your "get-by" thinking is putting a glass ceiling on your ministry.

Your first step toward full funding is to prepare an official budget. More on that in chapter 8.

8. Poortalk dishonors God.

What is poortalk? It's a mentality of wishing you had more money, usually expressed in complaining or hinting. Simply put, it's whining about money.

Most Christian workers have participated in a missionary pity party at some point. Picture the scene. It's late at night at the mission conference. Two missionaries have been talking for an hour over coffee in Styrofoam cups. They have pontificated on every problem in the mission, particularly the leadership structure. Now their talk turns to finances.

"How's your income doing?"

"Good. Picked up a new donor last month—$100."

"Great! What did you say his name was? Ha ha, just kidding!"

"We lost two big churches last summer. Cindy might go back to work even though she doesn't want to. I feel bad for the kids. No toys for Christmas this year. Donors are getting less generous."

"Our personal allowance was only $16 last month—we're at 37 percent! I had to sell my memory-verse packet at a garage sale."

"That's nothing. Last month I didn't get an allowance at all. Headquarters sent me a bill!"

"This economy is just killing us Christian workers!"

"I tell you, these are the last days!"

David Myers and Thomas Ludwig call this kind of discussion *poortalk*. "Although poortalk is understandable, it is nevertheless debilitating. First, it makes us feel worse about our plight than is necessary. . . . Second, poortalk focuses our attention on ourselves, thus blinding us to the genuine needs of . . . others."[5]

Why do Christian workers talk poor? These are some motives that missionaries confess to me:

- Self-pity to elicit a response, such as "Oh, you poor thing. It must be so difficult to serve the Lord." Sniff. "Yes, it is."
- Poortalk is expected. Poverty and spirituality go hand in hand. I've heard whining from dedicated missionaries who seem to enjoy deep walks with God.
- Disguised financial appeal. "Maybe people will catch on that I need money."
- A bad habit inherited from parents or the mission environment.

What does poortalk communicate to your family, your friends, and particularly unbelievers? Pity? Plus, if financial struggles continue year after year, your friends wonder if the hand of God is truly on you. Your donors may wonder whether their investment in you is worthwhile.

I asked the chairwoman of a large church's missions committee how she felt about missionary newsletters peppered with hints about finances. She said, "It makes me feel bad, but I'm probably not going to do anything about it."

The apostle Paul had opportunities to whine about money. Instead, he wrote the following: "Not that I speak from want, for I have learned to be content in whatever circumstances I am. I know how to get along with humble means, and I also know how to live in prosperity. . . . I can do all things through Him who strengthens me" (Philippians 4:11-13).

When we were receiving missionary training, Alma and I found ourselves in dire financial straits, and I engaged in poortalk, hoping for sympathy. That's when Chuck Strittmatter, my supervisor, said, "Scott, you may be poor, but don't talk like you're poor." Ouch.

In the early days of The Navigators' ministry, when staff missed a meal because of inadequate income, Navigator founder Dawson Trotman told them to "put a toothpick in your mouth anyway" in order not to draw attention to their low income.

In Luke 10 Jesus sent His disciples on a ministry trip. He told them not to move from "house to house" (verse 7). Even today, in some countries beggars have an itinerary, moving from house to house. If Jesus' disciples had moved from house to house they could have been accused of selfishly seeking the most commodious lodgings. But Jesus did not allow His laborers to think like beggars or to be accused of taking advantage of their hosts.

Alma and I have made four personal commitments regarding poortalk to ensure we don't impede the gospel.

- We do not joke about a lack of money or "talk poor"—not even to one another privately, lest we reinforce the unbiblical idea that "God is broke" and there is not enough money in His wide world to fully fund us.
- We do not hint about our financial needs, particularly by asking newsletter readers to "pray for our finances." When we want people to give, we appeal face-to-face.
- We do not gripe about high prices. Once, Alma came home from the grocery store, and we began going through the sacks, complaining about the high cost of string beans, soap, paper towels, and blueberry-muffin mix. We grumbled about the US economy and the president, whom we blamed for the whole

mess! Finally, we caught ourselves. "What are we doing? We're whining in the presence of a sovereign God!"

- We do not compare ourselves with others—including donors. When we see the good fortune of "normal people," it's easy to think, *They sure have nice furniture. I wonder if we'll ever have a new sofa.* Even more subtle is comparison with other missionaries. At staff conferences whenever I saw a fellow missionary with a new car, I compared it with our "old car" and felt envy. But 2 Corinthians 10:12 helped me: "When they measure themselves by themselves . . . they are without understanding."

There is another dimension. Some missionaries fear that donors will discover they're fully funded and stop giving—so they keep up the poortalk. But I assure you that the donors won't stop. They will be delighted! One of our donors said, "Since you're up to budget, I guess we can quit giving!"

I said, "Then we wouldn't be up to budget!"

"Good point!" he said.

An honest answer to a question about your funding is appropriate. But hinting instead of honestly appealing, and whining instead of working, is poortalk. Drop it!

9. Focus on the giver, not the money.

Years ago I phoned an old acquaintance ("Norm") to see whether we could meet. We had seen each other only once in ten years, but he received our newsletters.

Before I hung up, I asked whether during our get-together I could explain our ministry and our support team. No obligation.

Silence! What had I said?

Finally, in a timid voice he answered, "Sure." But I couldn't get his hesitation out of my mind.

We had an enjoyable reunion at one of those fast-food places with 287 diet soft drink choices. As our visit was coming to an end, I cautiously asked Norm about his hesitation on the phone.

His eyes fell. He stared at the Diet Coke in his red plastic cup. Then he looked up, pursed his lips and mumbled something, his voice cracking.

Awkwardly, I broke the silence. "Norm, what's going on? You know I'm not here to twist your arm, right?"

"It's not you," he said, his eyes misty.

Then he poured out his story about another missionary whom he had formerly supported. "All he talked about was money. He was always hinting I should give more. It left a bad taste in my mouth," Norm confided.

I switched gears. "Norm, I'm withdrawing my request for support. I'm more concerned with your spiritual progress and helping you reconcile with this other missionary."

"Thank you," he said. "It's probably best."

As I drove away, I was grateful God had enabled me to be more concerned for Norm's walk with Christ than my support.

If we view our donors as ATMs, we violate the example of Philippians 4. Paul set the standard in Philippians 4:17: "Not that I seek the gift itself, but I seek for the profit which increases to your account." Though grateful for their gift, Paul was more concerned with the Philippians' spiritual progress. Donors must be treated with dignity—not merely so they will keep giving, but because they are fellow pilgrims with painful issues, like Norm's.

But how do we keep our motivation clear when we need support? For example, a wealthy Christian business owner comes into your circle of friends. You light up like a Christmas tree! You're tempted to pander to him, thinking that he might help you financially. But you feel like a hypocrite putting a *Beginning with Christ* booklet in his front pocket while taking a wallet from his back pocket.

Proverbs 19:6 states a truth about human nature: "Many will seek the favor of a generous man, and every man is a friend to him who gives gifts." You are not alone! Here's how I deal with the temptation. First, I admit to myself that I want this person's money. I used to deny that money even remotely motivated me to walk across the room to meet a person. Now I say, "Lord, I want his financial support, and I want it bad!" Honesty reduces pressure.

Second, I decide to do what is right for that individual, whether I get support or not. I pray, "Lord, I'd love for this person to support our ministry, but I don't know where he is with You. I want what's best for him. Please guide me."

I have a rhyme that helps me as I walk up to a prospective giver's house: "I put my hand upon their *door*, I quote Philippians 2:3 and *four*" ("With humility of mind regard one another as more important than yourselves; do not merely look out for your own personal interests, but also for the interests of others").

Third, I determine not to hint. People pick up on money signals, and it repels them.

If you are desperately behind in your funding, admit to yourself that you want to meet with a prospective donor because of money. At least you're authentic. In most cultures it is appropriate to set an appointment, but tell him *why* you want to meet.

Don't say it's for "fellowship" if you intend to roll the money grenade across the table. It's okay to invite a newcomer to support you; just don't trick him into it.

By the way, your motivation will never be 100 percent perfect. Jeremiah 17:9 says, "The heart is more deceitful than all else, and is desperately sick." It doesn't add, "except in the case of missionaries doing fundraising!" If you wait for perfect motivation, you'll not raise much support—nor share your faith, nor read your Bible.

10. Emphasize your vision, not your need.

In a *Peanuts* comic strip, Linus sits in a beanbag chair, staring at the TV. The announcer pleads, "This program needs your support." Second frame: "We need your donations." Linus is still sitting there, staring. Third frame, the announcer pleads desperately, "If we don't hear from you, we'll have to go off the air." In the final frame, Linus finally speaks. "So long!" he says.[6]

Too often, missionaries—like the TV announcer—view fundraising as the art of pleading for money more and more creatively. Let's change that distorted view by following Paul's 4-P model in Romans 15:

- Paul's *Passion* (15:20)
- Paul's *Promise* (15:21)
- Paul's *aPPeal* (15:24)
- Paul's *Personal* Relationships (15:24)

Passion

Romans 15:20: "And thus I aspired to preach the gospel, not where Christ was *already* named, so that I would not build on another man's foundation." This is Paul's passion—his dazzling vision: To preach where Christ was not named. Seven words!

When you share your "dazzling vision," are you passionate? I'm not talking about hype. You need not buy a plaid sport coat and imitate obnoxious TV quizmasters. Any personality type can show genuine zeal. American poet Ralph Waldo Emerson said it well: "Nothing great was ever accomplished without enthusiasm."

What if your ministry is not yet successful? Most people want to give to a ministry that has God's fingerprints all over it, even if it is not large or successful. Win donors' support by sharing the difficulties.

Promise

In Romans 15:21, Paul explains the foundation behind his passion by quoting Isaiah 52:15: "For what had not been told them they will see, And what they had not heard they will understand." A scriptural foundation or promise gives you confidence during dark days. I've made it a habit to review my personal Scriptural promises during my quiet times in the morning and whenever I board an airplane—and in the middle of the night when dark thoughts come.

Appeal

Romans 15:24: "Whenever I go to Spain—for I hope to see you in passing, and to be helped on my way there by you." The Greek word for "helped" as used here is *propempo*, which means "practical assistance." Although the phrase "helped on my way" appears indirect today, the Romans would have understood clearly that Paul was not asking for prayer support! He hoped they would outfit him for his mission to Spain—with food, provisions, money, and partners to travel with him. Custom dictated that you never let a traveling rabbi pass through your town without helping him on his journey.

Personal relationships

Romans 15:24: ". . . when I have first enjoyed your company for a while." Paul wanted to hang around and enjoy his giving partners, rather than hurry off with their money!

· · ·

Like Paul, lead with your vision—not your financial need. Here is your outline for your next appeal:

- Your ministry passion
- Your promise (scriptural foundation)
- Your appeal
- Enjoy building a personal relationship

A few comments about articulating your ministry:

- Don't merely describe your mission organization, but explain it in such a way that you bond with the donor. A winsome missionary couple called on us to ask for support for their ministry in Africa. They described the ministry with polished brochures. But they didn't share their personal spiritual journeys—no personal war stories, and no vulnerability. It was institutional. Had we bonded better with this couple, we might have joined their team. But they missed an opportunity to elicit our personal friendship. Your donors must respect your mission agency, but they must also have an emotional bond.

- As you describe your vision, avoid missiology talk. The primary person who would enjoy your missiology is your organization's vice president of missions. But he is not the one you are appealing to! Prospective donors want to know if you are changing lives.
- Don't explain your ministry—illustrate it! Tell stories about real people in your work to help your listener become passionate about what you're trying to accomplish. (Storytelling is a learned skill. Find storytelling tips in chapter 16.)
- To be articulate, you must prepare! I joined a missionary for an in-home appeal. This older couple really liked "Bob," but they talked voluminously about their grandkids, their church, their car problems, their arthritis—really boring, but we tried to listen attentively. Finally, the wife leaned over, patted her husband's knee, and said, "Now, dear! These young men have not come to listen to us ramble."

  "You're right," he said. He straightened up in his chair, looked at Bob, and said, "Enough about us. Tell us, what do we need to know about your ministry?"

  Bob and I came back to life from our overstuffed chairs. I said to myself, *It's showtime! Bob will mesmerize them with his ministry dreams!* Bob began, "Well, uh, we are hoping to exegete the city and develop, uh, you know, uh, discipling units . . . uh . . . We're actually trying to facilitate an outreach to the E-3 segment . . . uh, using the Engel scale of, uh . . ."

  Bob fumbled the ball. Within two minutes the couple resumed telling about their grandkids. Bob was not prepared—nor mesmerizing. Ask yourself: (1) What is my opening line in my personal testimony? (2) What is my opening line in describing my vision?

According to the *Chronicle of Philanthropy*, more than 1.5 million organizations (of which one million are religious) are registered as 501(c)(3) charities in the United States. Plus, there are tons of nongovernmental organizations around the world. What makes your message unique? Why would giving partners choose you rather than a gazillion other organizations?

In fundraising you can do everything "right," but if your attitude is un-Christlike, what is the point? If we are recruiting giving partners to *advance the gospel*, we must *model the gospel*. Unfortunately, fundraisers have a sullied reputation—even Christian fundraisers.

Adopting the ten attitudes in this chapter honors Christ and relieves fundraising pressure. Which one or two is the Lord is speaking to you about? Bring them to Him in prayer over the next few days.

Developing Your Strategy

You are now ready to create your fundraising strategy, confident you are building on a biblical base. As you work through this section, jot down your ideas of tactics and the names of people who ought to hear your story. It is at this stage where the enemy of our souls will work to defeat you. Take your time. Pray step by step as you create your plan.

5

SIX BAD ASSUMPTIONS

ONE OF THE GOALS of this book is to help you develop a personal funding plan. But before you create your plan, it is time to identify bad assumptions that can derail you before you even start.

1. There's no money out there.

A missionary who had just returned to the United States for a new assignment was anxious about funding. He asked a well-known Christian businessman for advice and was told, "Don't stay in full-time ministry; there's no money out there."

At the same time, I was told, "There is no money in Africa." And in a similar theme, a ministry CEO publicly predicted, "America will continue to be the major source of funding for African, Asian, and Latin ministries." Is the sky falling in every place except America?

Consider the following:

- Americans give over $375 billion to charity annually, the greatest share going to religion.[1] But historically that is only 1 to 2 percent of Americans' gross income according to the IRS. "No money out there"?

- I asked an African friend whether there was money for ministry in Africa. He smiled and said, "The 'health and wealth' pastors certainly think so."
- In 2010 Brazil was the number-two sender of Protestant missionaries in the world, with 34,000 sent.
- Every entrepreneur in the solar system has his or her eyes on Asia.

Gordon-Conwell Theological Seminary estimates that 400,000 international missionaries were sent in 2010 (127,000 from America). Though some of them may be bivocational and many might not be fully funded, that still means money from many nations funded 273,000 non-American gospel-workers sent in 2010. There *is* money out there—even for you, no matter what your country is. I do not believe there is a shortage of money but only a shortage of great, well-articulated vision. If God calls you for Christian service, He will provide giving partners—even in a struggling economy.

But your potential donors might not know *how* to support you. Many only know how to give to a basket on Sunday morning or to needy relatives. Take time to show them how to support you in an ongoing way.

2. Meetings raise long-term money.

When missionaries think of fundraising, they often visualize a fellowship gathering where strangers come to see photos, eat apple pie or Kenyan samosas, and hear about missions. Magically, after two or three meetings, the missionary leaves for his assignment fully funded.

Sorry! Meetings rarely raise much long-term money. In a Navigator study of 736 people attending group fundraising meetings, only 9 percent pledged monthly (compared with 46 percent on face-to-face appeals). In Africa and Asia, missionary group meetings are well received; however, gifts are overwhelmingly "one-off"—similar to a Kenyan *harambee*, where the community comes together to help one who has suffered a tragedy.

How can such enthusiastic meetings inspire such meager monthly support? Maybe it is the universal "let George do it" syndrome. Imagine you are sitting in a group holding a plate of pie. Now the host hands you a pledge card. *Hmmm, monthly support? What if other expenses come up for me this year? I better keep my options open. I'll bet George sitting beside me will give. He looks well-off. Maybe I'll give a small one-time gift to show I'm supportive. Or maybe not. Wonder if they'll serve ice cream with this pie?*

Group meetings are a good way to thank donors, create enthusiasm for your vision, and recruit newcomers for your mailing list. But you won't raise much monthly support. Go face-to-face.

3. Churches are your best prospects.

In previous generations, mission-workers funded most of their budget from churches without needing to build deep, bonding relationships with them. But those days are gone. No longer does a church welcome you with open arms just because you are a missionary. Even if your kids sing at the Sunday service and the congregation applauds wildly, all you're likely to get is a small honorarium.

If you can develop a mutually beneficial relationship with a home church, you might find it providing 10 to 25 percent of your support from its mission budget. But you will be disappointed if you hope to recruit lots of churches with whom you have only a casual relationship.

A church might willingly support you if your ministry takes you to a region the church is keen on—perhaps a country that is in the news because of a disaster or because doors are opening miraculously, as Russia's did in 1992. And sometimes the church will support a local ministry because of proximity. Don't overlook that.

I don't mean to be negative on church support, but think soberly about how you spend your valuable fundraising time. Ask God to grant you favor with a home church or "sending church," but focus on individuals rather than churches. (More on churches in chapter 13.)

4. Mr. Big Bucks will raise it for you.

A missionary friend excitedly told me that a Christian businessman had agreed to raise his remaining support goal of $1,000 per month. The businessman told him, "Why should you have to do this money stuff? You're good at ministry; I'm good at money. I'll recruit a team for you!" Two years later the missionary lamented, "I have yet to see one dime!"

"Mr. Big Bucks" sounds promising, but don't hold your breath. Even though he is genuinely concerned, he doesn't know how to recruit a mission support team, and he doesn't have time to do it. The fact that he succeeded in business doesn't mean he can raise support.

But Mr. Big Bucks may be a gift from the Lord. First, train him in biblical fund-raising (do the Bible study found at scottmorton.net with him) and help him work *your* plan. If you struggle to find potential partners, ask him to introduce you to his friends one at a time—*after* he has made *his* giving commitment.

5. Raising support is like taking cough syrup.

Some missionaries view fundraising with the same enthusiasm as slurping down a tablespoon of green, syrupy cough medicine. But it doesn't have to be this way. Many mission-workers have come to enjoy fundraising. Several say, "After I got over the jitters of asking for an appointment, the meetings with potential partners went extremely well—even when they didn't give. I actually ministered to them." Raising personal support does more than bring in money. For example:

- *It forces you to grow professionally.* At the debriefing from his year in Russia, a missionary ("Joe") said, "Russia changed my life." I was surprised because at the outgoing training a year earlier, he was so noncommunicative and tentative that I doubted he would raise his funding. But here he was; he was different. "What changed your life?" I asked. "The culture, the Russian people?"

  "No," Joe replied, "the fundraising! It pushed me outside my comfort zone to share my heart with people. That stretched me, but it was good."
- *It enlarges your view of God.* When people who you didn't think cared one whit support you, you get the idea that God has big plans for you. Missionaries tell me they are humbled by generous gifts from unexpected people whom God has touched.
- *It expands the vision of your partners.* Sadly, many believers around the world do not have a God-sized vision for expanding the Kingdom. But when they read your interesting newsletters, their world vision grows. You help them think in Kingdom ways. And when they give, their hearts go along with their money (Matthew 6:21).
- *It gives you opportunities for ministry.* Reporting on your ministry with donors face-to-face may take thirty minutes, but they will share their lives with you for another two hours if you listen well. You can help them walk with Christ.
- *It helps you realize that God's hand is on you.* One discouraged veteran missionary was considering quitting, but he decided to give fundraising one last shot. Frankly, I was skeptical—he had endured so much pain. After returning from sixty days of face-to-face appointments he said excitedly, "God recalled me to ministry!"

  I asked, "How? Did he speak with you on a mountain? A dream perhaps?"

  "No," he said, "thirty-six friends committed monthly support! God recalled me through their yeses!"

If you cannot get over the cough syrup view of fundraising, something is wrong. Take time in the Bible study at scottmorton.net and talk with trusted friends. Let the Lord recall you in His marvelous ways. Choose to view fundraising as an adventure with God.

6. Visibility raises money.

Years ago a well-known evangelical leader confided that even though he was loved by thousands as a conference speaker, his funding was decreasing. Highly visible with the Christian public, he had over a thousand people on his mailing list—and he sent creative, interesting letters.

"What is wrong?" he asked. "Our funding keeps going down even though I am speaking more and more."

Some organizations hope to raise funds through attractive websites, frequent emails, and expensive annual reports. They seek to raise *awareness*. Their communication pieces may include a "soft ask," but they do not raise serious money because

- money does *not* follow visibility and
- money does *not* follow information.

Visibility and information don't raise money—they *cost* money. People don't give merely because they are *aware* of you. They do not go to bed at night burdened by your lack of support. They are thinking about *Seinfeld* reruns or worried about their kids' schooling or how to get their teenaged daughter to a nunnery. Even though they love you, they will not support you unless they are *asked to make a stewardship decision*. The bottom line: You must inform and *ask*.

A former mentor, Navigator Chuck Singletary, humorously misquotes James 4:2 from the King James Bible: "Ye have not because ye *phone* not!"

Now that you know what to avoid, you are ready to develop your funding strategy.

6

THREE BENCHMARKS FOR AN EFFECTIVE STRATEGY

MANY GOSPEL-WORKERS TELL ME their situation is unique; "normal fundraising" won't work for them. True, every situation is unique, but the basics of biblical fundraising must not be tossed aside.

We begin with this classic pyramid diagram showing four categories of people who are needed for your mailing list.

- *Anchor donors* give large amounts, usually annually rather than monthly. Ask each one face-to-face for 5, 10, or 15 percent of your goal. Because not all of them will say yes (or give what you ask for), you'll need five to ten anchor donors. Anchor donors may not be needed for short-term assignments, but as your budget grows, anchor donors are essential to reach full funding.
- *Monthly donors* are the heart of your giving team. Gifts need not be large, just faithful. Teach them to give monthly if they have no history of it. Half or more of your support should come from monthly partners.
- *One-off or sporadic donors* give now and then. Be sure to thank each one immediately. Move them up on the pyramid by inviting them to join your monthly or anchor team over time.
- *Non-donors on your mailing list* are friends and contacts who have not yet given or are deeply lapsed givers. They receive your mailings and are being cultivated to give in the future. Invite them to start support at least once a year. Some may never give—that's fine.

Special note for short-term assignment workers: Much of your support will likely come from the one-off or sporadic group—and that's okay. Think of this as your "Kickstarter group." Many will give once (even without a face-to-face meeting) to encourage you in your ministry. But if you go into a second or third year of service, you will need to focus more on monthly and anchor partners.

Now imagine your giving and nongiving friends marching upward on the pyramid. Many donors will start at the lower section, but as they embrace you and your ministry more, they will move up to monthly giving; eventually a few may become anchor donors. Some will not move up, but many will. This gives you a framework for sorting out what to do next in your fundraising year by year.

Using the giving pyramid as our guide, let's examine three benchmarks common to fully funded mission-workers.

1. Concentrate on face-to-face appeals.

Mass appeals, such as email blasts or Kickstarter campaigns, generate one-time gifts, but for monthly support, you'll do much better going face-to-face.

The chart below reflects a study conducted before Mark Zuckerberg was in high school. Nonetheless, based on my interviews with gospel-workers from many cultures, the face-to-face yes-rate percentages are even higher today. In some countries, 80–90 percent of people are saying yes to face-to-face appeals.

BASELINE STUDY OF AMERICAN NAVIGATOR STAFF (7,401 APPEALS MADE IN 1992)

Type of Appeal	"Yes" (monthly support)	"Yes" (cash or annual gift)	Total
Face-to-face	46%	14%	60%
Phone/letter combo*	27%	18%	45%
Personal letter*	14%	18%	32%
Group meeting	9%	11%	20%

*Personal hard-copy letter to specific friends—not strangers

Note that the total face-to-face yes-rate of 60 percent outshines other types of funding appeals. The three less personal types of appeals (phone, letter, and group meeting) generated results, but not nearly as high as face-to-face interaction. The letter/phone combination appeal produced a 45 percent yes-rate—not bad. But keep in mind those appeals were to well-known acquaintances and friends. Otherwise that yes-rate would have been much lower.

Group meetings are great for building enthusiasm for your mission, but only 9 percent of meeting attenders agreed to monthly support.

Mass-mailing appeals are not included in the chart, but gospel-workers report that mass-mail appeals generate almost zero responses for monthly support, and only 10–15 percent of them generate one-off cash gifts.

Face-to-face must be at the heart of your funding plan. This is a no-brainer!

Now, what about social media? I do not have survey data on the yes-rate for social media, but having counseled gospel-workers from many cultures, I can tell you that nothing comes close to the 60 percent yes-rate of face-to-face appeals. Perhaps Skype would approach it, but I have no data. I have tracked email appeals informally and find that only 1–2 percent say yes to monthly or annual support—and that is often a follow-up to a personal encounter.

Too many of us want fundraising to be short and painless. But face-to-face appeals are time consuming. As I said in the introduction, we are building and blessing giving partners, not merely collecting money. The bond you establish while sitting in your potential giving partner's home, trying to ignore their nervous cat and their kids spilling Kool-Aid on you, lasts a lifetime.

Sometimes missionaries say, "I've spent hours trying to raise support, but it hasn't worked. Maybe I'm not called to ministry."

Answer: In all your funding work, how many face-to-face appointments did you have? Most of the gospel-workers who are discouraged in fundraising have not done many face-to-face appeals. Before you give up, set five more face-to-face appointments! Then reevaluate. Don't be too quick to conclude that God is not calling you.

2. Build a wide mailing list.

My coworker Rob Mahon from Albuquerque says humorously that the secret to successful fundraising is found in the children's chorus "Deep and Wide":

Deep and wide, deep and wide
There's a fountain flowing deep and wide.

Rob reminds us that Jesus had a deep personal ministry with a few—the three, the Twelve, the seventy, the 120 in the upper room—but he also had a wide public ministry with the crowds. Deep *and* wide.

Rob's deep-and-wide strategy ensures you will never run out of prospective givers! Genuinely make acquaintances with as many people as you can, and add them to your mailing list. As they hear more and more about your vision, they will one day gladly hear your appeal for support.

Well-written newsletters are your spokesperson to stimulate interest in your vision. As you tell your story to a wider and wider audience, you are developing the interest of more and more people who might later give. Even if they never give, you have ministered to them through your newsletters. In 2008 my friends at Mission Aviation Fellowship (MAF) concluded an informal study of their missionaries. Among other findings were the following statistics:

- Ninety-one missionaries with mailing lists averaging 362 people received 95 percent of budget.
- Eighty missionaries with mailing lists averaging 610 received 103 percent of their budget.

That's not a huge difference—although it means the difference between being below and above budget. That's important. But here is what got my attention from their study. Their mailing list sizes are large. Many gospel-workers who are struggling have eighty or 120 people on their mailing lists. That is too small. Shoot for at least two hundred people—four hundred if you are married.

Once I added a couple to our mailing list whom we did not know well—they were practically strangers. For three years they received our newsletters (three to four times per year). Twice I sent a personal, handwritten letter, and we stopped once at their home for a brief visit. After three years we needed to raise additional support. I phoned to ask for an appointment, but they were going to be out of town. On the spot I explained why I wanted to visit and asked whether I could send a follow-up letter. Fine. Within a few days we received their commitment of $60 a month. I couldn't have made an appeal if I hadn't added them to our mailing list three years earlier.

A second reason for a large mailing list: You never know whom God has appointed to share in your support. Missionaries testify, "We never dreamed 'Miss Q' would support us." Because it is impossible to predict who will support you, let as many as possible be aware of your ministry.

I can hear you saying, "I'm maxed out on relationships now!" Remember, you are not doing intensive ministry to 98 percent of your mailing list. Also, it may be that you need to spend more time in your "wide" ministry. I'm not asking you to work harder, just differently.

To expand your mailing list, don't ask, *Would this person give?* Wrong question! Ask yourself, *Would this person glance at my newsletter?*

So how do you add people to your mailing list?

- Have a sign-up list at conferences or seminars.
- Seek friends outside your mission agency.
- Ask casual acquaintances whether you could have the privilege of adding them.
- After church, take an acquaintance for coffee.
- Serve in your church, especially teaching adult classes.

This is how I do it—I say to a new friend, "I've enjoyed our visit. Can we stay in touch? We send a newsletter four times a year that tells about God's work in our ministry. I think you might enjoy it. I would love to send it to you."

To an old friend: "I don't think I have been sending you our newsletter about our ministry. That's my mistake. I'd love for you to hear what God is doing—it's exciting. May I send it to you four times a year?"

Some missionaries purge their mailing lists to cut cost and clutter. This is not wise. Do you do that in evangelism?

However, sometimes a name grows cold, and you can't remember who they are. Try this: Track them down on Facebook. Or phone them. Politely give them a chance to "unsubscribe," but chances are you will reenergize a friendship!

Over the years I was tempted to remove two names we never heard from. But I stuck to my conviction to remove people only if (1) they asked or (2) they died. These two did neither! Last December, in response to our year-end mailing, we received gifts from both! Wow! I thought they didn't care. Now we are reconnecting with these old but silent friends.

Jesus limited the number of His close disciples but *not* His financial benefactors. Luke 8:2-3 names three women who supported Jesus: Mary, Joanna, and Susanna. Then it says, "*Many others* who were contributing to their support" (emphasis added). *Many others!*

You have *intensive* (deep) ministry with a few, but you also need *extensive* (wide) ministry to "many others." Deep and wide!

3. You must ask.

A gospel-worker was puzzled about his lack of support because he seemed to be doing everything right—he wrote good letters, he was articulate, and he was even a good listener. "I talk about my budget all the time!" he said.

Finally it came out. Though he talked about his budget, he was not asking, nor was he giving a commitment card to potential donors. Talking about money is not the same as asking.

We tend to idealize those ministries in which the money is supplied without asking—"God did it!" we say. But when people give in response to our halting appeals, is that any less God's doing? Many veteran missionaries are silently waiting for those dozens they've led to Christ, those dozens who have attended their Bible studies, those dozens with whom they've served on church committees to start giving. But the giving won't start until these missionaries *ask* in a meaningful way.

Automobile pioneer Henry Ford once purchased a huge life-insurance policy from a man he hardly knew. Ford's close friend, a life-insurance agent, stormed into Ford's office and demanded, "Henry, why didn't you buy that policy from me? We've been friends for years!"

Ford's reply: "You never asked me."

Missionaries are headed for disappointment if they assume that ministry success guarantees full funding. Money doesn't always follow ministry—money follows asking!

A missionary stayed overnight in the home of a couple from our Sunday school class. I inquired, "Does your missionary friend need financial support?"

The couple glanced at each other. "We suppose he does. He's returning to Africa for a new assignment."

"Are you supporting him?" I asked.

"No, we're not," they replied.

"So you know your missionary friend needs support, but you're not giving?" I pressed. "Why not?"

My friends smiled awkwardly and said, "Because he didn't ask."

"Osmosis" fundraising—standing close to donors but not asking—doesn't work. People can't read your mind. You must ask—even your friends!

Here's a classic story about asking. In 1984 a thirteen-year-old New York girl named Markita Andrews sold 25,000 boxes of Girl Scout cookies. Hearing of her incredible success, Disney Productions featured her in a sales training film, and IBM flew her around the country to address its sales force.

Here's what this eighth grader said: "You can't just chat; you have to ask for an order!"[1] I'm not suggesting that raising support is like selling Girl Scout cookies, but the principle of asking for a decision instead of hoping or hinting certainly applies.

Your time is too valuable to waste doing unwise fundraising. Put these three benchmarks into your funding plan.

7

SOCIAL MEDIA AND EMAIL IN FUNDRAISING

Cake or Frosting?

OKAY, BIG QUESTION: If Jesus were with us today (instead of two thousand years ago), would He use social media? Let's come back to this question at the end of the chapter.

Technology changes so rapidly that what I write now is old-school even before my second draft. Social media that is wildly popular today falls from favor when a new electronic star is born. But you needn't be on the bleeding edge of technology to make it work for you. Here are five suggestions for using social media and email in fundraising and donor ministry.

1. Embrace the unique power of social media.

Social media enables you to broaden your base of potential donors and communicate instantly and easily. Here's how:

- *Broaden your base of potential donors.* A frequent obstacle many missionaries face is a small contact list. Social media helps you reconnect with old friends and develop "contacts" into friends. A few years ago a missionary candidate burst into tears because she was "completely out of contacts." But she had six hundred Facebook friends. Hmmm.

- *Instant communication.* Within seconds your ministry project can be propelled through the solar system. And within seconds you can receive responses such as "Yes, I will pray for you!" or "Yes, I want to give!"
- *Easy communication.* Sending prayer updates with snappy photos about your ministry has never been easier—even instantly sending video of the Bible study happening right now. But be careful about confidentiality. Do your Bible study members want their faces transmitted through the solar system? Also, regarding travel, be careful about broadcasting dates when your house will be empty.

2. Understand the limits of social media.

Below is the classic ladder of communications effectiveness from the Harvard Business School. This chart does not describe fundraising communications specifically but communications effectiveness in general. Social media is not listed because this diagram was created before social media developed. I've penciled in where I think social media fits on this chart. Where would you rank social media?

I place social media applications in the middle of the chart with Skype (and similar apps) higher not because of research but because Skype is more emotionally compelling.

LADDER OF COMMUNICATION EFFECTIVENESS

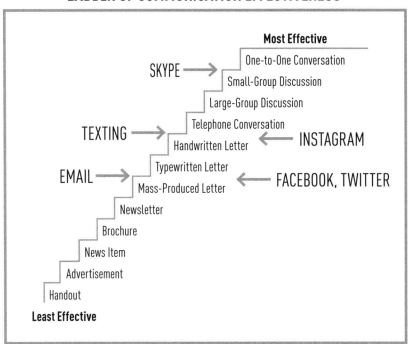

Just because a communication tool is fast or new doesn't mean it makes a deep impression. Yesterday I put up some "likes" on Facebook and thought briefly about the people involved. Briefly! Today I can't even remember who or what I "liked." But I clearly remember whom I met face-to-face yesterday. For fundraising and deepening friendships, face-to-face continues to be most effective.

What about email? I was director of The Navigators' development department when email became popular. Our hopes soared as we anticipated sending thousands of personal letters *for free*—as opposed to expensive hard-copy letters. We soon found out that open rates for religious organizations averaged 27 percent. But the percentage of readers actually sending gifts is extremely low. According to a report by Nancy Schwartz, the yes-rate for email appeals is .06 percent—this means that in an email blast of 10,000, only six would send a gift.[1] Other reports show similar results—all less than 1 percent. Studies are also being done now to show that giving increases when various media intersect—such as a Facebook post referring to a YouTube video that in turn refers to an email appeal. Experiment with several types of communications, but understand the limits of what you can expect.

What do these limits of social media mean for your fundraising? First, the bad news. Raising *monthly* support via social media or email is not effective—except possibly for Skype. Committing to monthly support is a big decision; an email or Facebook post asking for monthly support is a bridge too far.

Exceptions occur. Some missionaries tell me excitedly about new monthly donors they recruited by "email only!" But upon investigation, their three or four email yeses come from close friends or family who would have supported them anyway. And I suspect that the size of each commitment is lower than it would have been with a face-to-face visit. And what about bonding with the donor? In a face-to-face appeal you deepen your relationship because it is a physical dialogue.

Video conferencing is an unknown in funding, but it has huge potential to recruit both monthly and anchor partners. When gospel-workers living overseas or far from home run into funding shortfalls, I recommend they Skype with potential donors instead of waiting to fundraise when they return home. The advantage of Skype (and similar apps) is emotion—the donor sees the missionary face-to-face, albeit electronically. But the Skype interaction must be a dialogue in which the missionary can listen and minister to the donor. Try it! You will be a pioneer. At this date I know of no funding data collected for Skype appeals. Make something happen!

Now the good news! Readers will respond to *one-off* projects (not monthly support) via electronic media. For example, for fifteen years Craig Parker, a Navigator in Boston, has sent email appeals for special projects—including a student trip to Croatia. His goal was $5,000. Gifts were sent to The Navigators directly. His results:

- Appeal sent to 1,137 email addresses (contacts built up over twenty-five years): 77 bounces and no opt-outs, resulting in 1,060 net addresses.
- Ninety-six responded with a gift—a 9 percent response! This is huge for an email appeal, since the averages nationally are less than 1 percent!
- Total given was $10,097.
- Average gift: $105. Excellent!
- No criticism from readers.

Craig's appeal required scrolling, but there were no distracting attachments to open. It included student photos and a "thermometer" to gauge progress. He traditionally asks for no more than $20–$25 to attract new and younger donors.

Craig's responses are much higher than institutional mailings because he has become well connected to his mailing list friends over many years. I know Craig is grateful to the Lord for his email funding results. The gospel advanced.

Social media can give a huge assist to your funding efforts, but it has huge limits as well. It is not a substitute for the basics of fundraising. I encourage you to try some creative strategies, as Craig Parker has done. But I also know that this is the frosting—not the cake—of Craig's fundraising! He has a solid donor base built up by face-to-face appeals.

3. Crowdfunding sites recruit new giving partners for start-stop projects.

In 2013 crowdfunding raised $3 billion through websites such as Kickstarter, Indiegogo, and GoFundMe. According to Philanthropy.com, crowdfunding will raise $93 billion by 2025.

Gospel-workers look with envy at the millions raised for someone's "garage project" or for digging a well in Africa to provide clean water. Because they are start-stop projects that capture donors' imaginations, sites devoted to these projects bring tons of money from strangers in a short time.

Today I cruised a crowdfunding website and found a for-profit appeal with a goal of only $350 to publish a calendar featuring models wearing old-fashioned clothing. I also found a newly invented bicycle bell that raised $331,938 from 5,827 backers in two months—16.5 times the $20,000 goal. Crowdfunding works! But realize that crowdfunding donors are in the bottom part of the partner-development pyramid: one-off or sporadic donors. Can you move them up?

For ministry, the best crowdfunding projects are those that stimulate donors' imaginations and provide practical solutions to help one desperate person going through an emergency. Donors visualize an impoverished village child filling his jar with clean water that gurgles from a pipe in a dusty village square. Or they visualize helping a single mom to complete her education. The project must be practical, emotionally compelling, and credibly presented.

Crowdfunding sites have the advantage of attracting strangers to your ministry— potential donors you would never find. "Web-ites" from around the world cruise giving websites every day, looking for worthy projects.

Should you use crowdfunding? Keep the following realities in mind:

- Crowdfunding promoters take a fee—as high as 20 percent.
- Money does not go directly to your ministry; it goes to the promoter via the website and then to you.
- Response is low. One I checked today showed a response rate of .001—one out of 1,000. At that rate, fifty thousand website cruisers would be needed to raise $2,500 (fifty donors each giving an average of $50).
- You may not be given the names of those who gave, or you may be charged an additional fee.
- There is no tax benefit for the donor (mainly in the US).

Let's compare these findings with Craig Parker's appeals. One year he gave readers the option of sending him gifts either through The Navigators or through GoFundMe. Results:

- Sent to 1,317 people, mostly from his Navigator mailing list.
- Of these people, 141 gave through The Navigators (a 10.7 percent response). Outstanding.
- The total given that way was $37,212—an average gift of $264. Excellent.
- An additional 79 (6 percent) gave through the GoFundMe link for a total of $7,393—an average gift of $94.
- GoFundMe charged 5 percent and gave him the names of the donors.

The GoFundMe option stimulated seventy-four additional readers to give. Wonderful, even though the average gift was smaller ($94 compared with $264). Readers like choices. In Craig's words, "I have used this approach [email or GoFundMe] annually for fifteen years—for spring-break trips, conference scholarships, and summer trips—and have always met my goal. The most I have ever asked for is $25. I usually just ask for $20."

One reason Craig gets such positive results is that he has built up a loyal mailing list over twenty-five years. And he is passionate about reaching students. That lies behind his success. You may not receive the same great results, but I encourage you to experiment in funding your passion.

4. Social media plays an important role in your funding strategy—but not the major role.

Despite all the good social media can do in funding, don't be naive. Social media alone cannot carry the weight of your funding or communication strategy. Don't ask social media to do something it is not designed to do. In my seminars I tell gospel-workers that social media is only the frosting; hard copy is the cake. A hard-copy letter will sooner or later be read, but email is easy to delete! You have social media friends who say they "never read hard copy," but are they donors?

My twentysomething tech-whiz assistant Katie says, "Move people offline as soon as possible to your hard-copy newsletter, the phone, and face-to-face." She also suggests seeking phone numbers and postal addresses from your social-media friends to build more permanent friendships.

Human interaction is still at the top of the communication effectiveness chart. To ask for an important decision, choose face-to-face where you can read body language and engage in dialogue. Did you propose to your spouse via Facebook?

Don't overdo it. A friend received twelve reminders on April 15 (the day taxes are due in America) about a social-media funding campaign—twelve! Ridiculous!

5. Obey time-tested rules for emailed ministry newsletters.

Most of the guidelines for hard-copy newsletters apply to social media generally. Here are some reminders.

- Do not send your letter as an attachment. Readers promise themselves they will "open it later"—which is never. Put your letter in the body of the email.
- Keep it short. Don't make the reader scroll constantly.
- Capture the value of social media by telling short, straight-from-the-battle

stories. For example: "I just got back from a Bible study with three nonbelievers—listen to what George said . . ."

- Include a photo of you in action. And write a one-sentence caption under the photo—not just "Bob and me with the dog." Readers are in a hurry, but they will glance at the photo and read the caption.
- Use a service like MailChimp. They supply templates you can easily master to create an attractive letter. Their metric reports tell you instantly who opens your letter.
- Utilize the secret of one: one topic, one photo, one prayer request, one story. A newsletter is not a list of your activities—that's for your mom.
- Don't overdo it! How do you like those constant senders?
- Don't mention money except to say thank you. But once or twice a year, send an unapologetic appeal for your ministry via both hard copy (see chapter 14) and social media—particularly email.
- Include your mission logo and contact information clearly.

How often should you send email newsletters? I suggest four to six hard-copy letters per year, plus email blasts for prayer requests and sharing on-the-spot news. That could be twelve connects or more per year—plus whatever you do on other social media.

Is this a generational thing—older people prefer hard copy but younger people prefer electronic? Not always. A missionary friend in the UK told me of a twenty-something donor who is inundated with social media. He "longs to hold a 'real letter' in his hands." Katie says the same. "I delete tons of stuff on email, but a personal letter lying on my kitchen counter? Sooner or later I will seriously read it. It does not go to my trash bin."

But it *is* a generational thing regarding how younger donors give. Most want to give online—not by writing checks.

• • •

Let's go back to the question: Would Jesus use social media?

Yes! And no! Yes—because God loves to communicate. In John's Gospel, Jesus is called the Word—a message from heaven! Can you imagine the number of Twitter followers Jesus would have picked up after turning water into wine? And how many "likes" He would have elicited for healing the man born blind? Would He have sent an e-vite to Zacchaeus for lunch?

Like today's social media, Jesus had intriguing ways of communicating. He wrote in the dust during the interrogation of the woman taken in adultery. He plastered a muddy mixture over a blind man's eyes. And He told stories—*short* stories.

But would Jesus have taken selfies while walking on water or feeding the five thousand? I think not. Unfortunately, social media is often used to promote self-accomplishment or how bright your kids are or what you are having for lunch.

Jesus also touched people *physically*—Facebook can't do that. Jesus spoke with emotions of anger, frustration, and even humor. One-hundred-forty Twitter characters can't do that. Jesus bonded with his giving partners by *being with them physically* (Luke 8:1-3). You can tweet all day and still be lonely. Mark 3:14 sums it up: "And He appointed twelve, so that they would be *with Him* and that He could send them out to preach" (emphasis added).

With Him! Physically with Him! Physical presence increases the joys and heartaches of relationships—and we were created for relationships, not chat rooms. Social media can assist, but it cannot substitute. The late Johnny Cash summarized it in song: "Flesh and blood need flesh and blood."[2]

At the risk of sounding old school, I must warn you about obsessing about social media. Social media cannot bring you the hoped-for joys of relationship, nor does it prevent loneliness. It allows you to live in a narcissistic world revolving around getting "likes." It undermines your self-esteem if your kids or cats aren't as smart or cute as your friends' kids and cats. Can you leave your phone alone for two hours?

In the popular newspaper cartoon *Dilbert*, Dilbert is asked how many Facebook friends he has. "Seven," he replies. Then he is asked, "Have you ever invited these people to your house?" Dilbert's answer reveals social media's destructive blind spot. "Why would I want to do that?" he answers.

Indeed. Social media is the frosting—not the cake.

8

HOW TO SET YOUR FUNDRAISING STRATEGY

AT LAST! You've made it to the "meat and potatoes" of fundraising—writing out your fundraising strategy on paper. Having it on your computer is fine but not enough. Without the plan written on paper staring back at you, you will postpone, postpone, postpone.

And the plan must fit *you*. Just as David did not fit into Saul's armor, do not copy someone else's plan. Get your strategy from the Lord. Following these six steps will help you develop a wise strategy.

Note: For a short-term mission strategy, go directly to chapter 20. The suggestions here are for longer-term gospel-workers.

1. Discover your current reality.

"Know well the condition of your flocks" (Proverbs 27:23). I'm amazed at the number of missionaries who don't know how many donors they have or the exact amount of their monthly budget.

I was helping a missionary develop his funding strategy, but we weren't getting anywhere. He nodded in agreement to my suggestions, but mostly he was staring blankly. I felt like I was talking to a BMW dealer about trading in a Volkswagen hippie van. Finally I asked, "You haven't put much time into studying your names, have you?"

"No, I haven't," he confessed awkwardly. So I assigned him three hours to study his list and pray through his names one by one to find his top twenty-five. Three hours later he returned brimming with confidence—and a workable plan! In only three hours he went from uncertainty to confidence about becoming fully funded.

Knowing the "state of your flock" takes time. Can you answer these questions?

- How much donor income have you received over the past twelve months?
  $_____
- What is your monthly donor base average? $_____
- In the past twelve months how many people gave monthly? _____ Once or twice? _____
- What was the average monthly gift size for monthly donors? $_____
- What is your total budget (exactly)? $_____
- How much of that is your salary (personal allowance)? $_____
- How many donors have given at least once in the past thirty-six months?
  _____
- In the past thirty-six months, which donors made monthly pledges but are not following through (or gave once or twice and stopped)? _____
- How much (exactly) do you need to raise? (This is your "holy number"— the answer you give when people ask, "How much do you need to raise?")
  $_____

In analyzing your data, be patient—it is not a waste of time. Studying your current reality makes it easier to develop your plan. When you do this analysis thoroughly, you will discover ideas for what to do next.

2. Determine your fundraising goal prayerfully.

Please don't dishonor Christ by merely picking a funding goal out of the air: "Oh, we need about $1,000." How much do you need *exactly*? If you are fuzzy about your goal, you will not sound credible to donors. No one will take you seriously, not even the Lord.

Determine your funding goal on the chart below. If your mission agency has already determined these figures, filling this worksheet is easy. If, on the other hand, your agency lets you determine your budget (with their approval, I hope), go to scottmorton.net to find a worksheet for both personal allowances and ministry costs. This takes work, but it is necessary.

If the amount you need to raise (your holy number) seems overwhelming, resist the temptation to lower it; let the holy number sit for a couple days and review it with your supervisor and, if you're married, with your spouse (obviously). Don't be alone in your funding goal.

DETERMINING YOUR MONTHLY FUNDRAISING GOAL

Your monthly budget, as approved by your mission agency (cash projects not included). All figures are monthly. Use your own local currency.

	First Draft	Adjusted
A. Salary/Living Allowance	$ _____	$ _____
B. Ministry (Entertain, Travel, etc)	$ _____	$ _____
C. Benefits (Insurance, Pension, etc)	$ _____	$ _____
D. Administrative Charges	$ _____	$ _____
E. Other	$ _____	$ _____
F. Total Monthly Budget	$ _____	$ _____
G. Current Monthly Donor Base Average	$ _____	$ _____
H. Monthly Goal (Line F minus line G)	$ _____ (Your holy number!)	$ _____

In the "First Draft" column, insert your first-draft amount for each line item. Make adjustments in the right column after reviewing with your spouse or a friend and supervisor. Your ministry may use slightly different terms for each line item.

Feel free to lower your salary line if you have outside income. Do *not* reduce your total simply to avoid raising more support.

Your ministry might preset your budget, in which case this budgeting exercise is not needed. But to be a good steward, you ought to create a personal household budget. Without a personal household budget, you'll stop raising support at 80 percent because you somehow manage to pay your bills. You will assume you have enough, but you'll have no margin, and you won't be able to save.

In fact, I hope this doesn't discourage you, but now I am going to recommend that you *add another 10 percent* to the funding goal you have been working on. Create a 10 percent margin. Here's why:

- Some giving partners will not follow through even though they pledged to support you in all sincerity.

- A few monthly partners will not give every month.
- You will experience emergencies and additional costs that you or your agency could not anticipate.
- With margin in finances you can be more generous and spontaneous.

To create your salary–personal allowance budget, download a sample detailed budget worksheet at scottmorton.net. Writing cash appeals is covered in chapter 14. List "one-time" cash projects here.

One-Time Cash Projects		
Project Description	Amount Needed	Due By
_____	_____	_____
_____	_____	_____

Tips on budgeting:

- If you don't believe every dollar is needed, you will not seriously try to raise it. But if you believe that every dollar on your budget is necessary (including savings), you'll work to raise it all.
- Don't guesstimate budget amounts. Look at last year's expenses and set realistic amounts based on history, not guesswork.
- Does your budget include money set aside for a vacation, family fun, or new furniture? Single guys, there are other foods besides ramen noodles!

Am I overemphasizing budgeting? No! Good fundraising starts with knowing exactly how much you need to raise. But more importantly, please understand that you are a *steward* before you are a fundraiser. Luke 16:11 warns, "If you have not been faithful in the use of unrighteous wealth, who will entrust the true riches to you?"

3. Determine how many giving partners you'll need.

To determine how many giving partners you'll need, simply divide your holy number (line H in the budget chart on page 83) by your current average monthly gift size.

For example, if your average monthly gift is $50 and your holy number is $1,250, divide $1,250 by $50, yielding 25 additional donors at $50 each. If you feel future average gifts will be $75 per month, then divide $1,250 by $75. You'll need 17 new donors at $75 monthly to hit your holy number. Got it?

If you can secure some $100- to $200-per-month partners and a few annual commitments of $2,000 to $5,000, you will not need as many donors.

How many face-to-face appointments will be needed to recruit twenty-five new monthly donors? About fifty; based on my funding experience in many cultures, about half of potential donors say yes to face-to-face appeals.

Raising cash for a start-up or one-time project is easier than generating monthly support. Build your monthly base first. (Cash appeals are dealt with in chapter 14.)

4. Identify your top prospective givers.

How do you find fifty potential partners to meet for appointments? Here's where missionaries often lose common sense. Instead of considering people they already know, they search for referrals with strangers. But this is unneeded extra work. Why look to strangers when your friends and acquaintances will gladly hear your story? Start with those you know. Try referrals only after you've exhausted your own contacts.

Where to start? With your mailing list. Here is a discipline I follow:

- I prayerfully browse through the names on my mailing list, person by person, asking the Lord to impress upon me which people I ought to visit. My mailing list has seven hundred entries. That's right—seven hundred. This is where a large mailing list pays off. (If you have only a few names on your mailing list, browse through your cell phone and Facebook directories. If you still feel you have no one to go to, review the mailing list chart on page 86.)
- As I review the names one by one, I ask, "Would this person be willing to hear my story of ministry?" The question is subjective, but I'll pull out a few names and transfer them to my top-twenty-five worksheet, going beyond twenty-five as needed. Don't ask, "Would this person give?" That's the wrong question. Your role is to give them an opportunity to hear about your calling and let them decide whether to support it.
- After I have pulled out up to seventy-five names, I review the names again, asking God for wisdom on which ones to connect with first.

Here's how this process worked with Joe, a discouraged missionary who took me to lunch because he thought he was out of contacts. "I need referrals," he lamented. His emotions were winning the day. Over his Philly sandwich Joe and I filled out the chart on page 86. (Jot in your own numbers beside Joe's.)

Mailing List Chart		
	Joe	**You**
Total number on general (widest) mailing list:	247	____
Minus current monthly donors:	−25	____
Minus annual or consistent donors:	−15	____
Minus nonbelievers:	−10	____
Minus family members:	−15	____
Minus other missionaries:	−25	____
Minus people who don't like you!	−5	____
Minus those you've asked face-to-face in past two years:	−15	____
Subtotal:	−110	____
Subtract subtotal from mailing list total:	137	____

To his surprise, Joe found 137 friends on his mailing list who had not heard his story face-to-face in the past three years! They had received appeals through email and hard copy, but Joe admitted, "I guess they didn't take those seriously."

If you're just starting out in missions, then nearly everyone on your mailing list is a candidate. If you invited them face-to-face to give years ago, start again! They will welcome you. The late Ron Nikkaido, a Canadian missionary, said, "I want to give every person on my mailing list the privilege of saying no to my face." Most said yes when Ron visited them!

Write down the names of the friends and acquaintances to whom you hope to appeal. You can do this on a computer spreadsheet, but you'll save time if you transfer your prospects to the "Top 25 Potential Partners" worksheet at scottmorton.net. Seeing your top twenty-five in one place on a piece of paper makes the job seem manageable.

To recap: Don't ask, "Who would be willing to give?" Ask instead, "Who would be willing to hear my story?"

5. Plot your prospective donors on a map.

After you've written down each *who* on your top twenty-five list, the next step is to figure out *where* they are located. It is difficult to schedule your calendar until you've identified where your top candidates live. Plot them on a map.

A cluster of two or three in one area is certainly worth a trip. One anchor donor possibility (someone who can give $5,000 to $10,000 or 10 to 15 percent of your budget or more) is worth a trip.

6. Draft your action plan.

By now you have

- clarified your holy number,
- discovered the number of donors you'll need,
- identified your top twenty-five (or fifty or more), and
- plotted them on a map.

It is time to draft your action plan. Download and print the financial appeal action plan from scottmorton.net.

The first draft of your action plan needn't be perfect. Analyze your plan using the six checkpoints from this chapter. I include the plan on page 88 so you can more easily identify actions to take having just read through the explanations above.

FINANCIAL APPEAL ACTION PLAN

Be specific!

Amount to Raise (Holy Number) $_____ Monthly $_____ Additional Cash

Due by _____

1. Current number on Mailing List: _____ Increase to _____total by _____(date)

I will increase my mailing list through these actions:

- _____
- _____

2. I will appeal to the following donors for anchor gifts.

An anchor gift would be 5–10 percent of your total monthly budget. Anchor donors could include a few current donors increasing their giving significantly. Anchor donors usually prefer to give annually rather than monthly.

Name of potential anchor donor	Location	Amount to ask	By this date
_____	_____	$_____	_____
_____	_____	_____	_____
_____	_____	_____	_____
_____	_____	_____	_____
_____	_____	_____	_____
_____	_____	_____	_____
_____	_____	_____	_____
_____	_____	_____	_____
_____	_____	_____	_____
_____	_____	_____	_____
_____	_____	_____	_____

3. I will make _____ face-to-face appeals (top twenty-five).
4. I will make _____ letter/phone/Skype appeals (people on top twenty-five who are impossible to visit in person).
5. I will invite _____ current donors (listed below) to increase support.

_____ _____ _____
_____ _____ _____

6. If needed, I will network with _____ (a helpful donor friend) and ask them to arrange appointments for me to appeal to friends of theirs.
7. Other _____
8. I will trust the following people to start giving through "prayer alone."

_____ _____

9. I will send a weekly report to my fundraising coach (name: _____), who will hold me accountable to work my funding plan.

Signed: _____ Today's Date: _____

Signed by fundraising sponsor: _____

Effectively and Respectfully Asking

If you Google "fundraising asking" you will find tons of material from tons of experts such as "Making your ask irresistible," "Asking without losing your friends," or "How to make a big, fat fundraising ask." It's overwhelming. In my seminars, questions about asking predominate. But despite the curiosity, asking is not a mystery—it includes four parts. First, you identify whom you will ask; second, you set an appointment, usually with a phone call (that is the scariest part). Step three—the ask itself—is almost a joy. And the fourth part is following up to find out the decision of the potential partner.

But we must not reduce asking to a formula. Your relationship with potential donors is the unknown. If you follow these tried-and-true basics in the next six chapters, I am certain you will find asking a joy.

9
HOW TO ASK

"ASKING" IS A MYSTERY for many gospel-workers. The many webinars and books devoted to helping leaders learn to ask show that it is an area of uncertainty. Here are five simple tips to keep you from overthinking this important step in the fundraising process.

1. Ask for one thing.

A missionary returned to the United States and launched a support-raising campaign for his new ministry assignment. He secured sixty-three personal appointments from friends on his mailing list—many who had given one-off gifts previously. But only twelve pledged monthly. Why so few?

After many questions, I finally asked, "What do you say when you make your appeal?"

He said, "I give three choices: monthly support, a cash gift, or prayer. Most choose prayer!"

Bingo—too many choices! Ask for *one thing*. What exactly do you want the donor to do?

We've already learned this lesson in evangelism. There comes a time to ask a seeker, "Will you receive Jesus Christ?" We don't also ask, "And will you join my church? And will you stop smoking?" Give one choice.

2. Slow down! Make sure you have their attention. Be prepared.

I have seen gospel-workers and experienced ministry leaders make these anxiety-related mistakes:

- Asking before you have had feedback from the donor. Slow down. First, give the donor a chance to share how he *feels* about the project. Take your time.
- Letting the appeal get lost. Funding guru Jerold Panas told me this classic anecdote about a nervous leader he was coaching. The leader was determined to make a bold pitch, even though he was anxious. During the dinner presentation he gathered up his courage and said in one breath, "We'dliketo askyoutogiveonemilliondollarspleasepassthesalt." The appeal needs to stand by itself during the conversation—naked and alone, so the donor knows she is being asked. Don't run it into other conversation. Oops! Let your appeal stand alone!
- Running the stop sign. After you have made the ask, stop talking! I mean *stop talking*. Silence must now hang over the room. You will be tempted to break the silence because it seems awkward to you. But it's okay. It is now the donor's turn to speak.
- Not knowing what to do if the donor says no.

3. Ask donors to pray about their decision.

I do not ask, "Will you give?" I say, for example, "Will you pray about a gift of $100 to $200 per month toward our discipling ministry?" I want giving partners to seek the Lord about how He wants them to use His money. Most say that yes, they will pray about it. I then thank them sincerely and ask whether I may phone them in a week (or less—don't wait too long) to see how God has led them in this decision. If the appeal is for a five- or six- or seven-figure gift, more time will be needed.

4. Use a response device (pledge card).

A young missionary was ecstatic about his success in raising monthly support to be a short-term assistant at a mission headquarters. He had contacted thirty friends face-to-face, and twenty-nine agreed to give starting August 1.

August 1 arrived. No money. September 1. Still no money.

In trying to solve this mystery, I asked what kind of response card he used.

"I don't need a card," he said. "My friends know what to do."

October 1. Reluctantly, he sent out pledge cards with return envelopes to his twenty-nine pledgers. The money arrived within thirty days.

Why a response device? Because even well-meaning friends need a vehicle to express their intentions. Out of sight—out of mind. Even if your partners can easily give online, you still need a response device to leave with them. An exception: No card is needed when you invite a massive gift from a major donor for a corporate project that requires several weeks of consideration. Of course, during these weeks you are checking back with them and discussing how the gift can be made.

The apostle Paul used a response device of sorts. In 2 Corinthians 9:5, he says, "So I thought it necessary to urge the brethren that they would go on ahead . . . and arrange beforehand your previously promised bountiful gift." Paul sent collection brethren!

Once I gave a presentation on behalf of fellow gospel-workers Bob and Sally, a married couple assigned to Indonesia. They invited twenty friends to their home, and I gave the appeal for support. When the party was over, as we were leaving, Bob thrust out a pledge card, looked me in the eye, and said, "Scott, I'd like to ask you and Alma to join our finance team!"

I laughed, "Good joke, Bob! I'm the speaker, not the giver!"

But he insisted, "No, Scott! We're serious. You know us well. Will you pray about joining our monthly team?"

I shrugged, reluctantly took the pledge card, and grumbled to Alma (who didn't grumble) all the way home. "We're already supporting everyone we can," I reasoned.

The next morning I put Bob's card on my desk. After a few days, I noticed my attitude changing. Because of that card, we couldn't get Bob and Sally and Indonesia out of our minds. Alma and I soon returned the card with our pledge.

A pledge card is your silent advocate. Don't overlook its value.

Make sure your mission account number or banking number are on the card so your donor knows how to make the gift. Your pledge card must also explain how to give electronically. And include a return envelope for the post (if used in your country).

5. Ask for a specific amount or range.

A short-term missionary was apprehensive about fundraising, but she stepped out in faith to make face-to-face visits, and God blessed. Of her top twenty-five prospective givers, twenty-four committed monthly support. She was excited, but she said, "There's a problem. The twenty-four commitments total $960 monthly, and my budget is $2,900."

"Did you ask them to give a certain amount?" I asked.

"No," she blurted out. "I'm just glad they are giving!"

She now had to raise an additional $1,940 from people she didn't know as well. If she had asked specifically for $100 to $200 per month, she likely would have raised the entire amount.

Never ask potential partners "just to give." Ask them to give an amount or within a range.

A friend from Wisconsin receives many missionary appeals. She told me, "When I am asked to 'give,' with no amount suggested, I don't know what to do. Tell me what will really help you—immediate cash, $100 monthly, $5,000 annually?"

Even Moses asked specifically. In Exodus 25:1-7 the Lord commanded Moses to raise a contribution for the tabernacle "from every man whose heart moves him." In verses 3-7, the Lord lists fourteen specific items needed for the tabernacle—gold, silver, bronze, scarlet material, goat hair, rams' skins dyed red, porpoise skins, and so on.

By listing individual items, the people could more easily participate. If Moses had simply said, "Please give!" the Israelites would not have known what to do. But if you happened to have one of the fourteen items, such as a porpoise skin brought from Egypt, you could participate.

Let your donors know specifically what is needed, just as Moses did. They will seriously consider what you suggest. Vague appeals communicate uncertainty and confuse givers.

But is suggesting a specific amount or range too pushy? Not usually. Years ago, Alma and I asked Mrs. X and her daughter to help with our $150,000 devotional guide ministry, due August 1. She had given $500 gifts previously. We were having a delightful overnight visit in her Florida winter home.

The next morning I asked whether she would pray about giving $25,000 to expand the devotional guide ministry. Immediately she burst out laughing, "$25,000? Ha-ha-ha. I can't give $25,000. Ha-ha-ha-ha!" Her daughter also laughed.

I felt stupid, but I did not recant. I explained that most of the donors to the project gave $10 to $25 and that we needed a few people to undergird the ministry with larger amounts. She understood and said she would "do something" by the August 1 deadline. But $25,000? Ha-ha-ha!

We spent an enjoyable morning with her and her daughter, and as we prepared to leave, she slipped a check for $2,000 into Alma's hand. And by the deadline she had sent additional checks totaling $10,000. I'm glad I didn't ask for $2,500!

If donors can't give as much as you suggest, they'll tell you. But they may be inwardly flattered that you thought they could give that much. In my experience, donors are rarely offended if you ask for too much.

For appealing to major donors, check chapter 12.

Now it is time to review the nuts and bolts of the appeal process.

10

PHONING

Setting Up a Fundraising Appointment

NOW THAT YOU have identified your prospective donors and plotted them on a map, it's time to set up face-to-face appointments. This is a difficult part of fundraising for gospel-workers of any culture. Many say, "I enjoy fundraising—except for setting up appointments."

Why is it so hard? Because this is when rejection is most likely.

Though phoning is a traditional way to set appointments, it is not the only way. You can also text, email, visit in person, send a Facebook message, and more. Be creative, but be wise. A text or email might not communicate the importance of the appointment, and people will find it easy to say no.

Securing an appointment is a leap of faith, but follow these suggestions and you'll do fine.

1. Make an outline and pray.

If you phone, don't read a script, but don't rely on spur-of-the-moment wit, either. An outline allows you to forget yourself and concentrate on the listener.

Rehearse your phone outline a few times to the mirror, a friend, or—if you really want help—your spouse. I can hear extroverts saying, "Nah! I can wing it." Sorry, but you'll be more effective with an outline. I learned by bad experience that I'm not naturally articulate. Most of us aren't.

At the end of this chapter, you'll find a sample phone outline. Then go to scottmorton.net for a blank outline to create your own talking points. Keep your outline beside you when you phone.

2. Make sure you have the listener's full attention.

If your listener is preoccupied with kids' bedtime chores, you won't have her undivided attention. After a brief greeting, I ask, "Do you have a minute to talk? Are you in the middle of something?" Your listener will tell you if it's a bad time.

3. Mention money when you ask for an appointment.

If you do not mention financial support when securing the appointment, it is awkward to mention it during the appointment—you'll be as nervous as an interim pastor on Stewardship Sunday. Instead of enjoying the conversation, you'll be preoccupied with looking for a money opening, such as, "Speaking of high prices, let me tell you about our financial situation." Don't lead your friend to believe you are meeting for fellowship when you intend to make a financial appeal.

However, don't say so much about money that the listener thinks you are asking him to make a financial decision on the phone.

A missionary friend preparing to go to Indonesia was 0-for-7 in securing appointments from his best prospective givers. He was discouraged! He had been up-front on the phone and had explained in detail that he was seeking financial support.

I suggested that he cut back his financial words because the listeners likely thought he wanted them to make a financial decision right there on the phone.

He changed tactics. He still mentioned money but was clear that he was not expecting a financial decision on the phone. His next five phone calls resulted in five appointments and eventually five pledges!

The goal of the phone call is to get an *appointment*—not a gift! If my friend hesitates to give me an appointment, I say, "There is no obligation. It would be an honor to tell you about my ministry whether you are able to give or not." I want people to feel free to say no without jeopardizing our relationship.

4. Confirm date, time, place, and directions.

Appointments are tough enough without going to the wrong meeting place on the wrong day. Get the appointment on your timetable with their contact information in case you are delayed.

5. Be your *enthusiastic* self.

On the phone your listener cannot see you, so your voice alone must carry your spirit. Don't imitate "Mr. Energy" or "Miss Perky," but don't slip into the bad habit of a monotone or low-energy voice. Are you excited about your ministry or not?

6. Expect to get an appointment.

A group of young preachers sought counsel from the legendary British preacher Charles Spurgeon. They said they were not seeing many people come to Christ and wondered whether Dr. Spurgeon had any counsel. He said, "Surely you don't expect someone to come to Christ every time you preach, do you?"

"Of course not," the young preachers chorused.

Slowly Dr. Spurgeon replied, "That is your problem!"

Similarly, on the phone, we either expect God to act, or we don't. A negative, apprehensive demeanor invites a negative, apprehensive response. That's why prayer is so important before you begin. Remind God of His promises. If God has called you to ministry, how dare you be unexpectant!

7. Keep the door open.

If your friend says no (even after you've said, "There is no obligation"), have a plan. Instead of breaking into tears, affirm your friend. Perhaps he feels badly that he can't meet you. I say, "I understand. May I keep you on our mailing list so you can stay informed about our ministry and know how to pray for us?" A *no* to an appointment does not mean a *no* forever, but only a *no* for now. A handful of our current partners said no originally.

8. No stalling!

Saturday morning. A missionary prepares to phone for appointments. After checking social media, he retires to a semiprivate part of the house with his cup of tea. But he forgot sugar.

Back again. He clears space on his desk but checks social media one last time. Finally, he pulls out his top-twenty-five list and studies each name to decide who is "easiest."

Having decided on his first call, he searches for his phone outline. Can't find it. He checks his backpack stashed in the kitchen. "Honey, any oatmeal cookies left?" he asks his wife.

She icily replies, "Aren't you supposed to be phoning so we can *buy* oatmeal for cookies?" Hmmm.

Having found the phone outline, he revises it. That finished, he tidies up the desk . . . prays . . . picks up the phone . . . dials four digits . . . hangs up. The first name was not right.

Second name. Dials the number. Perspiration beads ooze from his forehead. It's ringing. Once. Twice. No answer. Three times. Four. Five.

In relief he hangs up. "Praise the Lord! Time for more tea."

If you've experienced a phoning exercise like this, please know you are not alone. Try these suggestions:

- Set aside a start/stop time, say, from 7:00 to 8:30 on Tuesday night. Tell yourself you're stopping at 8:30. Having a predetermined ending point is motivating and forces you not to waste time. But you will probably go beyond the end point.
- Get your top-twenty-five list, phone numbers, and phone script organized beforehand—including tea and oatmeal cookies.
- Ask a friend or your fundraising sponsor to pray for you during the phoning—even have the friend come to your house.
- Invite another missionary to phone with you wherever is convenient for both of you. Or Skype so you can observe each other on the phone. OYOFR (on-your-own fundraising) can lead to discouragement.

Sample phone script

Because human nature is similar around the world, the following sample script has been found helpful in over a dozen cultures when adapted to local contexts. The example presupposes that "Jim" does not know the missionary deeply but has been receiving his newsletters.

Greeting
- "Hello! Is this Jim?" (Or, "May I speak to Jim?")
- "This is [your name] from [your agency or church]." Establish the context for how you know them. They might not recognize your name alone.
- Chat briefly; exchange pleasantries.

Transition

- "Jim, do you have a minute to talk? Is this a good time?"
- If it's a bad time: "Could I call you back in a few minutes [or "in an hour" or "tomorrow"]?"

Ask for appointment

- If it's a good time to talk: "As you know, I'm on the staff with [agency] in [location]. We're in our _____ year of ministry and are excited about what the Lord is doing."
- If your relationship is casual to distant, but Jim is on your mailing list: "Have you been receiving our newsletters? . . . Great! I hope you like them."
- "This month I'm in the process of developing my support team. Part of my ministry [or, if you are starting out, "my first official assignment"] is to develop a group of partners who will join us in prayer and finances."
- "As I thought about who I'd enjoy having on my team, your name came to mind!" [Chance for humor here!]
- "I wonder if there would be a time within the next week or two that we could meet for about an hour? I want to tell you about what God is doing in my ministry and show you some photos of people who have met Christ—it is amazing! Then I'd like to tell you about our finance support team."
- Alternately: "You have shown a significant interest in our ministry in the past through your gifts and prayers. And we are grateful. I wonder if there would be a time within the next week or two that we could meet for about an hour? I want to tell you about what God is doing in my ministry and show you some photos of people who have met Christ—it is amazing! Then I'd like to leave an invitation with you to join our finance team."
- If they hesitate: "There is no obligation whatever. It would be an honor to tell you about our ministry and catch up face-to-face."

Close

- If yes: Confirm the appointment date, time, and directions to the meeting location.
- If no: "I certainly appreciate your willingness to consider this, Jim. Maybe we could talk again in a year or two. . . . In the meantime, I'll continue to send our newsletter for prayer. Our major prayer request is _____. When you think of us, that's the prayer need. Thank you!"

Texting or email language

Here is a sample text to get you started: "Let's meet! Want to tell you about my new ministry at _____. How about Friday 15th at White Castle on 30th Street? Noon? My treat."

. . .

Go online to scottmorton.net to create and download your personal, customizable phone outline. Use words and phrases you are comfortable with. Knowing your outline will help you serve and enjoy the other person. The outline has only four elements: greeting, transition, ask for appointment, close.

11

HOW TO MAKE A FACE-TO-FACE APPEAL

You've survived the toughest part of raising support—setting up your face-to-face interview. Now you're ready to meet your potential new giving partner! What should you take with you to the appointment?

- Directions to the meeting location and the donor's phone number
- Presentation folder and leave-behind materials
- Response card and a return envelope

And make sure you've prayed!

Now, anticipate the meeting in five segments, as in the diagram on page 104.

Box 1: Get acquainted or reacquainted.

Don't do all the talking! Avoid running your mouth just to dispel nervousness—blithering disease, a British friend calls it. Insecure missionaries fill silences with words, but that's a good way to stick your foot in your mouth. A nervous missionary,

1

GETTING ACQUAINTED
OR REACQUAINTED

Transition:
"As I mentioned
on the phone..."

2

EXCHANGE SPIRITUAL
JOURNEYS

"Before I tell you about my
ministry, may I explain how
it all began..."

3

WHAT PROBLEM ARE YOU
TRYING TO SOLVE?

"How do you feel about..."

4

ANSWER: GOSPEL
STRATEGY STORIES

"Any questions about
what I do?"

5

INVITATION TO BECOME
A MINISTRY PARTNER
(PLEDGE CARD)

"May I check back with you
in a few days?"

in the home of a potential donor, asked whether a photo on the wall was a father or grandfather. "No, it's Martin Luther King Jr.," came the icy reply. Blithering disease strikes again.

Don't rush into your presentation. Relax. Ask get-reacquainted questions. For example:

- What has been happening since last I saw you?
- Tell me about your family.
- Tell me about your job.

If you're in your friend's home, observe photos and home decor. Ask questions. Be a learner. Do not make disparaging comments about their cat. If you're relaxed, they will relax.

Transition

If you've arranged to meet for only an hour (such as a business lunch), be sensitive to time. I say, "I want to honor your time. We have an hour—is that still correct? . . . So as I mentioned on the phone, perhaps I should start by telling you how this all began . . ."

Don't wait until they inquire about your ministry. My personable young former assistant was asked by her hosts, "Lisa, was there something you wanted to show us?" Good question, because they'd been happily chatting for over an hour.

If you are in a private home, ask to rearrange the seating so everyone can easily see your presentation notebook or photos. Sitting around a kitchen table is better than being buried in a soft billowy sofa across the room from the listeners. If you show a video on your computer, you must rearrange seating. At a restaurant you will be even more limited, but be creative and make it enjoyable.

Box 2: Spiritual journey and calling.

Share how you came to Christ and how God called you to ministry. I say, "Before I explain my ministry, let me tell you how it all started. My spiritual journey began the day our neighbor, Emil Johnson, drove his 1949 Chevrolet pickup into my dad's barnyard . . ."

In listening to hundreds of funding presentations over the years, I find nothing is as riveting to potential donors as the testimony of the gospel-worker sitting in front of them. If you connect deeply with them on your personal testimony and how God led you into your ministry, you will likely receive support—and wonderfully deepen your friendship. Jeremiah 51:10 says, "Come and let us recount in Zion the work of the LORD our God!"

But some mission-workers say, "My testimony is boring." Nonsense! How can the work of God be boring? Perhaps you think *you* are boring, but God's work in your life is never boring. To make your spiritual journey more engaging:

- Be vulnerable. Don't candy-coat your abusive family or divorce.
- Tell how Christ changed your life, not merely that you are glad about heaven.
- Use a verse of Scripture that has spoken to you deeply.
- Give examples of your life before and after your decision to walk with Christ. Include humor. Be vulnerable.
- Know your first and last sentence.
- Limit your testimony to three to five minutes.

Next, ask your listener about his or her spiritual journey. This bonds you to your listener deeply but is risky if someone doesn't have a Christ-story or doesn't know how to express it.

What if you have heard someone's story before? I say, "Ben, I know you told me years ago how you met Christ, but it has been a long time. Tell me again your spiritual journey."

I asked a Navigator donor in Illinois to share his spiritual journey—even though I had never met him before. Afterward, he had tears in his eyes. I asked whether something was wrong. "No," he said, "I am so glad to share my testimony. No one ever asks me how I met Christ—not even my pastor."

Next, explain how God called you to this ministry. Use a Scripture life verse. Take only a minute.

Box 3. What problem are you trying to solve? Your mission problem.

Before you describe the *how* of your ministry, explain the *why*! Use statistics, quotes, or charts to connect your listeners emotionally with the problem.

Don't merely read your statistics. Point to one and explain it, then add a personal story. For example, on the trend of secularization: "A few Christmases ago I went into a music store to buy a CD of Handel's *Messiah*. I sought out a friendly young clerk with multiple body piercings. I asked about *Messiah*, thinking he would point me to the proper bin. Instead, he frowned and asked, 'Is that a new group?'"

To promote dialogue, I ask my listeners what examples of secularization they see in their worlds. Get your listeners involved in the discussion, not merely listening to your speech.

Don't feel obligated to explain every quote or statistic in your handout. What about a video? Sure, but it must be short and compelling.

What is your ministry strategy to attack the problem you are trying to solve? It is tempting here to simply read your organization's mission statement, but be careful. A few years ago I passionately quoted our Navigator calling to a potential donor. He just stared at me and finally asked, "Yeah, but what do you *really* do?"

I was embarrassed. I paused, then said, "To know Christ and to make Him known."

Immediately he smiled and said, "I get it. Good."

Mission statements are insightful, but they are laced with philosophical assumptions that outsiders are not privy to.

Box 4. Ministry strategy and stories.

Describe your ministry strategy by telling stories about people, not by giving a philosophical treatise. For example: "We have a guy named Bob in our ministry. Last year, he ridiculed the idea of studying about Jesus. But Friday night, he dropped in during the Bible study and told us he hated his dad." Then tell more about how Bob is getting interested in Christ.

Tell two or three short stories about changed lives or seekers like Bob. But come back to your strategy. For example: "As you can see from these stories, our strategy is to get a Jesus Bible study going in every residence on campus. My primary role is mentoring thirty leaders of these studies—and some are pretty inexperienced. We have a good start, but we have eighty-two residences still to go. Please pray."

What if your ministry is not going well? Tell stories about the spiritual journeys of people in your ministry—successful or not. Unsuccessful stories often move people to pray more than successful ones such as the story about Bob above. Describe your vision and be vulnerable.

Should you use a paper handout or an electronic display for your presentation? Yes to either. A display gives both you and the listener something to stare at besides one another. Constant eye contact can be threatening.

Transition: Clear the deck. "Any questions?"

Invite your listeners to ask questions. I say, "Well, that's what I do with all the energy I have. Any impressions or questions?" Hopefully, they will have a question or two. Do *not* go to the close until your listeners have had a chance to express themselves about your vision.

Box 5. Close (invitation to give).

Invite your potential partner to join your support team. Suggestions:

- Get their full attention. I've watched nervous missionaries inadvertently submerge their appeal into the flow of conversation so that the listeners don't even know they've been asked. Pause, look them in the eye, and ask: "Bob and Nancy, you've heard about our ministry, and I've explained our financial goal. Now it's time for me to ask you an important question. [Pause.] Will you pray about joining our team at $100 to $200 per month?"

  Stop! Once you've blurted out the question, there will be a few seconds of silence. You'll be tempted to fill the silence with words, but don't. Your mind will race. *I've offended them. Why don't they say something? I should have sent a letter. Why is he looking at me like that? Maybe I should have kept my job at the newspaper. They're angry. Somebody say something. I'm sweating. Nancy looks unhappy. Now she's looking at Bob. They're going to tell me they never want to see me again. They'll probably say no. I don't blame them.* Actually, only three seconds have passed.

Don't break the silence with inane comments such as "Actually, we don't need support that bad" or "Maybe you prefer just to pray." It is their turn to speak. Don't water down your appeal.

- Be prepared for disclaimers. For example, "Our church just had a funding drive for a new fellowship hall" or "Our kids' school fees are due." Rather than deflating like a four-day-old balloon, acknowledge the disclaimer but do not remove the appeal. You could say: "A new church building sounds wonderful—the Kingdom is growing! For our ministry, we are asking people to pray about giving above and beyond their current levels . . ."

  A disclaimer is not a *no*. Bob and Nancy want you to know that they can't support everything. Similarly, in evangelism, when a friend is seriously considering Christ but gives a disclaimer such as "What about those who have never heard?", we don't stop explaining the gospel.

- If they say they will pray about support, affirm them and review the response card in detail. Some missionaries downplay the response card or send it in the mail later. That's a mistake. Handle the card with great care to demonstrate its importance.

- Close with a Scripture about giving. Teach about giving wherever you can, even in little snippets. I say, "Thank you for bringing this before the Lord. I've suggested $100 to $200 monthly, but 2 Corinthians 9:7 says we are not to give 'grudgingly or under compulsion, for God loves a grumpy giver'—no, I mean a *cheerful* giver!" This little humor gets the point across and makes people smile. "Whatever your decision, I trust it will be cheerful as unto the Lord." Listeners appreciate being reminded that the decision is between them and the Lord.

- Arrange to check back for their decision. You could say, "Can you send the card back to me by the 14th—seven days from today?" or "I will phone in a week to see how the Lord has led or if you have questions. We launch our ministry September 10, and I need to have my funding team in place by then."

- *You must call back.* If I don't hear in seven days, I phone them. This week I met with a mission-worker who told me he made twenty-one face-to-face appeals last month with only one yes. "Did you phone all twenty-one back?" I asked.

"Only four," he said sadly.

Phoning back is tough. Many donors postpone making stewardship decisions, and you might have to check back many times. Make your deadline clear, and give them the reason for the deadline (for example, the students are back).

- If they say no, thank them and ask whether you can continue to send your newsletter for prayer. If you think they want to give but are temporarily overstretched, suggest that you will check back in a year or so.

Building friendship.

Now it's time to stop talking about yourself. After making an invitation to give, I say, "We've been talking about my work all evening. Tell me, how are things going with you?" Ask about their careers, family, and church—their spiritual journey, particularly if you got a fuzzy response on their testimony earlier. I say, "Tell me, what lessons are you learning in your walk with Christ these days?" Or ask, "What can I pray for you as I think of you the next few days?" Rarely does anyone ask them those questions! Remember, you are meeting with them not only to gain a support partner but also to encourage them in their faith. As Paul reminded the Corinthians, "It is in the sight of God that we have been speaking in Christ; and all for your *upbuilding*, beloved" (2 Corinthians 12:19, emphasis added). Additional suggestions:

- Have a few materials to give away—your missions brochure and perhaps a spiritual growth booklet.
- Close with prayer unless it would embarrass them—as it might in a restaurant. A brief prayer is almost always appreciated—*brief prayer*. Break the stereotype of long-winded missionaries.
- If the visit was in their home, immediately send a short thank-you note for opening their home to you. Don't mention money unless they already pledged.

12

HOW TO APPEAL TO MAJOR DONORS

When gospel-workers hear the term "major donor," they usually think one of three things:

- Do I need major donors? (Yes you do!)
- I don't know any millionaires. (Major donors need not be millionaires.)
- How do I find big donors? (They're closer than you think!)

If you are a career missionary with a budget climbing higher each year, you will not be fully funded without major donors. Gospel-workers who are fully funded year after year always have a few major donors. It's not optional. Sorry.

But it's not impossible either.

What is a major donor? Some organizations define a major donor as someone who can write a check for $100,000. But individual missionaries should think in terms of $3,000 to $25,000.

You can develop major donors by imitating Nehemiah, a fearful but courageous fundraising leader.

1. Find your passion.

During Nehemiah's day, the Jewish nation was exiled in Persia (present-day Iran/Iraq). Nehemiah was cupbearer to Artaxerxes, the Persian king, sampling the king's drinks to check for poison. A high-risk job!

During the month of Chislev (November 15 to December 15) around 445 BC, an entourage from Jerusalem led by Hanani visited Persia. Nehemiah "asked them concerning the Jews who had escaped and had survived the captivity, and about Jerusalem" (Nehemiah 1:2). They replied that the Jewish remnant were in great distress. The walls of Jerusalem were broken down, and the city gates were burned.

Their report devastated Nehemiah, and in verse 4 we see him weeping and mourning "for days." But his mourning drove him to prayer. Verses 5-11 capture Nehemiah's prayer of confession for himself and his nation. He also reminded God of His promise to Moses to bring them back to "the place where I have chosen to cause My name to dwell."

Nehemiah's passion (undergirded by God's promise) went beyond sentimentality or patriotism. It drove him to mourning and to prayer.

Passion is where your fundraising begins.

A high school graduate in Minneapolis made a funding appeal to a realtor friend of mine (David) for a sports-ministry trip to South America. The young man was sincere, but he lacked passion. David said, "You don't really want to take this trip, do you?"

"Yeah, I do," came the nonchalant reply.

"Nah, I don't think you do!" David countered. "You just want to get away from your folks for a few weeks to have fun. Isn't that right?"

Blushing, the young basketball player gathered his courage and thundered, "I want to go on this mission trip to serve God!"

"Great!" David said. "Now finish your presentation like you believe it, and I'll gladly support you." David told me later with a wink, "Just wanted to see if he believed his own stuff!"

How about you? Do you believe your own stuff? Are you driven to prayer and mourning? To repentance? To claim promises? To leave your comfort zone to boldly make your appeal? If you are not willing to raise money for your passion, do you truly have a passion—or just a hobby?

To discover your true passion, ask, "What makes me sad or mad?" When Nehemiah got the news about Jerusalem, he became sad and wept. He was also mad about the walls being down and about Judah's enemies dominating his Jewish countrymen.

If the calling of your organization does not make you sad or mad, is there an *aspect* of it that does? Maybe you need to tailor your job to a certain aspect of the cause that grabs you. Or maybe it's time to review your passions and dreams. This may signal a career change, but that's okay. Life is too short to feign passion for a cause that does not motivate you. Poet Ralph Waldo Emerson said, "Nothing significant is accomplished without enthusiasm."

2. Pray much.

It was now the month Nisan, March 15 to April 15—four months after Nehemiah heard the devastating news about Jerusalem. His praying for Jerusalem was not a quick once-or-twice appeal to God. Although he may have wanted to spring into action, Nehemiah held back and prayed for four months. While on his knees in prayer, he waited on the Lord and developed a plan.

I wish I were better at sustained prayer. I mourn and pray primarily when I'm in a scrape. But here's what helps: I've written my life mission on the prayer page of my journal; I look at it almost every day. Also, I review my life goals every time I get on an airplane. As I take my seat, I pull up my life goals screen and pray through it. What a joy!

Keep your passion before you. Pray about it every day.

And pray also in the heat of opportunity. In Nehemiah 2:2, the king noticed Nehemiah's sad, fallen countenance. That was a no-no in the Persian court. The hired help was not supposed to let personal problems come to the surface. Remember the hassle Queen Esther endured to get an audience with the king? Same palace.

So Artaxerxes discovered Nehemiah's sadness. But instead of panicking, Nehemiah "prayed to the God of heaven" (2:4).

Long-term sustained praying (1:5-11) as well as spur-of-the-moment praying (2:4) typified Nehemiah. He backed his passion with prayers—long ones and short ones.

Like Nehemiah, you can do that. Do you pray about your work every day? Ask God to sustain the work of your hands (Psalm 90:17). And then pray before each encounter with potential giving partners—that your passion will become their passion also.

3. Take a risk.

When King Artaxerxes confronted Nehemiah about his fallen countenance, Nehemiah said, "Why should my face not be sad when the city, the place of my fathers' tombs, lies desolate and its gates have been consumed by fire?" (2:3).

This was courageous. Only seventeen years previously, the Persian government had denied the rebellious Jews permission to rebuild the city.

We know it was risky because Nehemiah says parenthetically in 2:2, "Then I was very much afraid." Similarly, you may be fearful to appeal to a major donor. Okay—fear is normal. Take a risk like Nehemiah and tell "the king" what is on your heart—as fellow missionary Glenn did.

Glenn made his first major donor appeal to a friend over lunch, smiling confidently. However, during his presentation, Glenn noticed a constant faint tinkling noise in the background. When he finished, he discovered he had been "white-knuckling" his coffee cup out of terror; he was rattling it against the saucer. He also noticed he had not eaten his meal.

Despite his fears, Glenn finished his appeal, and the donor said yes. Then he asked Glenn, "Are you sure you're asking for enough?"

Don't let terror prevent you from sharing your dazzling vision with a major donor—only relax your grip!

4. Ask big—ask specifically.

If your goal seems like a lot of money, maybe you are stuck in a small-money paradigm—don't base your appeal on what seems like a large amount to you. It is likely small to a major donor.

Nehemiah boldly told Artaxerxes exactly what he needed. He didn't water it down. "Send me to Judah, to the city of my fathers' tombs, that I may rebuild it" (2:5). He asked for the following:

- time off from serving as cupbearer in the Susa palace (implied)
- permission to build
- letters of passage to ensure safety during the eight-hundred-mile trip
- timber from the king's forest to build the gates

Obviously, Nehemiah had made a thorough plan during his months of mourning. And then he asked specifically for resources to accomplish that plan.

By contrast, imagine a huge fundraising thermometer in front of a church showing 30 percent of the goal raised. Two church members are studying the thermometer. One says excitedly, "What's it for?"

The other replies, "Nothing in particular! I just thought we could use extra funds!" In other words, "Send money; I'll explain later!"

If you received a request for money without an explanation, how would you feel? Explain to your major donor candidates exactly what you need and why—no filler, no fluff, no organizational clichés. Don't worry about the amount being too large or the vision too preposterous. But do worry about your request being too vague!

A professional athlete was asked for $5,000 for a missions project. The total goal was $15,000, but the missionary couldn't bring himself to ask for that. Some months later the athlete confessed that he would have given the entire $15,000 if he had been asked.

Ask big—ask specifically.

5. Get to the point—be succinct.

Nehemiah didn't ramble with preambles. He stated his passion in one sentence: "Send me to Judah, to the city of my fathers' tombs, that I may rebuild it." How refreshing. Too often our appeals are wordy and vague. Or they are visionary "happy talk" without explaining how we will spend the money.

Major donors are busy and don't have time for you to meander like the Niger River. They know why you are there—get on with it.

Years ago my friend Don, a no-nonsense homebuilder from Minneapolis who has received many charitable appeals, told me: "Scott, tell missionaries to just come out and ask! Don't beat around the bush!"

For my regular budget I say something like this:

Bob and Sally, in my new role we must raise an additional $24,725 by the end of December to start the new year fully funded. I will contact many friends who will likely give $20–$30 per month—and that is wonderful. But we need a few people to anchor the team at $5,000–$10,000–$15,000 per year. I would like to ask you to pray about being one of them.

Then be still.

For a special project (after explaining the project and answering questions) you might say:

Bob and Sally, to reach our goal of $42,350 to put a Bible in the hands of every student on the coast campuses, we will need a major gift. May I ask you to pray about supporting half of this project—$21,175?

6. Build genuine friendships.

Note this phrase in Nehemiah 2:5: "If your servant has found favor before you." Because Nehemiah had won the respect of Artaxerxes during his years of service, the king was willing to consider Nehemiah's appeal.

Now and then you hear of a major gift given on a "cold appeal." But the largest gifts are given by donors who have a good relationship with the asker and the organization he or she represents.

Years ago Campus Crusade launched the "Here's Life, World" campaign and appealed for $1 million gifts. Of donors who gave $1 million or more, their first gift to Crusade averaged $15—most likely to a Cru staff from years before. That shows they were faithfully cultivated in friendship over time. Well done.

Don't have time to build relationships with donors? You might as well say you don't have time to accomplish your calling. Ask your board or leadership team to help you prioritize your work. Plan to give 20 percent of your time to funding and donor ministry.

Why 20 percent? Over the years when gospel-workers (especially organizational leaders) asked me how much time should be given to fundraising and donor ministry, I stonewalled because I didn't have a Bible passage to guide me. They were looking for specifics, but my nonspecific answer, "Let the Lord lead you," was not helpful. So I came up with 20 percent—one day per week. That's what I aim for in my own fundraising when I fall behind or when working on a project. Once you reach 100 percent of budget (or better, 110 percent), you can cut down to 10 percent.

But city leaders or regional leaders will need to keep it at 20 percent or more because they need to raise more than their personal ministry budget—things such as emergency funds for their staff or initiative funds to expand ministry.

Caution: A major donor told a member of our department, "I appreciate your coming to see me. But I'm also grateful that you are sensitive to my limited time. I'm not looking for a new best friend."

7. Wisely answer questions.

In Nehemiah 2:6, the king questions Nehemiah. "How long will your journey be, and when will you return?" Obviously, Nehemiah had anticipated this question and gave the king a "definite time."

You are not ready to make an appeal until you have anticipated questions and prepared specific answers. Get the facts! Generalities are a sign of lazy thinking. For example, if a donor asks, "How will the money be used?" or "When will you complete the building?", you must respond with specific answers. To say, "We will use it wisely!" or "Sometime in the next twenty-four months!" is too general. Do your homework.

8. Avoid buzzwords.

Because the Jews had been refused a building permit, Nehemiah had to be tactful. Wisely, he never used the "J-word" but instead referred to Jerusalem as "the city of my fathers' tombs."

What negative buzzwords will your prospective donor react to? For example: fund drive, pledge card, building campaign, leveraging our ministry. The more you listen to your donor friend and the deeper your relationship, the better able you are to identify what he likes and what is a turnoff.

9. Bring emotion.

"The city of my fathers' tombs" is an emotional phrase. If you have lost your father, you know where he is buried, right? My dad died in 2007, and I frequently visualize the lonely one-acre cemetery on windswept Iowa farmland where he is buried. And it floods my mind with emotion. When Nehemiah mentions the "city of my fathers' tombs," Artaxerxes, too, would think about the tomb of his own father—emotional.

I used to believe that donors gave out of intellect more than emotion. But now I see that emotions are a huge driver for giving decisions—even for major donors.

10. Give glory to God.

Nehemiah was quick to give glory to God: "And the king granted them to me because the good hand of my God was on me" (2:8).

It is tempting to take credit when we have worked hard. Like Nehemiah, do your part, but give credit to whom it is due.

Application

Now it is time to list potential donors who could be invited to give $3,000 to $25,000 or more. Do names come to mind? Don't ask, "Do I know any rich people?" Wrong question! And do not ask, "Will this person give?" Wrong question! I have yet to meet a gospel-worker in any part of the world who does not know a few people who ought to be invited to give major gifts—"wealthy" or not. To be specific, I ask them to list people they know who likely have good cash flow—business owners, doctors, dentists, salespeople, or government leaders. Start there.

Besides that, I have yet to meet a gospel-worker who does not know at least one or two "Artaxerxes"—genuinely wealthy people. All of the names that come to mind when you think of these categories should be on your mailing list. Start there. Do not go outside your world until you have given everyone in your world a chance.

Ask this: "Who, in the wide world of acquaintances the sovereign God has given me, ought to hear my story?"

How do you know whether they can give a major gift? You don't! You are not looking for millionaires. Certainly Artaxerxes would have qualified as a millionaire and looked the part. But today, if someone looks rich, they could be living in, wearing, or driving their wealth. It is fruitless to try to determine giving potential by external appearances. Let the Lord surprise you!

One more tip: After anchor donors start supporting you, introduce them to your national director so he or she can thank your donor personally and start to connect them with the broader national work. While I was development director for The Navigators, I found that most donors will not give more than $5,000 to $25,000 toward an individual missionary's personal support, but they might give $100,000 to your national work if the relationship is cultivated. And they will still support you! Fundraising teachers in other ministries agree it is true in their organizations as well.

13
APPEALING TO CHURCHES

I DON'T MEAN TO start on a negative, but you need to know that you will be more successful in your fundraising if you focus on individuals rather than churches.

In some missionaries' minds, fundraising means traveling to fifty-two churches in fifty-two weeks, making presentations to strangers. Friendly, smiling strangers, but strangers nonetheless. If you gave a good talk and your kids sang at the Sunday service, you would get support. That strategy may have worked years ago (though I question it), but it will not work today.

Why not? Churches, especially larger churches, are becoming more deliberate in the types of ministries they support. Some focus on evangelism ministries; others may prefer church planting in developing countries, while still others prefer pioneering in the 10/40 window across the Middle East. Plus, most churches prioritize mission candidates who grew up in their fellowship over a stranger from outside it.

Yet the myth persists that church solicitation is your best strategy. Sorry.

The exception is the missionary with an attractive overseas ministry. Churches show more interest across the water than across the country. One missionary in Kazakhstan has seven supporting churches. Another, with a secret ministry in Eastern Europe years ago, had twelve. But if you're trying to reach college students in your own country or businesspeople downtown, you sit at the bottom of the missions committee's list—in baseball terminology, you are a "cellar-dweller."

Now that I've discouraged you, here are suggestions to recruit church support.

1. Focus on your home church or a "sending church."

Even nondenominational mission-workers need a church home. But you will have a tough time raising money if you move frequently from church to church. A pastor told me, "If future missionaries constantly church-hop during their formative years, don't count on much church support."

It's possible you grew up in a church that does not believe in missions—no warm emotional home there! If that's your situation, develop an "anchor church" where you feel warm ties with the members.

2. Develop an advocate.

For years, our church in Minneapolis supported Greg, a missionary who had grown up in the church. His father was a stalwart pillar. But I noticed that Greg received only token support—he was a cellar-dweller. When budget time rolled around, Greg's name again went to the bottom of the list without even a discussion. So I asked whether anyone knew him. Silence. Someone volunteered that he had been active in the church years ago. No one knew about his massive ministry among the secularized in Latin America. Despite my arguments, he stayed at the bottom of the list and soon was dropped.

Greg had no advocate! Old-timers in the church appreciated him, but they did not get word to the committee.

Because missions committees change, because decision-makers in the church change, you must have an advocate who has influence. Without an advocate, you'll soon be a cellar-dweller. Committees give to those they know.

How to find and maintain advocates? The best thing you can do is to serve in the church whenever possible. That way, you will meet church decision makers. Make new friends, serve wholeheartedly, make yourself useful and well-known. Out of that you'll not be an unknown to the missions committee and you'll easily find advocates.

3. Keep the decision makers informed.

Besides not having an advocate, Greg did not work hard to keep the church informed. Listen to this former Cru staff member, a pastor's wife and missions committee member:

Over the years I have noticed a trend. Missionaries that send regular prayer letters and communications with the church are viewed as being "a part of our ministry." The others eventually become a casualty. Regardless of the effective ministry they may or may not have, their frequency of communication was monumental in [our support decisions]. Please encourage your staff to regularly send even short letters (emails) to let their supporters know they are alive and on the field of harvest. Otherwise, I guarantee that they will be in "the hole" in their support raising.

Make sure your letters get into the hands of the missions committee and the decision makers. One missionary discovered his letters addressed to the church were not being delivered to the missions committee for years!

Besides sending letters, you need to attend the church mission festivals, even if they occur at inconvenient times.

4. Church appeals are a process, not an event.

It will take several encounters to be approved by a church for support. On your first visit, you might only find out whom you should talk to about the application process. The second trip might get you the support application form. On the third visit, perhaps you will meet the missions pastor or the missions committee chair. On the fourth visit, you might make a presentation.

Don't give up. These decision makers are handling other people's money, and you must jump through their hoops.

Throughout the process keep talking with the decision makers. One missionary friend said it takes five visits to be accepted for support.

5. Do the paperwork.

With individual giving partners, paperwork is not so essential. But with a church, paperwork is nonnegotiable. How well you've done your paperwork indicates how well you do your ministry.

6. Speak the church's language.

Find out what the church likes to give to. For example, if they are keen on church planting, explain how your ministry aids in church planting (if it does). Or if the church is interested in recruiting national leaders, show how your mission does that.

Do your homework! If your mission does a ministry the church is not interested in, refer them to an appropriate organization.

7. Know what you're talking about.

Churches are disappointed when you are not knowledgeable about your mission organization. Here are questions you may be asked:

- How many countries are you in? How many staff?
- How was your organization founded? (Tell a folklore story.)
- Do you plant churches?
- How do you train national leaders? (This is a hot button for many.)
- What percentage is deducted for administration?
- What does your mission believe about charismatic gifts?
- What does your mission believe about Christian liberties?
- Is your mission a member of the Evangelical Council for Financial Accountability?
- We support nationals for one-fifth your cost. How can you justify your high budget?

8. Serve in the church and show up at services.

If you are local, then of course it is easy to attend or join a church, to teach a Sunday school class or serve on a committee. But if you don't live locally, then deliberately plan to visit your home or sending church as frequently as possible. And let the decision makers know you are available to teach, give a progress report in the service, or meet with the missions committee. Offer to help—preferably in your area of gifting. If desperate, offer to watch the two-year-olds in the nursery. Church decision makers notice your attendance and your willingness to serve. Don't underestimate it!

9. Exempt giving candidates one by one from no-ask policies.

Some churches will not allow you to appeal to individuals in the congregation if they support you through the mission budget. The purpose is to protect the congregation from unscrupulous outsiders slurping up cash.

Such a position is understandable. If you or I were the pastor, we would probably agree. Here is how I dealt with it. I asked the missions committee chairperson, with whom I had a good relationship, if the policy meant I could not appeal to Ted, who had been in my early-morning "Yawn Patrol Bible study."

"No, of course it doesn't mean Ted," she replied.

What about Brian, whom I was personally discipling?

"Brian's okay," she said. And so on down the list of twenty people I wanted to appeal to individually.

Identify those you want to appeal to and exempt them one by one. The policy—designed to protect the church—need not harm your funding.

10. Prepare a formal résumé.

Below is a sample format if the church does not provide one. Also have available a doctrinal statement, agency literature (don't overdo it), a commitment card and envelope, and your annual budget.

This is an introduction—not your presentation for support. But they may ask for this ahead of time.

Caution: If possible, do not give a missions committee your budget ahead of time. You should be there to explain it in person. Inexperienced committee members compare your budget with other missionary budgets (and sometimes their own salaries!), but they're comparing apples and oranges. It's best to explain in person.

	RÉSUMÉ OUTLINE FOR A CHURCH
Page 1	Color photo (include family if married)
Page 2	Your calling to ministry and your spiritual testimony
Page 3	Ministry experience, education, and training
Page 4	Description of ministry target and problems your ministry attempts to solve (be sure to tell a story about one person in the group you hope to reach)
Page 5	Your ministry strategy and expected outcomes (organizational literature available)
Page 6	Financial explanation and appeal (with commitment card and envelope)

11. Ask for a significant amount.

Missionaries customarily ask for modest amounts from individuals, but because a church is a collection of many individuals, ask for 10 to 50 percent of your budget, depending on the size of the church and your relationship with it. Consider a church a potential "anchor donor."

The reason I suggest up to 50 percent of your budget is that some churches in some situations like to consider a missionary their own. Therefore, they may want to take up the bulk of your support. That may mean you'll need to realign arrangements with your mission agency as well.

I encouraged a young short-term missionary from Wisconsin to ask her home church for $800 per month—30 percent of her budget.

She told me, "They never give more than $50 and never outside the denomination." But she was willing to give it a try because it was the church she had grown up in.

The big day came. Gathering courage, she blurted out $800 per month. The missions committee was aghast. "Young lady," they said, "we have never supported people outside our denomination and never for that amount."

She didn't flinch. She reminded them that this was her home church. "Will you pray about $800 per month?" she repeated.

Kathy eventually headed off to France with $800 in monthly support graciously given by her home church! Policies are not set in concrete. Think bigger.

Next, how to make written appeals for cash.

14
HOW TO WRITE APPEALS FOR CASH
Print and Electronic

LETTER APPEALS FOR cash hold a significant place in your funding strategy. Let's review the pyramid diagram from chapter 6 that outlines three types of giving partners. In this chapter I am addressing primarily the bottom of the pyramid—the one-off or sporadic giving group and the non-donors on your mailing list.

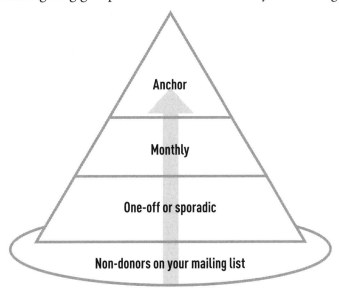

Why are these two groups so important? Because it is difficult to meet your full budget with anchor gifts and monthly giving only. You must have extra cash gifts to reach 100 percent. Plus, a cash appeal letter to your non-donors gives them the opportunity for greater involvement in the Kingdom through your ministry. Also, some donors—perhaps many—will not give monthly or anchor amounts with their first gift. Once they have given their initial gift, they might move up the pyramid.

Your cash project appeal letter should go to *all* pyramid levels. Invite your anchor and monthly donors to give an extra gift, but focus your appeal to non-donors and sporadic donors.

How often should you send a cash-appeal letter? Once a year minimum, especially to non-donors. But an additional midyear cash appeal can also be sent if your readers have heard news from you since the last appeal. You can also send a cash appeal for an emergency overseas trip that has just come up or to seize a local unexpected ministry opportunity.

Before you send your appeal letter, remember these cautions:

- Cash appeal letters recruit *little or no* monthly support. Monthly support is best raised face-to-face.
- Write genuinely. Tell the truth. Do not beg.
- Email responses are *significantly* lower than postal-letter appeals, but the average gift is higher.
- Though I recommend one page for general newsletters, your printed cash project letter can be two or more pages—take as many pages as you need in order to tell your story well. Longer letters frequently elicit a better response. But keep your letter focused on your project—this is not a letter to your mom.
- Email appeals must be short and pithy—one screen.
- In both email and hard-copy appeals, explain how readers can give online.

Before you hit "send" or "print," use this checklist to evaluate your letter. This checklist applies both to hard-copy and email appeals except where specified. At the end of the chapter is an interview on making email appeals more effective.

1. Did I include a response slip? (Hard copy only.)

If you do not include a response slip, fewer readers will say yes. A response slip gives the reader a vehicle by which she can express her commitment.

One missionary told me, "My donors are familiar with our mission's receipting system; they don't need a response device." Oops! Don't mistake loyalty for knowledge. Donors may love you, but they still need a response device in hand. Serve them by making it easy to respond.

Response slips fulfill another purpose: As your slip lies quietly on the donor's desk amid papers, bills, and articles she intends to read but probably never will, it is your silent advocate reminding her to make a stewardship decision. Seven days ago when she read your letter, she intended to make a decision but set it aside. Now your letter is out of sight and out of mind. But your faithful response slip will soon remind her.

For email appeals, you do not have a silent advocate. Instead, send a brief reminder. You can also send an email follow-up to your hard-copy list reporting how much has come in and encouraging readers not to forget your project!

Write your response slip *before* you write the letter, because it forces you to answer the question "What action do I want the reader to take?" You are not asking for prayer or recruiting for a summer trip. You want your reader to do one thing—to make a special gift, at God's leading, by the deadline. Multiple goals inhibit response.

Here are elements every response slip ought to have—does yours?

- Offer *only* money choices—not a checkbox for prayer support, literature requests, or an invitation to camp. For example:

    $_____ Cash today $_____ Monthly commitment

- Include a range of gifts or amounts you want the reader to consider—including an "other" choice. For example:

    __ $500 __$250 __$100 __ Other: $_____

- Clearly state the name of your project and the purpose. Readers often discard the letter and keep only the slip. The slip reminds your donor of what her gift will accomplish. It is the last thing she looks at before she gives.

- Clear instructions about how to give both by check and online. Double-check addresses, banking numbers, and account numbers for accuracy.

- Give the deadline by which you need the money in hand—and the reasons for this deadline. A rationale for the deadline increases motivation. For example: "Please send your gift by August 30—that's the day students arrive on campus."

- Include a return envelope with a physical letter. It need not be postage-paid. Your people are not likely to say, "Gee, no postage—I'm not going to give!"

- Include the name and logo of your organization with official contact information.

- Include a place for the donor's address, phone, email address, and additional contact information.

2. Does my letter focus on my cash project only?

You have only one topic—the appeal itself. Additional news diffuses the urgency.

In a comparison of Navigator cash-project letters, those that added an appeal to a regular newsletter got a 3.5 percent gift response. Those who sent an appeal only—no other news—got a 14 percent response.

Will readers be offended if you talk only about giving? If they hear from you *only* when you need money, yes! But if you write four newsletters per year plus the appeal letter, then only one in five is about money. That's not offensive (assuming you don't hint about money in your regular newsletters).

See from this example why it's important to focus on one topic.

CASH-PROJECT FOCUS

Having multiple topics eclipses the main focus. Delete the first two paragraphs.

As I've raised support these past ten months, God has been faithful. While my support crawls in, I have enjoyed finishing my thesis, visiting family and friends, and working with my new staff team.

Recently I began studying the Gospel of Mark with my neighbor, Joe. I'm amazed at Joe's insightful questions. It's fun to watch him begin to understand the Gospel.

I'm writing today because I need your help on a special project that will impact students for Christ—a scholarship fund to send students for spring break training in godly living!

Start with this paragraph.

Here's the real topic of the letter: money! Limit your letter to this topic.

3. Do I mention early in the letter why I'm writing?

An engineer from Illinois told me, "With all the mail I get, if I don't see the purpose in the first paragraph or two, I lay it aside."

Avoid the temptation to "warm up" to your readers! Don't ease into your appeal the way you ease into the cold waters of a swimming pool. Tell them immediately why you're writing. Here is a good first paragraph:

> Dear Friend,
>
> I'm writing today to invite you to become a partner in our second missionary journey to one of the most needy parts of the world—Peru! On March 20 at 10 a.m., we board a flight to Lima for a four-week special assignment. But I must not go alone! Your help is needed.

This first paragraph doesn't ask for a gift; it simply announces the purpose of the letter. Don't waste readers' time with a long preamble. If you mix your appeal with other topics so the readers won't feel pressure, perhaps you are embarrassed to ask.

4. Did I clearly state the financial goal?

Readers appreciate knowing *how much* you need, *when* you need it, and *why* you need it. Being vague about the amount frustrates your readers and lowers your response.

5. Did I offer the readers a range for giving?

Prospective giving partners can't read your mind. They don't know whether to pray about giving $5, $50, $500, or $5,000. Donors like to know what they could do that will help. And they appreciate knowing *why* you are suggesting that amount or range. For example:

> As you consider our $8,700 challenge, will you pray about a gift of $75 or $150? That will provide discipleship training kits for one or two students.
>
> Gifts of $500, $1,000, or more are also needed. $1,000 covers airfare, and $500 sponsors one gospel-worker at the discipleship training camp.
>
> Will you pray about one of these amounts? Of course it is up to you. Gifts of all sizes will be cheerfully accepted as they are cheerfully given— "God loves a cheerful giver" (2 Corinthians 9:7). Thank you in advance for whatever the Lord leads you to do.

Don't set your range too low, because people give what you suggest. And have a logical reason for the gift size you suggest. Don't merely pick a number out of the air. A veteran missionary asked his readers to consider sponsoring one or two days of his ministry trip to Africa—$163.89 for one day or $327.78 for two. Many gifts were exactly those amounts.

6. Did I communicate urgency—a due date?

To communicate urgency, answer two questions:

- Why do I need the money?
- Why do I need it now?

These two questions force you to think and pray about what to ask. Your appeal will be much more credible and honoring to the Lord.

If your answers are fuzzy, perhaps you don't need the money. "To pay my bills" is not a good answer. Here's a better answer: "So we can launch a new evangelism thrust starting August 26—that's the day students return to class. We want to be ready to tell them about Christ."

Do you see the urgency—and the vision?

Is a deadline too pushy? No. Most people are like the legendary American bandleader Duke Ellington, who said, "If it weren't for deadlines, baby, I wouldn't do nothing!"

Send your letters out six to eight weeks before your deadline. One missionary wanted to send his letter in December for a project due the following June—six months later. That's too far. Readers will forget about it.

7. Did I tell readers how to make a gift?

Don't assume that readers know how to give a gift—even though they get a response slip. I explain it in the P. S. because a P. S. usually will be read—*even in emails.* For example, in a hard-copy letter:

P. S. To give, please fill out the enclosed card and return it with your check, payable to The Navigators, by June 10. To give online, please go to navigators.org and click on "Find Staff." Thanks in advance.

In email appeals, since there's no accompanying card to add detail, you must be especially clear about how to give.

8. Did I tell a ministry story?

When I am asked to review appeal letters, I find that even veteran gospel-workers frequently omit a stirring ministry story. It takes work to write a good one. But it is worth it. Why?

Giving is emotional as well as intellectual. It is not enough to *explain* your financial project. You must stir emotions. Tell a story about your God-conversation with "Joe" at a late-night Bible study in a dormitory lounge with pizza boxes strewn around. Or describe an evangelism encounter with a small-business owner at the village market amid dead fowl hanging from stalls.

People don't give to bail you out; they give to help you reach those students with pizza or those villagers. The old adage is true: People give to people.

Compare the two examples in the diagram "Explaining vs. Illustrating a Ministry" on page 132. Jesus told stories to spur listeners to action! In Matthew 13:11-15, Jesus says, "That's why I tell stories: to create readiness, to nudge the people toward receptive insight" (MSG).

9. Did I personally hand-sign each letter? (Hard copy only.)

Personally hand-sign each letter—*legibly*! If you are asking for their help, the least you can do is sign their letter.

In an age of technology, a handwritten signature shows personal attentiveness—"I value you!" Use thick blue ink so your signature is obvious. It is worth your time.

Legibly? Yes. Famous baseball player Reggie Jackson once saw a rookie player hurriedly scribble his name on a baseball for an admiring fan. Jackson rebuked him, saying, "Signing your name illegibly dishonors your family. Write it proudly." Well said.

What about adding personal handwritten notes? Yes! Write notes especially to those readers whom you hope will give their first gift. Make your comments heartfelt.

10. Did I apologize? Hope not!

Starting with an apology devalues your readers. For example:

- "We've been so busy in the ministry that we don't have time to write each one of you personally."
- "You are probably inundated with financial appeals at this time of year . . ."

EXPLAINING VS. ILLUSTRATING A MINISTRY

EXAMPLE 1

I lead two Bible studies at Dixon Paper Company. I'm committed to reaching women in the marketplace. I'm excited that these professional women will be effective in multiplying their lives as they reach out to others.

I want to continually be effective in reaching women in the workplace. That's why I can't wait to go to the "Reaching Today's Businesswoman" seminar next month.

An important and exciting ministry, but the reader gets an explanation instead of an illustration.

EXAMPLE 2

It's 11:30 A.M., Tuesday. I finish packing my turkey sandwich and bundle up to drive 20 minutes to Dixon Paper Company. As I enter the office, I can hear five phones ringing and one angry customer cussing out the sales rep for delivering cases of gray 25 lb. instead of ivory. Four tired-but-smiling professional women enter the corner lunch room, and we chit-chat for 10 minutes.

"We're on page 10," I remind them. Eyes dart down or away when I ask, "So, what do you think it means here when Jesus says, 'I am the truth'?"

Silence. Then Tricia broke the quiet, "How can you know that He is right? I mean, my husband thinks you should follow your instincts. That works just fine for me."

In order to keep reaching out to women like Tricia, I need to continually learn. That's why I can't wait to go to the "Reaching Today's Businesswoman" seminar next month.

The same ministry activity as the example on the left, but illustrated. This engages the reader and helps him or her visualize what you do.

11. Did I add extra handouts? Don't do it!

Adding extra literature cuts down your response rate. Giving decisions are based not on volumes of information but on an emotional connection. In Exodus 25:2 God told Moses to raise a contribution "from every man whose heart moves him."

For email appeals, avoid inundating your readers with nice (but unnecessary) attachments. One attachment about your organization is okay.

12. Did I whine?

How do you like those "Woe is me!" letters? Emphasize your vision, not the sad state of your financial affairs.

In conclusion, following the letter appeal guidelines in this chapter will not guarantee funding. Kingdom ministry is not accomplished by formulas. Poorly written letters sometimes get excellent results, and "correct" letters sometimes flop. But following these tips will make your letter more understandable and more motivating. Your project must have God's fingerprints on it.

Email Appeals

I interviewed Dave Kassing, who has thirty years of experience as a no-nonsense direct-mail manager with The Navigators' development department, about email appeals.

Q: What gets results in email appeals?

A: In contrast to hard-copy appeals, short emails are better—not five-hundred-word treatises. Think of your appeal as a longer text message or Twitter post describing an upcoming ministry event. For example: "Our fall freshmen retreat at Lake Winnebago is set for September 15–19. Now it's time to replenish our Freshman Fund and award $50 discipleship-retreat scholarships to as many incoming freshmen as possible."

Q: What response rate should we expect?

A: Much lower than hard-copy appeals—but the cost is much lower too! On a recent email appeal to 57,000 nationwide contacts, we received 114 gifts totaling $25,853—an average gift of $227. That is higher than hard copy, but the response rate of 0.2 percent of the 57,000 sent is 20 times lower than hard copy. However, the $25,853 income has no mailing expense.

Q: How often should a missionary send an email appeal?

A: Don't send an appeal in every email blast—send other news, too, at least four to five times between appeals. But you can certainly appeal twice a year (or more) for special projects such as trips. If you have just come from an exciting meeting and a financial need has been discussed, send an immediate appeal—keep it pithy and help the reader feel he or she was with you at the meeting.

Ministry to Your Giving Partners

If your goal is simply to "get money," then you can skip this section. But please don't! I hope you will choose to minister to your giving partners. In his excellent book *The God Ask*, my colleague Steve Shadrach has described the partnership between God, you (the asker), and the giving partners. This diagram is adapted from his book and used with his blessing.

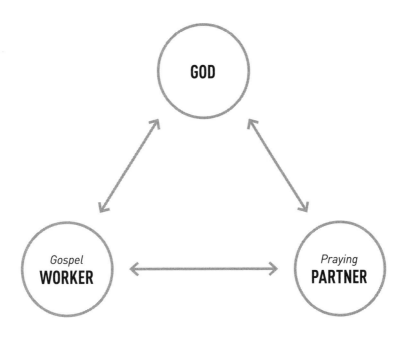

Secular fundraising mostly leaves God out of the picture, but we as gospel-workers must not. The partners are ultimately giving to Him. This implies that your role as the asker is also to minister to your giving partners, seeking to draw them ever closer to the One to whom they ultimately give. We are not looking for mere financial transactions but for spiritual transformations with those whom God has brought into our worlds.

But from a pragmatic point of view, why go through all the work of bringing giving partners through the front door of your ministry if they dash out the back door within a year?

15

DONOR MINISTRY

Bringing Your Givers Closer to You and to the Lord

SOME USE THE TERM "donor maintenance" to describe their relationship to their donors, but *maintenance* refers to things, not people. A computer guru *maintains* a database. The service rep *maintains* the copier at the office. Giving partners are not ATM machines! They are human beings who struggle with food allergies, job security, and kids' potty training. They need appreciation, information, and encouragement—not maintenance.

Donors "feel" your motives. We do not minister to donors merely to keep them giving. Our goal is to help them mature in their relationship with the Lord and their outreach to others. As former Navigator president Lorne Sanny used to challenge us, "Every donor a laborer." Keep in mind the diagram in the introduction to this section—donors are part of the spiritual triangle.

Here are seven suggestions to help you succeed fabulously in donor ministry.

1. Accept donor ministry as part of your calling.

If you have chosen to accept the gifts of others, then you have also chosen to accept responsibility to inform, encourage, and minister to those who support you. It is just as important as your other ministry work. Stop resenting taking time to write donors, send thank-you gifts, and keep your mailing list up to date. Plan it into your schedule.

In Philippians 4:17 Paul says, "Not that I seek the gift itself, but I seek for the *profit* which increases to your account" (emphasis added). Besides affirming the Philippians for sending financial support, Paul was committed to the spiritual "profit" of his giving partners. Can you imagine Paul resenting having to communicate with his giving partners?

2. Personal attentiveness wins hearts.

In *How to Win Customers and Keep Them for Life*, Michael LeBoeuf researched why customers quit buying. Here are his findings:

- 3 percent move away.
- 5 percent develop other friendships.
- 9 percent leave for competitive reasons.
- 14 percent are dissatisfied with the product.
- 68 percent quit because of the business's attitude of indifference toward the customer.[1]

True, these figures are for businesses and not mission organizations, but we can still learn from them. This excerpt of a letter to The Navigators' vice president reinforces LeBoeuf's findings:

Dear Mr. Libby,

I am writing to let you know that we will no longer be providing support for [a missionary family]. I realize that [they are] busy spreading the Gospel.

[But] occasionally it would be nice if—instead of another generic form letter . . . we could receive a personal note or letter.

The writer had written this missionary seeking advice on a personal issue, but he heard nothing. Several months passed, but he received only a generic postcard asking for funds. He continues:

Originally, I was just not going to make any further contributions. . . . [But] I at least owe someone the courtesy of explaining . . . my actions. I guess we just reached a point that we felt like we were being taken for granted and were just being "left out in the cold."

What went wrong here? Why didn't the missionary respond with a thoughtful answer to his personal question—or better yet, a phone call? *Personal attentiveness* would have solved the problem. Management consultant Tom Peters highlights the need for personal attentiveness after he sent a meal back in a restaurant.

> I had ordered the vegetarian plate, which turned out to be a lump of bland pasta with a glob of nondescript melted cheese on top. . . .
>
> The owner quickly came by the table. The first words out of her mouth were . . . about money. She'd remove the meal from the tab.
>
> Well, fine.
>
> But . . .
>
> The issue wasn't money. . . .
>
> Something was missing.
>
> That something spontaneously arrived when our waitress next stopped by the table. She said she'd worked for another restaurant that always toyed with its nightly vegetarian entree, and that triggered a five-minute conversation about vegetarian cooking and the like.
>
> What she provided was . . . *attentiveness*. The most powerful force in the universe? Perhaps.[2]

Your generic newsletters must not be your only communication with giving partners. Remember the diagram. Donors are partners with you and God. *Personal attentiveness* must be part of the relationship.

3. Segment your list.

Some on your mailing list don't need to hear much from you; others want to read your daily diary! Don't treat everyone the same.

This chart shows how I segment my list into three groups and how often I communicate with each.

	Jan.	Feb.	Mar.	Apr.	May	June	July	Aug.	Sept.	Oct.	Nov.	Dec.
General (3)	X				X			X				
Donor (3+4=7)			Y				Y			Y	Cal.*	
Prayer Warrior (3+4+5 =12)		+		+		+			+			+

I mail a hard-copy general newsletter three times a year. Everyone gets that—donors, non-donors, family, nonbelievers, strangers I met on the airplane—everybody. This letter is written so that strangers and nonbelievers will understand—it's not cluttered with Christian lingo. If the postal service in your country is unreliable, of course, you must communicate electronically. But hard copy makes a deeper impression than email.

Traits of general newsletters (X)

- One page, one side, one topic.
- Photo with a sentence caption.
- Each letter personally signed with a heavy blue-ink pen.

When I write a newsletter, I write to one person. I visualize my aunt Phyllis on her farm in northern Minnesota—a wonderful Christian lady and a no-nonsense pragmatist. You need only watch her decapitate and gut a chicken to understand that she does not countenance pretentiousness.

Writing with Aunt Phyllis in mind forces me to use plain words instead of ministry jargon. Also, she has farm chores to do and does not have time to wade through a tome from me.

Donors on my list receive two to three letters (marked in the chart with an X) in addition to the general newsletters.

Traits of donor-only letters (Y)

- More intimate than general letters.
- Share personal challenges in my ministry—more vulnerable.
- More intimate prayer requests. Donors generally want to know more than non-donors.
- Personally signed with heavy blue ink.

Traits of the prayer-warrior email group (+)

- Opted in to receive email prayer notices and trip reports.
- Not scheduled, but sent whenever I feel a special need for prayer or to report.
- One screen, no attachments.

Some readers might hear from me ten to twelve times a year (three general + three donor + five email prayer notices).

Note the "Cal*" in the chart. I send all donors from the past twenty-four months an appreciation gift-calendar at Thanksgiving in November. I include a warm, short thank-you letter (hard copy) expressing gratefulness for their partnership even if they have given only once. Though the letter is generic, I write personal notes on many.

So far, this segmenting is fairly tidy, but there's one more element that is messy. It's called "As I Think of You."

- I keep a supply of thank-you cards close at hand. If I think of someone during the day (frequently in my prayer time), I'll simply write, "I was thinking of you today." I'll add two sentences of news, and it's done.
- I sometimes send "as I think of you" notes by email.
- I randomly phone donors just to thank them. Usually I leave a voicemail.
- I text two or three donors while waiting to depart on an airplane or before I speak at a meeting.
- I respond to *every* personal letter I receive from a mailing-list friend.

What about electronic communication? Yes! Use email and social media in donor ministry. But heed this advice from Judith Martin, the American syndicated newspaper columnist "Miss Manners":

"Many people mistakenly think a new technology cancels out an old one." . . . People are charmed by handwritten letters, she says, precisely because they are rarer.

"You glance at an e-mail," Martin says. "You give more attention to a real letter."[3]

I agree. Just today I received a short handwritten thank-you card from a missionary. I'll give again! Research now shows that people in their twenties and thirties are returning to hard copy. A 2012 study featured in the *Guardian* gave half its participants a story on paper and the other half the same story on screen. The result? Digital readers didn't feel that the story was as immersive and therefore weren't able to connect with it on an emotional level. Further, those who read on paper were much more capable of placing the story's events in chronological order.[4]

4. Say "thank you" frequently, quickly, and creatively.

I learned to say, "Thank you" from my mother. When visiting neighbors, if we kids did not thank our hostess, we were marched back to say, "Thank you for the delicious dinner, Mrs. Jones."

But today, Alma and I notice that we usually do not receive prompt thank-you notes from missionaries to whom we send a first gift. Not that we demand to be thanked (we give to the Lord), but it would be nice to hear whether they received the gift.

You know the story of the ten lepers (Luke 17:12-17). One leper, when he realized he was cleansed, came back to Jesus to glorify God out of appreciation. Jesus asked, "Were there not ten cleansed? But the nine—where are they?"

You can't fake appreciation. Either you appreciate your donors, or you don't. If you don't, you must repent. Is *repent* too strong a word? I don't think so. Ingratitude is a serious sin. Hebrews 12:28 says, "Therefore, since we receive a kingdom which cannot be shaken, let us show gratitude, by which we may offer to God an acceptable service with reverence and awe." Gratitude is the only possible response to a God who has done so much for us.

Why don't missionaries show more appreciation? Here are possibilities:

- *A "they owe us" mentality.* Some missionaries think support is owed to them because they have chosen to go into "full-time" (unfortunate term!) ministry.
- *Failure to study donor reports.* Do you glance at or study your donor reports? At the end of each month, I schedule a McDonald's luncheon with my printed-out donor report. With pen in hand, I circle names of new donors, restarted donors, donors who jumped from $25 to $30, and those who skipped two months consecutively. What poverty of values causes missionaries to browse through their donor reports carelessly?
- *No administrative capacity.* Without clerical help, missionaries may be so overwhelmed they can't communicate with donors, even if they have good intentions.

Here is a personal attentiveness must for every gospel-worker: When you receive a donor's first gift, phone or text that person *within forty-eight hours* to say thank you. Demonstrate to your new donor that you are excited to have her on your support team—you are excited, aren't you?

In addition, I have a "new partner" thank-you letter ready to send in my computer.

I insert the donor's name and amount, print it, and mail it within forty-eight hours. I include a helpful booklet on prayer that I sign on the inside cover. This goes to any first-time donor, monthly or one-off.

Immediate affirmation endorses good work. Jesus immediately affirmed those who took a chance on Him—such as the sinful woman who wiped His feet with her tears (Luke 7:47) or the Roman centurion whose servant Jesus healed. He said, "I say to you, not even in Israel have I found such great faith" (Luke 7:9).

We immediately affirm our kids. Why not our giving partners?

5. Keep accurate records.

In order to give personal attentiveness, you must study your donation reports well. Look for address changes, support increases, and support stoppages. You can learn much about your donors by studying their giving patterns—especially over twelve to twenty-four months.

When I discover that a donor has not missed a month all year (twelve for twelve), I sometimes send a note telling that person I noticed his or her faithfulness—"Well done!"

The donor record/prayer page on page 144 is designed to help you start your own record keeping. Do it electronically and customize it to fit your situation.

As in your personal finances, so in your donor records: "Know well the condition of your flocks, and pay attention to your herds" (Proverbs 27:23). Make time to study your partners (though not necessarily at McDonald's!).

6. Write well.

Most of the communication between you and your giving partners will be written rather than verbal. That means you must write well. Sadly, many missionaries think that good writing is optional. Wrong.

But take heart—you do not need to write like Ernest Hemingway! You will be amazed at how quickly you can improve your writing. (Follow the simple suggestions in chapter 16.)

· · ·

To conclude, why do donors stop giving? A few years ago, Bruce Swezey studied missionary donors as part of his graduate degree. He asked, "Why do donors stop supporting Navigator missionaries?" Here are his results:

DONOR RECORD/PRAYER PAGE

Donor Name _____

Address _____

City _____ State _____ ZIP _____

Phone _____

Email _____

Personal History

_____
_____
_____

Testimony/Spiritual Background

_____
_____

His Job/Her Job

_____
_____

Notes

_____
_____

Prayer Record

_____
_____
_____

Financial Record

Year	Pledge	Jan.	Feb.	Mar.	Apr.	May	June	July	Aug.	Sept.	Oct.	Nov.	Dec.	Total

Communication Record

Visits _____

Gifts _____

Phone Calls _____

Other _____

WHY DONORS STOP GIVING

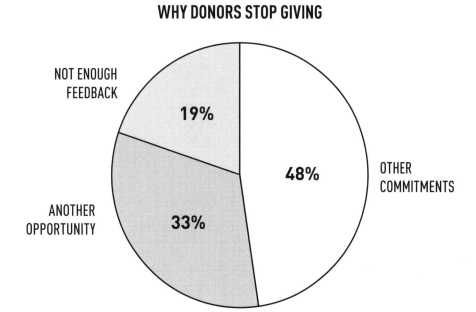

Nineteen percent—one in five!—stop because they did not receive enough news. If you have sixty donors and don't communicate faithfully, twelve will stop supporting you.

Thirty-three percent of the donors were "satisfied" but stopped supporting a Navigator in order to support "another opportunity." Can anything be done about that? Yes! Think about it—these donors are not bonded deeply enough to your ministry to say no to another giving opportunity. They are hanging on to you with a weak grasp! When a more attractive giving opportunity comes along, they kiss you good-bye in a heartbeat.

I'm grateful to consultant Dwight Maltby for the helpful diagram on page 146. Notice where gospel-workers drop the ball: not telling partners they made a difference—donor ministry!

7. Listen!

Maybe I don't need to remind you of the importance of *listening* as part of your ministry to giving partners—if you are in gospel ministry, you are likely already a good listener. I hesitate to say this, but I find that the longer people serve in ministry and the higher they rise in responsibility, the more tendency they have to talk instead of listen—they have so much to say! Including me!

When you are with your giving partners, tell them about your exciting work, but

LIFE HISTORY OF DONORS

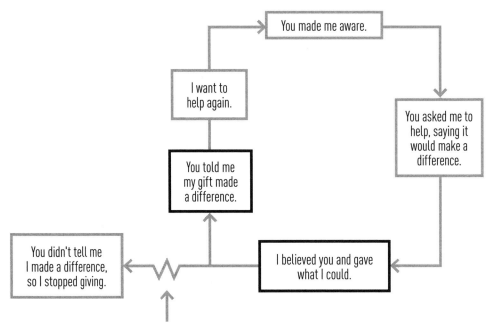

This is where missionaries drop the ball.

also leave plenty of time to hear about them. A friend told me of a gospel-worker she supported who came for an overnight visit to her home (good idea!), but did not ask her or her husband a single question about them, their family, their struggles, or their walks with Christ. "He only talked about his stuff," she said sadly.

We can do better than that! Here are a few questions that your giving partners hope you will ask—even though they may not have great answers!

- Tell me about your careers—what do you like about what you do?
- What do the next ten years look like for you? New jobs? A move to Florida?
- What is happening at your church? What do you like about your church fellowship? Are you involved in ministry there?
- Are you involved in Bible studies with neighbors or nonbelievers?
- What is happening in your walk with God? What is He saying to you? Any word from heaven these days?
- Any struggles you are facing these days? What issues or decisions are on your minds?
- As I think of you the next few weeks, what can I pray for you?

You don't have to give insightful counsel to your giving partners—just listen without judgment. It is more important that you be *interested* than *interesting*. The less you talk about yourself, the more your giving partners will find you a brilliant conversationalist and want you back for more!

Maybe today's donors are too fickle or too demanding, but whining will not change them. Instead, help them believe they are vital partners to advance the gospel. Get serious about donor ministry. Consider the famous proverb: People will forget your name and what you do, but they never forget how you make them feel.

In the next chapter, we'll look at donor ministry through newsletters.

16

WRITE NEWSLETTERS PEOPLE LOVE TO READ

WHAT IS THE NUMBER-ONE complaint about missionary newsletters? *They are too long!* They meander from topic to topic like a black-and-yellow bumblebee floating lazily from flower to flower. Giving partners around the world ask me to tell you, "Write short letters!"

Here is a dangerous trend that is not helping: Gospel-workers are writing not newsletters but flyers or brochures that are better suited for the church bulletin board. Their flyers have these traits:

- No salutation—no "Dear Mary."
- Graphically "busy." Too much to look at.
- Newspaper column format.
- No specific date.
- No closing signature.
- No single issue to focus on.

These brochures ooze with information but lack emotional connection. Do you want your readers to care about you? *Write a letter*, not a brochure or a flyer. Follow these tips.

1. One topic, one page, or one screen.

Limit your letter to one topic rather than describing seven things you've done since the last letter. A missionary newsletter is not a compendium of your activities.

Even though your donors like you, most will not wade through a long letter, whether on hard copy or on their computer screen. And most do not open attachments.

If you cannot delete anything in your letter, send shorter letters more often so you don't have to cram seven topics together in one small-print, five-screen tome.

What about family news? Include it in a short paragraph or in a P. S. A few close readers want to know every detail about your kids' schooling and Hector the cat. The rest of your donors care about your personal life, but they pray and give because of your ministry.

Alvera Mickelsen, in *How to Write Missionary Letters*, says, "Decide the thrust of your letter before you begin to write. A letter focused on one idea or incident is more forceful."[1] The exception to this rule is a cash-project appeal letter. Take as many hard-copy pages as you need to tell your story.

2. Include a photo (or two) with captions.

If a picture is worth a thousand words, put a photo in every letter! Many readers quickly skim your words, but good photos with captions get their attention.

How important are captions? Notice your own habits. When you read a newspaper or newsletter (even an electronic newsletter), your eye goes first to the headlines and photos. And when you look at the photos, you read the captions! It's human nature.

Which photos to use? Ask four questions:

- Does the photo tell a story?
- Do the colors contrast, or are they muddy?
- Are you in the photo? Readers want to see you in action.
- Can you see a close-up face (not the backs of heads)? Faces communicate emotion. Advertisers capitalize on this principle.

Write a newsy complete sentence to caption each photo. Don't merely say, "Bob and me." If readers merely browse your captions, they should grasp the thrust of your letter.

3. Allow plenty of white space.

A crowded newsletter with wall-to-wall words shouts to the reader: "This is going to be difficult!" Allow at least one-inch (preferably one-and-one-half-inch) margins. Should you eliminate words to widen your margin? Yes! Note the clean look of the sample letter below.

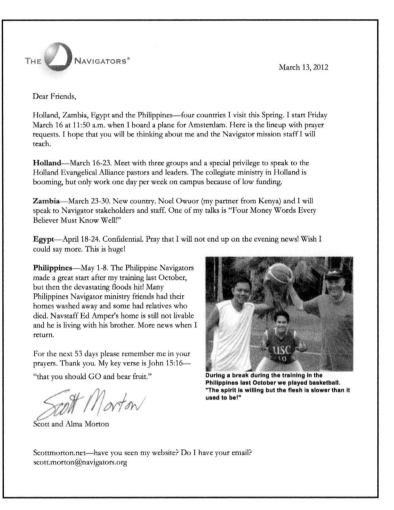

It is easy to skimp on white space when you have a gazillion different fonts, borders and icons to choose from—you want to use them all! Nevertheless, you must follow basic rules of graphic design, such as these classics:

- Use white space generously.
- Limit your fonts to two or three. Too many font styles communicates instability.

- Use serif typeface for body copy. The human eye, reading English, more easily comprehends serif fonts (like Times New Roman) than sans-serif (like Arial). Sans-serif is okay for headlines.
- Use a "ragged edge" for the right margin. You're writing a letter—not publishing a newspaper.
- Prominently display your organization's official logo. Don't alter it, lest you erode the organization's credibility and your own.

4. Find an interesting lead—a grabbing opener.

Writing to your mom, you can ramble about how quickly the summer passed, your annoying neighbors, and the hassle with Billy's fifth-grade teacher. But start your newsletter with an interesting story, a question, or a conversation. Also, avoid opening apologetically: "It's been a long time since we've written, but we've been so busy."

Compare the three newsletter opening sentences below. Which one grabs you?

1. Much has transpired since our last letter. We continue to sense the caring and encouraging work of the Holy Spirit in our lives.
2. Please excuse the impersonal nature of this letter, but I wanted to communicate my new address as soon as possible and give a brief update.
3. "Now I know I have a relationship with God!" Dagmar blurted out last Friday after our pizza Bible study in the dormitory. I was surprised because she . . .

Capture a ministry event like Dagmar's announcement in the first sentence of your letters. There is no such thing as a dull topic, but there *are* dull writers!

5. Use the power of story.

You might not recall the main point of last week's sermon, but you eventually remember a story the pastor told. Those who recorded Jesus' words remembered His stories—the parables.

Stories carry the DNA of your vision and make it pass-on-able. Without stories your newsletters drift from memory like a child's helium balloon at the state fair. But well-told stories stick.

What makes a story compelling? A threat, the possibility of disaster, a lion growling in the distance. The children's story *Goldilocks and the Three Bears* is a good example. Little Goldilocks has entered the bears' home—but we know the bears will return! Trouble is coming!

A typical newsletter says this: "Bob had a difficult background, but after attending our Bible study he trusted Christ." This story has potential, but no lion is growling in the distance. Say it this way instead:

> Bob missed most of our Bible studies, but when he did come he spewed out anger about his father's drinking problem. Because his father was a churchgoer, he angrily told us Christians were hypocrites.
>
> Last Monday, as we were finishing the study over cheap pepperoni pizza, Bob barged in and stared at me. Silence. *Is he going to cuss me out?* I worried.
>
> Leaning against the doorframe, he sighed. "I just got off the phone with my dad. I fear I'm becoming like him. What you say about Jesus makes sense . . ."

In the second version Bob has a personality. We feel tension. A lion growls in the distance. The punch line is held until the end.

Guidelines for storytelling

1. Briefly describe the background with word pictures. What kind of pizza? What did you smell, feel, and hear?
2. Describe a threat; build drama. "Bob barged in and stared at me."
3. Describe your personal emotions. "Was he going to cuss me out?"
4. A story need not be successful. Has Bob come to Christ? His uncertain future spurs readers to pray.
5. Don't reveal the ending prematurely.
6. Get permission from your story characters or disguise the names and places.
7. When the story is finished, move on. Beware of moralizing. Let the story do it for you.

It is difficult to *explain* your ministry, but you can *illustrate* it!

6. Eliminate unnecessary words.

Good writing is concise. As has widely been reported, the Lord's Prayer has fifty-six words, Abraham Lincoln's Gettysburg Address has 272, the Ten Commandments have 297, and the Declaration of Independence has roughly 1,300; but a government order setting the price of cabbage has 26,911 words.[2]

We enjoy speakers and writers who *prune, prune, prune*. Note how pruning leaps the action forward in these examples.

- "During furlough it has been very refreshing for us to have a series of visits and contacts from those we've ministered to in the past." (Twenty-five words)
- *Visiting those friends we ministered to in the past refreshed us during furlough.* (Thirteen words)
- "There were a great number of students crowded into the living room for our first study, which takes place every Friday night." (Twenty-two words)
- *Thirty-eight students crowded into our living room for our first Friday night study.* (Thirteen words)
- "It was kind of like the line I just read in Tozer's book *Knowledge of the Holy,* where he said . . ." (Twenty words)
- *As Tozer said in* Knowledge of the Holy . . . (Eight words)

Thomas Jefferson, author of the American Declaration of Independence, called "the most valuable of all talents, that of never using two words when one will do."[3] And George Orwell, in his essay "Politics and the English Language," advised, "If it is possible to cut a word out, always cut it out."[4]

7. Use action verbs. Avoid state-of-being verbs.

State-of-being verbs (*is, was, are, am, be*) stifle your writing. Replace them with strong action verbs. For example:

- There *were* fourteen students at the Bible study last week, and they *were having* pizza and a discussion on male-female relationships.

    Rewrite: Fourteen students *crowded* into the Bible study, *inhaling* three greasy pepperoni pizzas as they *debated* the Bible's view of male-female relationships.
- We *were able* to set up our first evangelistic dessert for business leaders last month.

    Rewrite: We *launched* an evangelistic dessert for business leaders last month.

Note the action verbs: *crowded, inhaling, debated, launched.* Watch for action verbs in your writing this week, and *plug* (good verb!) them into your writing.

8. Avoid jargon and shoptalk.

David McCasland showcases the problem of jargon in this example from an Australian magazine:

> Temperamental bowler, Rodney Hogg, smashed down his stumps after being given run out in Australia's first test against Pakistan at the MCG. Hogg was run out by Javed Miandad when he was out of his crease to pat down the wicket after a defensive no-ball play.[5]

The curious game of cricket! We worry about poor Rodney smashing down his stumps. American baseball is no better! "He wristed a Texas-leaguer into center." But Christianity has its own jargon, such as the following:

- "We *fellowship* at Open Bible."
- "I'm on *deputation* for *frontier* missions in the *10/40 Window*."

To discover your own "shoptalk," ask someone outside your ministry to check your letters.

9. Avoid generalities. Be specific.

Generalities are the refuge of a lazy mind. Here are words begging for detail:

- "Recently." When exactly? Three days ago, seven weeks ago, 1954?
- "Much has happened." What exactly?
- "Few/many/several/some." How many? Give me a number!
- "Had a great time." What made it great?

To convert generalities into specifics, ask, "How many? What kind? For example?" These questions force you to dive to the bottom of issues rather than float along on meaningless generalities. If your fact-gathering is weak, your writing is weak.

10. Use a specific date.

Your newsletter is not a brochure or a bulletin board flyer. Give it a specific date, such as "September 15"—not "September" or "Autumn."

I am asked: "What if I don't get the letter out by September 15? Dating it 'September' gives me thirty days of grace!"

With that logic, however, why not say "Autumn"? That gives ninety days. Or "2018"? Then you've got a whole year. A specific date gives urgency.

11. Avoid sermonettes.

If you don't have ministry news, it is tempting to write a sermonette. Sermonettes rank low with readers. However, a ministry-related personal lesson can touch a reader deeply. For example, if God is teaching you about disappointment in ministry, be vulnerable—what caused you to be disappointed? Include a verse of Scripture that God used in your life.

If you have a burning message from God, include an extra page or an attachment. Perhaps like this: "God is teaching me about humility through tough times in village evangelism and my reading in Acts. I have enclosed an outline of Acts 4–9 with my observations. Hope it speaks to you also."

The words "you should" or "you must" are red flags suggesting that you've gone to preaching.

12. Don't hint about money.

Say thank you but nothing else about money. A P. S. saying, "Please pray about our finances" is a thinly disguised appeal. If you want prayer for your finances, ask three or four prayer warriors privately.

13. Include your last name and contact information.

I know several Daves, so always include your last name and contact information for yourself, your mission, and where to send gifts.

. . .

In conclusion: Do you believe good writing is worth the effort?

Though your readers may never compliment you for pruning extraneous words, they will be grateful they don't have to rededicate their lives to Christ to wade through your newsletter. As American humorist Mark Twain said, "If the writer doesn't sweat, the reader will."

Why communicate well? The Trinity! God is an excellent communicator. During His time on earth, Jesus Christ was an excellent communicator. And the Holy Spirit is an excellent communicator. Sloppy communication dishonors the God we serve. And that's all the reason we need.

You can find more suggestions for effective writing online, but following these tips will take you to the 98th percentile. To learn more, check out *Writing Exceptional Missionary Newsletters* by my colleague Sandy Weyeneth.[6]

If you can make only one change now—use sparkling verbs. Words first! Graphics second.

All these suggestions for communicating well with your donors reflect the value I hope you place on ministering to them. When you communicate clearly and sensitively, you are drawing them closer to you and your ministry, and I hope they are drawing closer to the Lord as well as they team up with you. Sure, you need their financial support, but you should have the greater goal to encourage them in their walk with God as well.

Especially for You

The next six chapters address your unique situation in funding. While you will profit from all six of the special categories, select the chapter that best fits you and start there:

17. Especially for Organizational Leaders
18. Especially for Pastors and Missions Committees
19. Especially for Overseas Missionaries
20. Especially for Short-Termers
21. Especially for Single Women Missionaries and Their Supervisors
22. Especially for Gospel-Workers of Color and Their Supervisors

Certainly your funding situation is unique—there is no one like you! And chapters 17–22 touch as best I can on customizing biblical fundraising to your circumstances. But be careful of thinking of yourself as so specialized that the basics of biblical fundraising no longer apply to you. No matter what your situation, you must still apply the tried-and-true biblical basics—the "meat and potatoes," as we say in America—in your strategy.

Don't overlook chapter 17 for organizational leaders. Even if you don't lead other staff, this chapter will help you. Why? It will help you help your supervisor lead you! And if you lead only one person, this chapter is necessary.

17
ESPECIALLY FOR ORGANIZATIONAL LEADERS

I MAY LOSE some friends in this chapter, but this must be said, and said loudly: One of the biggest problems in missionary funding is poor leadership—not from funding specialists but from leaders on the line. That's you. In your defense, when you took your leadership role, you likely received no formal training in the financial implications of leadership.

Whether you are a CEO of a large ministry, a midlevel field manager, or a supervisor of one staff, you harm others when you blunder into these leadership-fundraising blind spots. Fasten your seat belt . . .

1. Silence about money.

It happened again yesterday. I was having dinner in the home of a missionary who was lamenting his poor funding (with his wife in full agreement). After an hour I asked, "What does your supervisor think?"

John rolled his eyes. His wife suddenly got up to clear the dishes. Silence.

Finally John said, "We talk about everything else, but he never asks about our funding—he doesn't care."

Trying to be encouraging, I suggested, "Perhaps he cares but doesn't know what to say."

John continued, "Maybe, but it *feels* like he doesn't care. He's not well funded either, and I don't think he feels confident talking about funding."

Dozens of missionaries tell a similar story. Spiritual leaders who are competent in other areas disqualify themselves with silence about money. Even though your staff don't talk about it, they live daily with financial tension:

- How will I replace a $500-per-month lapsed donor?
- Should my spouse go back to work?
- When will we get serious about saving?
- I haven't sent a newsletter in nine months.

Your staff are embarrassed to bring up the subject of money or fundraising lest they come across as unspiritual. It's the big, stinky elephant in the room, and they wonder why you haven't noticed.

Roger Hamilton, ministry partner development director for The Navigators, says, "Ignoring staff funding issues is like putting black tape over the 'check engine' light on your car's dashboard. You won't know about serious problems until it is too late."

My fellow leader, address the elephant! Keeping silent makes it worse. Though you might not be an expert, initiate talk about funding frequently—on home visits, at staff meetings, in new-member orientation, in communiqués. If you talk (not whine) about money, your staff will respect you more, and you will become known as a leader who cares.

Where to start? Talk about money at every meeting. Pull out your Bibles or electronic devices, and meditate on passages from the Scriptures about fundraising or money management. Then pray. When I study money passages with mission-workers, they are *always* energized. (For Bible studies on money, go to scottmorton.net.)

2. Failure to model.

If you are not active in fundraising—for personal support or corporate funding—you will have zero confidence to speak to your staff. Not wanting to be hypocritical, you say nothing (see #1). But your silence is not a sign of humility!

This is easily corrected. Simply do the basics—set an appointment, write a personal thank-you, phone a donor for no reason. Then simply and humbly tell your staff what you're doing in funding. And ask them what they are doing in funding.

Your modeling gives them permission to be active in funding also. Your questions about their funding shows you care.

Modeling in funding does not mean you must be the best fundraiser in the region! Be an example and let others pass you by.

3. Not knowing how to launch funding dialogues.

Here are six launching questions I ask missionaries (with their spouses):

- Tell me about your funding. What are your pressure points regarding money?
- What fundraising have you done in the past six months? Tell me what you did.
- How much are you trying to raise to be fully funded?
- Have you done face-to-face funding appointments in the past six months? Tell me about a couple of them—how did they go?
- Do you feel you have my blessing to take time for fundraising? How much time do you need? Let's look at your calendar.
- What can I do to help you reach full funding?

Ask these questions *without* offering fix-its! The answers you receive will give you more insights into your staff than three hours philosophizing at the coffee shop. Even if you're not a great fundraiser, you can spot obvious errors.

If the staff is male and married, his wife must be included and be made to feel free to speak up. Otherwise, you will get "spin." Husbands don't intend to spin, but they can't help it. Their wives are the key to getting accurate answers and understanding their pain level.

4. Exhortation only.

If your response to your staff members' financial pain is merely to exhort them to try harder, they will tune you out.

If you can't help them develop a strategy, point them to someone who can. Or steer them to your mission's training department—whoever is responsible for helping your staff in funding.

5. Failure to give your staff time and money for fundraising.

If you tell your staff, "Feel free to take time for fundraising," but neglect to help them block out time on their calendar, you have failed. They think you want them to add fundraising on top of everything else. This is what they hear: "Focus on your funding. But don't forget to recruit your team for the summer program! Be sure to meet with that new group from Oskaloosa! And take that two-week vacation—you deserve it!"

Conscientious missionaries try to do it all but cannot. Help them succeed by meeting privately with each team member to review his or her priorities for the next ninety days, *calendar in hand*. You will have to take the lead in directing your staff as to the exact dates he or she will take a fundraising furlough. Have them make a funding plan, then mutually agree on the dates to implement the plan. Don't merely give them permission to focus on fundraising—direct them to do it at dates you agree to. And when they are finished, have a debriefing and plan next steps. That's leadership.

If there is a funding coach in your region, include him or her. Agree together on what activities your staff will eliminate to ensure their funding plans will be carried out.

As you approve their plans, offer to pay for all or part of their fundraising costs from your leadership account. Yes, pay for their fundraising costs! It costs money to raise money. No leadership account? Raise it yourself or ask your supervisor. Push the system. Your staff are worth it! Don't allow them to be alone in their funding.

6. Settling for less than 100 percent.

Most leaders think they are doing their staff a favor by allowing them to raise less than 100 percent of their approved budget. But this silently spreads toxic carbon monoxide into the entire ministry. When staff members limp along on 60–80 percent, the following symptoms arise:

- Monthly bills are not paid in full. Staff are tempted to borrow from family or use credit cards.
- Saving from each paycheck is postponed and eventually abandoned.
- Staff seek to be around moneyed people with hopes of securing a gift.
- Poortalk dominates staff's minds. "Getting by" becomes the goal.
- Staff skip meetings because they have no money (but they tell you they are ill).

Just today I heard about some gospel-workers who were allowed to start their work four years ago without full funding. Now they are well below budget, discouraged, and the ministry is flagging. We can do better.

. . .

When you signed on for leadership, no one told you that "economic shepherding" was part of the job. But I'm telling you now! Your staff's funding problems are also your problems. That's part of leadership. Which one or two of these six issues is God speaking to you about? Determine that you will develop the leadership skills necessary to deal with the stinky elephant in the room. Bring up the *money* word and then truly listen.

18

ESPECIALLY FOR PASTORS AND MISSIONS COMMITTEES

A BRIGHT YOUNG couple bursts into your office: "God has called us to the mission field!" They are breathless with excitement. They've signed on with a reputable ministry. Their friends in the congregation have already committed support. Despite daunting financial obstacles, these young people can't be stopped.

But after a year of trying to sell a house, struggling with visa negotiations, working part-time at their jobs, whirlwind trips to the mission headquarters, and a frustrating experience in "deputation," they again appear in your office. But now they are disillusioned. Only half their support is raised. They don't know where else to go for money. They start language school in twelve weeks. They ask for help. What will you say?

If your church has already generously committed monthly support for this young couple, well done! The temptation will be to add to that as you hear their discouraging fundraising stories. But what can you do to ensure that they do not become dependent on your church every time they have a financial snag?

This is tough. Even if your church wants to make up the funding shortfall, that may not be wise. The advice you give will have a significant impact on the Kingdom and on the lives of these two dedicated people you love.

Here's what *not* to say. (For short-term missionary guidelines, go to chapter 20.)

1. "Just trust the Lord."

What does "trusting God" mean in fundraising? Other platitudes are equally unhelpful:

- "If you're called, the money will come in."
- "God's will done in God's way never lacks God's supply."
- "Where He guides, He provides."

At some level these platitudes may be true, but this young couple doesn't need philosophical exhortation. They need practical instruction on what to do next. Resist the temptation to sermonize.

2. "Visit more churches."

Unless the couple is 100 percent funded by your denomination, it is unwise to build a funding strategy around church support. What is the point of going to unknown churches weekend after weekend to drum up support from strangers?

It has proven more effective to build a funding team with personal appeals to friends and acquaintances rather than trying to make a favorable impression on many congregations with a ten-minute speech, followed by lunch in a crowded restaurant with the missions committee.

3. "Have a dessert!"

Though an evening dessert stimulates interest and a few send-off gifts, it produces little ongoing monthly support. The Navigators found that only 9 percent of those who attended funding desserts pledged monthly support. Lest you be tempted to think that is a good result, do the math. To recruit eighty monthly donors (a reasonable donor base), you'd need 720 people attending desserts.

The same study found that 46 percent of potential donors pledge monthly when seen one on one. A dessert works well to introduce the missionary to new friends and to solicit prayer support, but without one-on-one appeals, desserts cannot generate adequate faithful monthly support.

4. "God will bring in the rest once you get overseas."

I can't think of one situation where this worked. The apostle Paul set an example: He did not expect support from the people to whom he was bringing the gospel. A mission organization that permits a missionary to get on an airplane to go to a distant land to minister among suspicious people of a different culture while being underfunded is guaranteeing failure. It will affect the missionary for the rest of his or her life. Presumption is not faith.

5. "Foundations."

Foundation support is tough to get unless you personally know the foundation's decision makers. In America less than 5 percent of charitable giving comes from foundations. Another 5 percent comes from corporations, but 90 percent comes from individuals.

. . .

Now that we've identified bad advice, how about a different strategy? When the next breathless young couple comes to you with their missions dream, try this.

1. Assign them a Bible study on fundraising.

Tell them, "We are excited that God is leading you to full-time ministry. It is the policy of our church that everyone considering missions goes through a funding study with our missions committee representative."

A study at scottmorton.net, "International Fundraising Bible Study," has been used by thousands of gospel-workers just starting out in ministry. Give it to the new missionaries at your church, along with this book, to help them launch their calling.

Don't merely give money! Help your candidates understand funding from a biblical perspective so they can thrive for years. Even mature missions candidates do not automatically have a biblical perspective on fundraising.

Assign a motivated missions committee representative to interact with the candidates as they read the book and do the study. It will be a rich time of discovery.

Based on my experience, I recommend that candidates do ten to twenty hours of preparation in the Bible study. If they don't, send them back to finish. We must break the mold that funding is a minor activity.

2. Assign a funding coach to work with them week by week.

Ideally, a funding coach would be the same person who reviewed the Bible study with your candidates. A funding coach helps candidates develop their strategy, monitors their funding progress, and serves as their advocate to the congregation.

The coach checks with the sending agency to coordinate their schedule, monitor funding progress, and finalize the departure date. The coach also role-plays with the candidates as they practice their presentation. This is crucial—like practicing a sermon.

The coach becomes a sponsor, prayer warrior, critic, and chief encourager. Having an effective coach takes pressure off the pastor and missions committee.

3. The coach helps the missionaries develop a mailing list of 200 to 400 and a funding strategy.

If your candidates can think of only ninety-five friends to put on a newsletter mailing list, they should reconsider their suitability. Here is what to look for in a good strategy:

- A large mailing list of potential donors, prayer supporters, and acquaintances (at least two hundred people for a single missionary candidate and four hundred people for couples).
- Significant support from a "home" church.
- A focus on face-to-face appeals rather than group meetings, church visits, letters, or social media.
- Effective presentation materials. Materials alone are not the key, but they are necessary. The candidate should be able to make his or her presentation in twenty to thirty minutes.
- A simple reporting/accountability sheet. Without reporting results, little money will be raised, and candidates will become overwhelmed. Weekly or monthly reporting keeps candidates encouraged. Download the "Up Till Now Report" from scottmorton.net.

4. Help them find fundraising training.

What kind of fundraising training does the sending agency offer? Be careful. Some agencies are thorough, but others simply show candidates how to forward gifts to the receipting department. Search online for ministries that train missionaries in funding.

· · ·

In addition to your church's generous support, practicing these four steps assures you that you have done your part in helping your missionaries with the biggest task they face before they arrive on the field. Their missionary work begins the moment they tap into that Bible study you assign them. Their overseas ministry begins here—in biblical fundraising—not when they get off the plane!

19
ESPECIALLY FOR OVERSEAS MISSIONARIES

OVER THE YEARS, I've observed five mistakes that overseas (out-of-country) missionaries make in funding. These mistakes are not impossible to correct, but a change in thinking is required.

Error 1: Failing to organize your fundraising before you start your home assignment.

Home assignment (*furlough* is an unfortunate term implying "rest") also could be named "trying to accomplish too much in too short a time." Shorter, more frequent home assignments, rather than the traditional twelve months in four years, are more popular now, but funding pressure is not decreased.

Typically, toward the end of home assignment, fundraising panic sets in. Though half a dozen friends mentioned supporting you, no new money has arrived. You haven't been lazy—visiting family, bonding with supporting churches, visiting giving partners, taking a seminary course, recruiting short-term helpers, writing an organizational policy paper, attending missions conferences, and handling an ugly personnel matter assigned by your supervisor. And resting! One missionary told me he couldn't wait to get back to his majority-world country so he could regain his sanity!

How about this instead? Write your fundraising plan—including a detailed travel schedule—*before* you return to your sending country. Arrive home ready to execute your fundraising plan. Here are a few items to prepare before you board the airplane for home.

- A list of thirty-five to fifty people to ask for new monthly support (including email addresses, physical addresses, and phone numbers)
- A list of twenty-five to fifty of your top current faithful donors to thank in person
- Three to five appointments already tentatively set with anchor donors
- Your updated presentation and photos ready to share
- Three churches you will visit
- A plan to add twenty-five to fifty new people to your mailing list

About ten weeks before you return overseas, write a cash-project letter asking for the cash you will need for your return to the field. Don't rely on this letter to bring in monthly support—it won't. Early in your home assignment, identify and appeal to new prospective monthly supporters and anchor donors.

Also, before you arrive home, find a home-country coach who will hold you accountable to carry out your funding strategy—someone who will

- provide administrative help,
- find phone numbers,
- track down Facebook friends,
- set up meetings, and
- provide a reliable vehicle.

You must also work with your mission to ensure your home-assignment objectives are realistic. What seemed doable in discussion with your supervisor overseas becomes unrealistic upon arrival in your home country. Before you commit to grandiose plans, confer with your spouse (if married) and seek advice from other veteran staff.

Error 2: Failing to recognize your home country's communication preferences.

A furloughing missionary was discouraged about the meager response to his face-to-face appeals for monthly support. Bob had a sharp presentation describing his ministry in Asia. Yet he received only two yeses from fifteen appeals. I didn't know what to say to this discouraged brother.

I noticed that I could barely hear him in our private conversations. I also noticed he rarely looked me in the eye and then quickly glanced away. Finally, on a hunch, I asked why he spoke so softly.

"That's the way I speak in Asia," he said. "The loud, brash, American way of communicating is not well received there."

"True," I said. "But is it possible Americans are mistaking your Asian cultural sensitivity for tentativeness? They may wonder if God's hand is on you."

When Bob went back to speaking louder and looking Americans solidly in the eye, his results improved. (He changed back when he returned to Asia.)

You must be able to adjust your communication methods. Don't change your personality—just make sure that you communicate according to your listeners' standards. The apostle Paul said it this way: "I have become all things to all people" (1 Corinthians 9:22, NIV).

Error 3: Assuming that your donors' interest in your ministry is greater than their interest in their personal issues.

Missionaries come home bursting with God-stories about ministry, lessons they've learned, and deep things to share about cross-cultural living. They can't wait for their donors to ask penetrating questions about ministry.

But the donors rarely ask. And after a few minutes of listening to your story, they switch the subject to their kids, their dog, their church, and reality TV. Even though you traveled three hours to see them, they prefer to talk about themselves. They may even talk about another missionary they support and how wonderful she is.

Don't take it personally. Just last weekend we visited a giving partner who had supported us for thirty years but was still unsure about where we lived. Hmmm.

A missionary from Australia told me the attention span of his donors was twenty minutes—no more. So he lowered his expectations and communicated his key message in twenty minutes. Then he listened to his friends and tried to meet their needs for the rest of their visit.

Some donors have an insatiable capacity to hear your mission adventures hour after hour. Give them more time.

In my experience with millennials around the world, attention spans are not likely to increase anytime soon. Compress your communications tight—twenty minutes total, interspersed with dialogue!

Error 4: Failing to add names to your mailing list.

After ten years overseas, missionaries have learned a new language and have painstakingly built trust relationships. They are now finally ready for great ministry. But their budgets have risen 40 percent, and 20 percent of their donors have stopped giving. As they prepare to enter their most productive years of ministry, their support is drying up like a prairie iris in a hot Colorado wind.

Now what? They must lean on current donors to give more. "Can everyone increase?" missionaries plead.

Upgrading your donors should be a part of your strategy, but upgrading alone will not get you to full funding. While on home assignment, you must add new names to your mailing list *before* you need more support. Try these ideas on home assignment:

- Daily ask the Lord to grant you divine appointments with new people who will have a heart for you.
- Teach a Sunday school class for young married couples. (Graciously decline to teach kids' classes.)
- Attend various social functions of your home church.
- Ask five donors each to introduce you face-to-face over breakfast to two of their friends.
- When you speak at meetings, announce a sign-up list for your newsletter. Tell the story of one spiritually hungry seeker in your ministry and ask for prayer for him or her—not for the entire ministry. Invite your listeners to sign up for your newsletter to hear more about people like the person you described.
- Speak to civic-oriented service groups, such as Kiwanis or a young-professionals breakfast in your town.

Do not ask these new people for money. Merely add them to your mailing list. After they have received your newsletter for a year or two or four, they are aware of what you do and will gladly meet privately to hear more.

I say something like this: "I've enjoyed talking with you today, Burt. I didn't know we had so much in common. I wonder if I could add your name to our mailing list for our ministry overseas. We send a newsletter once a quarter, and this enables us to keep in touch."

I've added dozens of new friends to our mailing list in this way—many have become giving partners. Adding names to your mailing list is your year-round job—especially on home assignment. If you wait until you are low on funding, it is too late.

Error 5: Assuming your donors will support you on home assignment.

I've heard it a hundred times: "Our support drops when we are on home assignment." Tell your donors that a lengthy home assignment does not lessen your need for support. You are not on "vacation"! Write a customized letter to each donor, listing his or her support amount. Then explain the purpose of the home assignment and how it fits into your ministry. Like this:

> I'm writing to thank you for your generous support and to urge you to continue support during our home assignment the next twelve months. Unfortunately, some giving friends assume that our expenses are covered during our home assignments or that our ministry in Asia stops. Nothing could be further from the truth. On home assignment, we are still supported *only* by our giving team—the mission office does not subsidize us. Although our home ministry is different from what we do overseas, it is crucial to our success there.
>
> For example, here is what we must accomplish by next January . . .

Then follow up with a phone call to every donor to make sure they understand.

What if you find yourself low on funding and absolutely cannot return home for several months or years? Try this strategy in this sequence:

- Prayerfully identify five to ten potential anchor donors to help by increasing their support or giving additional periodic gifts.
- Arrange via email or Facebook a time to Skype these potential donors. Carry out the Skype as if you were sitting in the donor's kitchen.
- Explain clearly why you are in need of extra funds (currency surge or drop, increase in budget, family emergency, ministry opportunity to seize, etc.). Name the amount of your shortfall. Suggest an amount or gift range for them to pray about.
- Invite them to give as they feel led. Discuss timing of gifts.
- If you are unable to Skype, then arrange phone calls with a follow-up email appeal.

20

ESPECIALLY FOR SHORT-TERMERS

No matter what your age, I commend you for your courage to launch out in a short-term mission adventure. Whether your ministry assignment is two weeks or two years, you have the privilege of recruiting and blessing partners for the work of the Kingdom—some of whom have never supported a gospel-worker before.

Because the amount you are raising is less than that of career missionaries, you may feel you can shortcut the fundraising process. Don't even try. Funding your short-term ministry is just as spiritual as any other work you do. The Bible must be your guide—your cousin's wild idea to hold a bingo raffle is wonderful, but . . .

You are representing not only your family and your ministry organization, but also Christ—the One who is sending you.

Are you considering covering your costs from your savings account? The Bible certainly allows that, but I caution against it—for two reasons.

- Do you have other godly purposes for that savings? If it is earmarked for grad school, what will you do when you return?
- Are you using your savings to avoid fundraising? One young gospel-worker on a two-year assignment to Russia wanted to use her savings because she

disdained fundraising. When her mother heard her plan, she grabbed her by the shoulders and said, "Don't you dare fund your own ministry. Supporting you is the only way *I* will ever get to Russia!"

Don't ignore what many start-up missionaries have already learned. It is easier to do funding right the first time than to restart later when you're discouraged. Fundraising will test your character—and when you are driven to your knees, God will meet you in wonderful ways. Here are some tips as you begin.

1. Confirm that you are "called" for this assignment.

If the Lord is not the "unseen caller" behind your mission, what is the point of raising money? The scary part is that you may actually raise some!

Here are two crucial questions. First, are you going to the mission field to escape something? Some missionaries or pastors felt "called" mainly because they were petrified by a career in the secular world or were trying to dull the pain of a traumatic relationship. Mission work should not be an escape.

Personally, I have "peace" when I evade fearful circumstances or uncertainty. But it is not God's peace. As Jonah discovered, you can run, but you can't hide!

Second, are you going into ministry because someone (parent, pastor, or leader) says you should? Don't live someone else's dream. Be sure your call is from God, not people!

2. Find a fundraising coach.

Ask God to give you a coach who has the moxie to hold your feet to the fire. Someone who will ask, "Did you get your letters out last week?" and "Exactly how many phone calls did you make?" Look for a coach *without* the gift of mercy!

Your coach need not be experienced in missions. More important is his or her understanding of your fundraising plan and willingness to hold you accountable.

3. Study the Scriptures on fundraising.

You'll find "The International Fundraising Bible Study" at scottmorton.net. You might be tempted to skip or merely browse through this Bible study because you are "short-term." But be careful. Biblical fundraising is more about Christ-centered attitudes than funding skills.

I'm not suggesting you become a fundraising theologian, but invest ten to twelve hours in your professional development by learning what the Scriptures say about funding. Do the Bible study with your funding coach. Interact with him or her, especially on Scriptures you found puzzling. Be sure you discuss takeaways—your specific applications to apply from the study.

4. Build a mailing list of 200 to 400.

Yikes! Have I scared you into quitting? Build a large mailing list—two hundred people if you are single, four hundred if married. I don't have a scientific reason for suggesting this range—but I do know that gospel-workers with lists of 50–150 struggle to reach full funding.

Granted, you might not need hundreds of names if your mission is only two weeks in a nearby inner city. But think more broadly. Most of your contacts will not give, but they will be inspired and even drawn to the gospel as they hear about your mission. I'm not talking about two hundred or four hundred *donors*—just friends, acquaintances, or contacts who are willing to receive your mailings. Remember, your newsletter is not for donors or even potential donors only. Your letter will inspire everyone in your world, whether they give or not. You will touch people whom no one else can touch for the Kingdom. And some will pray faithfully for you.

Secondly, could this two-week adventure be the beginning of a longer mission career for you? If that turns out to be the case, hundreds of people already know about your ministry passion. You won't be starting from zero.

I often hear short-termers say, "I don't know that many people who care about missions." That is not the criterion. Add acquaintances who might know little about you or the gospel—they will learn and be blessed as they read your dynamite newsletter updates—even more if they give. Put down everyone you know who has a pulse!

"Everyone"? Yes, almost! God has providentially surrounded you with family and friends and acquaintances—Christians, non-Christians, family, former bosses, church friends, former church friends, neighbors, former neighbors, Bible study friends, workmates, and so on. (What about old girlfriends or boyfriends? No!)

Don't ask: "Will they give?" Wrong question. Ask instead, "Are they willing to hear about my adventure?" Most are. You will introduce them to Kingdom missions and maybe to the gospel via your letters. Put 'em down!

What about Facebook? You might be tempted to overlook your Facebook friends because you think of them as one big set—a monolith. But they are individuals with different interests, and each one is at a different place spiritually. Your letters will influence them in their walk with God.

In training new staff, Roger Hamilton, director of ministry partner development for The Navigators, says, "Set aside an hour to go *name by name* through your Facebook friends and cell phone directory. Ask yourself specifically, 'Would this person be willing to hear what God has called me to do?' Most will! If you are not sure, add them anyway."

One young gospel-worker told his funding coach, "I have no contacts!"

His coach asked, "How many Facebook friends do you have?"

The answer: "Six hundred."

The young guy and his coach began reviewing his Facebook friends one by one. Before they were out of the "A's" he had added ten names to his mailing list. As you take time to review Facebook friends and phone contacts one by one, you will discover angels you weren't even aware of (Hebrews 13:2).

5. Win support from a "sending church."

If you don't come from a believing family, finding a home church to send you out may be a challenge, but it is worth pursuing. More than financial help, a home church provides an emotional haven for encouragement and a sense of belonging. You might even help them develop a greater interest in missions.

6. Find others to fundraise with you.

Even if your "funding buddies" are in another city, arrange to fundraise together (perhaps at the same hours) so you don't feel alone. If you are living with your parents or in your old neighborhood, you especially need to find others to fundraise with you. I have seen many gospel-workers become discouraged in operating their funding strategy from their parents' home. I'm not sure why, but it's a trend.

7. Send a dynamite introductory appeal letter.

If your assignment is two weeks or two months, you can raise all your funding via a well-written appeal letter asking for "one-time" support. But for a one- or two-year term, you must first focus on face-to-face appeals. Send an introductory letter to your entire mailing list describing your new adventure. Tell them you will personally contact them soon. When you have reached 80 percent of your goal via face-to-face appeals, send an appeal letter inviting cash gifts to "push us over the top."

Don't be "just glad to get a gift." Sometimes, small one-time gifts are sacrificially given—that is wonderful! But help your giving partners also understand how to give beyond their first gift. Find a sample letter at scottmorton.net.

Resist the temptation to "talk poor" about fundraising—it is so common. Even your home church or faithful donors may unwittingly feed the poor-missionary "woe is me" mentality. If God has called you, He will fund you as you do your part. Your exciting task is to find out who your rope holders are!

Where to start? Take time to do the Bible study at scottmorton.net and walk through chapters 3 and 4 of this book. You'll be encouraged.

21

ESPECIALLY FOR SINGLE WOMEN MISSIONARIES AND THEIR SUPERVISORS

WITHOUT WOMEN MISSIONARIES, particularly single women missionaries, where would the advance of the gospel be? Through the centuries, women have boldly carried the gospel around the world, often with much hardship. And single women continue to make an impact today.

To list the contributions of single women gospel-workers would fill many books, but here is my favorite—Mary Slessor, Scottish missionary to Nigeria. We still draw inspiration from her.

Red-haired and blue-eyed, Mary arrived in Nigeria in 1876 at age twenty-eight and immediately sought to get "up-country." Once there, she was shocked at the superstitious tradition of killing twin babies. Native tribal people believed that one twin must have been fathered by an evil spirit and that the mother had committed a horrible sin. Not knowing which twin was of the devil, they killed both by leaving them in the bush to be eaten by wild animals or die of exposure. Sometimes the mothers were killed also.

Mary led a bold campaign to stop this cruel practice. The superstition was strong, but Mary Slessor would not give up. She once found five-day-old twins dying in the bush. The boy twin died, but Mary was able to nurse the little girl back to health.

In 1888 Mary was assigned to an area where previous male missionaries had been killed. Despite the danger, she believed that her message and the fact that she was a woman would give her an opening. She was right. She became known as the "White Queen of Okoyong."[1]

Could a male missionary have succeeded in Okoyong? Probably not. Women gospel-workers are often perceived as less threatening and more relational, thereby gaining openings more easily than men. We owe much gratitude to single female missionaries for the last two hundred years. Today, 4.4 million women from many nations serve in full-time Christian service, and two-thirds (2.9 million) are single.[2]

Despite their wonderful contribution, do single women missionaries face unique challenges in fundraising? Yes, and their supervisors do also. Here are three major challenges single women mission-workers face.

1. Blind spots of being relational.

As a generalization, women are the more relational of the two genders—that's a good thing! Women (generally) are more likely than men to pick up on nuances in body language and tone of voice and to remember details of conversation. This gives women the potential to be great fundraisers.

But any strength, if it goes too far, has downsides. For example:

- Feeling too much empathy can derail an appeal for support. Seeing that your potential donor has an old fix-up car and a daughter starting university might make you "feel" as if you shouldn't ask. But don't let your empathy prevent you from inviting them to join your support team.
- In the heat of the moment, you might feel that making an appeal will harm your relationship. Chances are that it will actually improve your relationship—but you won't know that until later. To combat this feeling, *memorize your appeal sentence* and be ready to share it at the appropriate time despite your emotions.
- Extreme "feelers" (male and female) find it difficult to condense. Sharing so much detail that listeners get lost in your stories hurts your funding appeals. Sure, you want them to know about the exciting evangelistic dinner last April, but be careful about running down rabbit trails or sharing your every

feeling at every moment of the dinner. Remember your listeners—do they want to hear every detail, or are they bottom-line people? When you are with a Type-A bottom-line person, cut to the chase, even if you feel awkward (Type A doesn't!). It is inconsiderate to expect a Type-A person to absorb as much detail as you wish to share.

- If you receive a no, it takes time to recover emotionally. Remember that a no is not necessarily an indication that the relationship is damaged. It usually means "no for now."

2. Feeling alone in fundraising.

I have seen it over and over around the world. Anyone engaged in fundraising alone can easily become discouraged. For women—even experienced and talented fundraisers—solitude in fundraising can be particularly demoralizing.

Find friends to fundraise with you, pray for you, and check up on you. Two Navigator staff women turn on their Skype just to watch each other phone—they briefly connect and then work on phoning—separately but still together! They stay jazzed when they see someone else doing it!

Who will pray for you during your fundraising? Who will hold you accountable? But make sure that your accountability partner keeps you accountable to your fundraising goals in detail; you're not helped by a partner who excuses you from difficult assignments.

If you rely on your supervisor to provide fundraising partners, you will be disappointed. If no structure is available, create your own.

3. The silver bullet—marriage to Mr. Wonderful.

Female gospel-workers around the world face the temptation to "wait for a husband to fundraise for me." Just today I received an email from a friend who said, "As my housemate gets married, I will continue to entrust myself to the One who knows, to the One who has not withheld good from me."

Though it's normal, dreaming of Mr. Wonderful gets in the way of your fundraising and your growth in Christ. My female mission-worker friends tell me that *objective realism* must be brought to the Mr. Wonderful daydream.

First, the guy you marry may be poor at fundraising—he may think *you* are *his* silver bullet! Second, dreaming about someone "doing it for you" is demoralizing and inhibits you from initiating funding activities. It makes things worse.

· · ·

Now, here are some suggestions for supervisors of single women staff members.

1. Listen to and trust your female staff.

Supervisor, you must attentively listen to your women staff as they share their feelings about fundraising. Resist the temptation to shut them off and to give Dr. Fixit solutions. Instead, validate their emotional struggle. One supervisor in America was so flustered by his single woman staff's crying over fundraising that he left the room without saying a word and sent his wife to console her.

Even if you can't understand her feelings, she must be listened to and taken seriously. Trust her. She is not manipulating you or pretending. She may be hurting.

2. Funding is not *her* responsibility alone—it is *your* responsibility also.

When a single woman joins your staff, work out a funding strategy with her *before* she launches ministry. One woman told me, "I knew what to do in funding, but I couldn't get to it because I was emotionally stuck. My supervisor accepted my emotions, but wisely, he didn't try to be a psychologist. He focused on helping me succeed at my funding plan, not on solving my emotional pain. That is what I needed."

Other ways supervisors can help:

- Join her support team with your personal giving—that demonstrates huge emotional support!
- Help her find other staff to fundraise with a funding coach (if not you), and connect her with other staff who are fundraising.
- Make sure she has adequate fundraising training and materials.
- Review her top-twenty-five list—ask about each prospective donor.
- Introduce her to two of your donors and ask them to support her.
- Go with her on funding appointments. Nothing communicates you are "for her" as much as giving your time.
- Make sure her budget is generous—not merely a "get-by" salary. Is money allotted for creating a warm, inviting home and taking a vacation?

Don't allow her to start ministry until she is fully funded, and don't allow her to lower her salary just to be done with fundraising. This may seem harsh, but in the long term it is actually a kindness.

3. Hold her accountable with specifics—not generalities.

Together, set up a fundraising calendar with specific deadlines. Do not say, "Take all the time you need for fundraising." That is *not* good leadership and will cause her to feel abandoned emotionally. Help her clear her schedule from other responsibilities; it is tempting to drop fundraising when a "bleating sheep" calls.

After I shared this material at a training seminar, a new female staff tearfully confided, "My supervisor thinks he is being kind by leaving it up to me to decide my fundraising deadlines, but it gives me pressure and guilt."

4. Fill in her shortfall yourself if you truly want her on your team.

If she has worked hard at funding and the money is still not there, fill her shortfall out of your personal or corporate funds. If you want her on your team, raise extra money and fund her yourself! This requires more of you as a supervisor, but the funding of your staff is your problem, too—not merely hers. Don't walk away from her if you want her on your team.

. . .

Single women missionaries have unique challenges in funding, but they are surmountable! If you are from a part of the world where women missionaries have a dismal track record in funding, don't give up. As Mary Slessor was courageous and persistent, single women missionaries around the world are succeeding, and you can too. Apply these guidelines and show them to your supervisor. But don't go it alone. Jesus said, "The worker is worthy of *her* support" (Matthew 10:10, slightly modified).

22

ESPECIALLY FOR GOSPEL-WORKERS OF COLOR AND THEIR SUPERVISORS

FIRST, A CONFESSION. I used to believe that ethnic-minority missionaries could reach full funding if they simply made a gazillion funding appointments. When they struggled, I'd say, "Try harder! Set more appointments!" Some did try harder, but they rarely got as many appointments as they needed. Furthermore, their gifts were often one-time, or they secured pledges that lasted only a month or two. But I remained convinced that *trying harder* was the solution.

As years went by, I noticed that missionaries of color were steadily leaving our American staff. Funding difficulties were mentioned as a reason, but so were other issues, so I persisted in my view that American minority staff could be fully funded if they kept making appointments.

My "solution" was challenged at a staff meeting near Los Angeles. Our funding team was headed into a restaurant when a curious middle-aged white guy asked, "What kind of group are you?"

The Navigators, we told him.

He nodded—he said he was a believer and "knew about that group." Then he asked, "What do you guys do?"

We told him we helped missionaries in funding, and he nodded again. "Oh sure, raising monthly support—I get it."

In an instant it occurred to me: An African American, Asian American, Native American, or Latino believer would not likely have understood what The Navigators were or what raising support was. The history of Anglo ministry since World War II had indirectly informed this white, evangelical stranger about ministry partner development. But other cultures in America—and around the world—do not have this history.

What I had failed to understand was that raising personal support is strange to non-evangelical, non-white ears. For example, an African American college grad phoned her grandmother to say she had been accepted to join The Navigators. Her grandmother was supportive—until she found out about raising personal support.

The phone went silent. "You mean they're not paying you?" the grandmother asked. "You come home right now!"

Family pressure also plays a big role. Parents of color often sacrifice so their kids can get an education and seek a professional career. The idea of their son or daughter becoming a lowly missionary with a mysterious "white" organization is incomprehensible—as is sending monthly support to a faraway "white" corporate headquarters.

A few months ago I was at Arceo's Mexican Family Restaurant in Colorado Springs for lunch with Marvin Campbell, an African American leader in The Navigators. He told me bluntly: "Raising personal support works okay for white, middle-class evangelicals, but not for ethnic-minority Americans—especially blacks."

I swallowed hard and reached for another tortilla chip. "How does that make you feel?" the ever-sensitive Marvin asked.

"Horrible," I muttered, "but tell me more. What makes you say it doesn't work?"

Marvin is a former Navy officer, and with typical Navy directness, he proceeded to explain the obstacles to raising personal support for ethnic-minority mission-workers:

- Ethnic minority gospel-workers do not usually come from evangelical backgrounds. They find it impossible to identify hundreds of believers to put on a mailing list.
- Non-whites have no history of giving monthly to parachurch agencies. Most non-white churches have never heard of The Navigators or similar outreach missions with origins in white evangelicalism. When they Google the ministry, they see a white organization.

- Non-whites (in general) earn less and therefore cannot give as much. Twice as many donors are needed.
- Many believers of color faithfully support their churches and local ministries. They keep the money in the neighborhood. Money to support a parachurch worker comes out of minimal "discretionary spending."

My mind raced with objections, but I kept still. Finally Marvin spoke. "We need to find alternative strategies. This is not working."

How would you have responded to Marvin? His critique is not isolated. Tim Keller, a highly regarded white evangelical author and pastor, acknowledged that the personal support system "marginalizes people who aren't white."[1]

In a study of 716 gospel-workers from seven evangelical outreach ministries, researcher Samuel Perry found that "the odds of raising one's full support were 66% lower for African Americans and Latinos . . . [and] the odds that they had to pick up a second job to supplement their income were twice that of white staff."[2]

The charge is also made that because staff of color struggle to raise full funding, they don't continue on staff long enough to be promoted to leadership. Without staff of color in leadership, the ministries stay white and funding challenges for ethnic minorities go on unaddressed. Critics admit that this is not done on purpose, but they argue that the system puts a glass ceiling on minority staff. I think there is some truth in this insight.

Some of these criticisms seem to be based on individual cases and could be debated, but the major conclusion cannot be ignored: The personal support strategy as currently practiced is *not* bringing gospel-workers of color to full funding. Let's not deny that.

But what can be done?

Encouragingly, since the Bible gives several examples of how God funds His workers, we can go beyond one method. The chart on page 192 lists twelve different funding models (including raising personal support) that have been or could be used in ministry funding. There are more methods than these twelve, and there is overlap between them. But let us not be naive. Just as raising personal support has upsides and downsides, so do these.

In considering your funding strategy, keep the following things in mind:

- Some models require unique special gifting which may not be reproducible. For example, starting a business or charging consulting fees requires unique gifting.
- Some models do not allow mobility (especially 1, 2, and 11).

	Funding Method	Upside	Downside
1	Business income (get a full-time job)	No fundraising; identity of staff understood; good penetration with gospel	Little time available outside of work; not as mobile or flexible with time
2	Bivocational ministry (get a part-time job)	Less fundraising; good cultural penetration	Two "bosses"; inflexible schedule; some gospel-workers don't thrive with multitasking
3	Fee for service (charge for your work)	Less fundraising; good cultural penetration	Mostly short-term clients; scramble to find clients; many staff aren't appropriately gifted to succeed in this
4	Special projects fundraising (focus on projects rather than monthly support)	Fundraising is less about "me"; donors like exciting one-off projects; staff are more motivated to fundraise	Scramble to put together several projects per year; support not usually ongoing
5	Central funding/pooled funding (field staff funds raised by headquarters with some funding raised by staff support)	Frees staff from fundraising, or staff raise a smaller amount of personal support	Limits field staff growth to amount raised; requires massive corporate fundraising effort; puts insulator between donor and end-receiver
6	Spouse works outside job	Frees staff from fundraising	Tired spouse; family stress; additional income may be overstated; childcare challenges
7	Major benefactor (find one or two major donors for all support)	Frees staff from fundraising	Risky if benefactor stops; no team providing prayer support
8	Church partnership (part-time staff at church; part-time with ministry)	Much less or zero fundraising; good cultural penetration	Two bosses; high expecta-tions; difficult to limit time spent at church; "job creep"
9	Live off savings	Frees staff from fundraising; good cultural penetration because mission-worker identity not an issue	Prayer and support partners team not built; no prayer partners; how long can savings last?
10	Third-party fundraising (find friends to fundraise for you)	Frees staff from fundraising; probably good cultural penetration	Puts insulator between staff and donors; third-party fundraisers recruit very few donors
11	Microenterprise business	Frees staff from fundraising; excellent cultural penetration; can hire those you want to disciple	Must raise start-up capital; time-intensive; chance of success risky; takes gifted entrepreneur to make it work; less mobile
12	Personal support (ministry partner development)	Builds a team of partners; forces professional development; funding is portable from location to location	Takes time; assumes a large mailing list; must be a self-starter; not all cultures have a history of this funding model

- All of these require hard work (except possibly 9) and taking risks. There is no easy street.

Which funding method should you choose—one that suits your preferences? No, a bigger issue is at stake. The apostle Paul emphatically stated that gospel-workers have the right to be supported financially by believers. He paraphrased Jesus in Matthew 10:10: "So also the Lord directed those who proclaim the gospel to get their living from the gospel" (1 Corinthians 9:14). But Paul would not *demand* his right to be supported by the very church he pioneered! Instead he said, "We endure all things so that we will cause no hindrance to the gospel of Christ" (1 Corinthians 9:12). And he added his insightful conclusion in 9:23: "I do all things for the sake of the gospel."

Which model to use? Which funding method advances the gospel the best in your ministry context? The decision about how to fund your ministry is not about your preferences—it is about the gospel. Do not let your feelings or experience in funding dictate your decision.

Back to Marvin: A couple of years ago I joined him on face-to-face funding appeals to African American friends of his. Marvin did a fine job of sharing his ministry. But their eyes glazed over when they found out Marvin's work was not through the local church or serving kids from the neighborhood. One began preaching to Marvin about "just trusting the Lord." (Marvin was remarkably restrained!) To get them to take Marvin seriously would have required several meetings and maybe Bible studies—maybe! I concluded to Marvin, "You will have to work longer and harder to get up to budget than an Anglo gospel-worker."

Marvin breathed a sigh of relief. He had been trying to tell me that for years, but I would not believe him. Now I do.

Marvin is not giving up. He continues to make progress in his funding. And as I continue listening to my minority brothers and sisters, I conclude that something must be discarded and something must be added.

- What must be discarded? On-your-own fundraising (OYOFR). The rugged individualism that works well in white American entrepreneurism doesn't work as well in raising support among cultural minorities (and, if we are honest, with many white evangelicals as well).
- What must be added? Teamwork fundraising with a dedicated-to-funding leader.

Teamwork fundraising is succeeding with The Navigators in Albuquerque, New Mexico. Their staff includes twenty-five gift-income staff comprising Anglos, Hispanic Catholics, single women, an African American couple, and volunteer staff. They work in diverse ministries—collegiate; military; within the Catholic Church; and among businessmen and -women, high schools, neighborhoods, and at-risk youth. By December 31 of each year, the twenty-five gift-income staff are all at 100 percent of budget. Here is what they do: Rob Mahon, the "dedicated-to-funding" city director, believes full funding of the staff is *his* problem—not the staff's problem alone. Rob owns the funding of the Albuquerque staff. He spends 30 percent of his time in finding and cultivating major donors, not merely for his personal budget but for the city budget. From this city budget he transfers cash to staff with shortfalls. Sometimes he transfers "match" gifts. And sometimes he offers incentives, such as $50 for each fundraising appointment a staff member conducts in thirty days (ten appointments = $500 cash transfer).

One reason Rob is able to be generous with his staff is that he hosts monthly citywide luncheons open to businesspeople all around Albuquerque. Rob would not say he is a gifted speaker, but he works hard to give interesting and entertaining biblical talks. The monthly luncheon promotes visibility of the work and cultivates major donors, enabling him to be generous with his staff.

What are the ingredients that contribute to successful funding of Albuquerque?

- The Albuquerque staff describe their organizational structure as a *family*—not a "team" or "ministry." As Rob reminds us, the word *Christian* is used only three times in the Bible and *saints* fifty times, but *brethren—family*—is used 225 times.
- Once a month, the Navigator staff and associates in Albuquerque gather for a supper to fellowship and pray together. Kids are included. Family!
- Once a month for two hours, the twenty-five gift-income staff gather for breakfast and one by one answer two questions: "What have you done in fundraising since the last breakfast?" and "What will you do in fundraising until the next breakfast?" The atmosphere is nonjudgmental, and they share failures as well as successes. Rob prints a brief worksheet for prayer with each person's funding goal. Rob also pays for the breakfast.
- Each staff is expected to have a funding plan on paper. They feel accountable not only to Rob but to each other. Rob says, "If *you* are working on your fundraising, *I* am working on your fundraising." He is

reticent to transfer cash to staff who do nothing. As a result, the staff work hard in funding.

- Albuquerque does not keep a pooled account. Each staff maintains his or her ministry account. Rob monitors each account to check on progress.

Humanly speaking, the success of Navigator ministry in Albuquerque—both in the diversity and in discipleship impact—is because of its leadership values that give individualized support to each staff person and because of a team culture in which the staff look after each other—teamwork in funding. And lest I forget, many Albuquerqueans are coming to Christ, and families are being discipled!

Is the Albuquerque strategy reproducible? Probably, but it requires thinking differently about how leaders and staff spend their time. Leaders must be "dedicated to full funding" for all your team—you must *own* the fundraising challenges of your staff.

Second, the "lone ranger" or OYOFR approach to funding must stop. But it is not necessary to move to a pooled fund—which often demotivates good funders who feel that they are picking up for slackers. Rob's attitude is, *Nobody is fully funded until everybody is fully funded.*

My staff leader friend, can you do the following? I think you can!

- Develop a family atmosphere with your staff.
- Build a "city budget" (or area budget) including all your staff plus additional projects.
- "Own" the city budget (or area budget) and raise 100 percent so you can share with your staff.
- Sponsor a once-a-month, nonjudgmental breakfast with only one agenda item—fundraising.
- Spend 30 percent of your time in funding and donor ministry.
- Take time to shepherd your staff economically and hold them accountable.

You may not be able to put the Albuquerque strategy fully into practice now, but this you can do: Discard OYOFR—on-your-own-fundraising! Whenever gospel-workers of any culture gather to work on funding together, good things happen. Add dedication-to-funding to your leadership.

For my gospel-worker friends, the application is obvious: With whom can you team up to fundraise together? You may not have a Rob Mahon in your area, but you

A Family Approach to Fundraising

Veteran Navigator staff Abe Chavez ministers to Hispanic Catholics in Albuquerque. Here are his insights on Albuquerque funding.

Q: Abe, is this "family" approach working?

A: Before Rob started teaching "family," Lizzie and I felt alone. Five months could go by without seeing another staff member. Nobody cared and nobody called. Now with twice-a-month meetings, we care about each other. Financially, Lizzie and I struggled for years, but now we are up to budget.

Q: Do you ever skip the funding breakfast—especially if you haven't done much since the last one?

A: [laughter] It is tempting to skip, but the atmosphere is nonjudgmental. We learned that environments of grace build relationships of trust. Lizzie is going now too. Much of what is shared we have heard before, but repetition is helpful. Romans 12:15 is our desire: "Rejoice with those who rejoice, and weep with those who weep."

Q: Can this model of funding succeed elsewhere?

A: Yes, it is not complicated. Family atmosphere is reproducible. Some ministry groups have good relationships, but they need to extend it to fundraising. I like to imagine God looking down on us and seeing how we relate as family—caring about each other in money matters. That gives Him pleasure. But when He sees a team not caring for each other—that brings Him grief.

Q: How is the fundraising going among Catholic Hispanics?

A: Years ago I didn't imagine that we would receive 50–60 percent of our support from Catholic Hispanics. Now it is happening! But . . . we are learning that we must spend time teaching them about biblical giving, both before and after they start giving.

Q: Do you have a special financial study you do with them?

can gather with a small group or even one staff friend so you are not alone. Don't wait for your leadership to construct a system. Start now to find partners with whom you can fundraise.

Something to drop and something to add.

Raising personal support is a biblical model, but the great negative is the "every person for himself" mentality. Let's drop that! And let's add the family concept of the New Testament! Instead of telling an ethnic-minority staff, "It's up to *you*!" follow Rob Mahon's practice in Albuquerque: "*It's up to us as a family!* We as a family can reach full funding together."

Here are some additional fundraising suggestions.

A: Not one specific study. We informally but frequently share the Scriptures on giving as part of discipleship, and we share what generosity means to us. When we invite them to give, they say yes to monthly support up to 70 percent of the time—and they follow through. Those who say no tell us, "We want to support you, but we will have to wait a few months." Many work two or three jobs. It's "no for now." We stay in contact, of course.

Q: What else are you learning in fundraising?

A: Several things. When I do fundraising, God shows up in my lap! He has a bunch of surprises when I do my part. Still, it is a step of faith to overcome inertia and contact people.

It blesses me when Lizzie comes along on our funding appointments. I can get into "tunnel vision" when I describe our ministry (I'm an engineer by training!), but Lizzie squeezes my knee under the table, which is my signal to stop talking! Then she asks a "feeling" question to get our friends involved again. She has great emotional IQ!

Lizzie also reminds me to do the callback. Our spouses are our complements in marriage. Why not be partners in fundraising, too?

Lay culture aside. If we think, *This culture won't give*, that is a slam against the culture—a condescending statement. I used to be skeptical that Hispanics would give monthly to our support, but we are choosing the biblical model that the "Levite" is to be supported by those they teach. Don't focus on the culture or the economics—follow the biblical patterns.

Broaden your list. Now I put everybody on my mailing list. I knew I was supposed to do that in years past, but I never did it until recently. You don't know whom God has appointed to support you.

Lavishly inform nonwhite donors.

Be ready for questions such as the following:

- Is your organization white? Your website looks white!
- Do people of color serve on your national board?
- What are you doing for the poor and disenfranchised?
- Why aren't you doing ministry through local churches?
- Why don't you pay a salary like most employers?
- What are you doing for my neighborhood? My church?

Misunderstandings are better resolved by talking in person humbly and forthrightly—not by email.

Remember the basics.

Any mission-worker, regardless of ethnicity, struggles with funding when they neglect the basics—things such as

- saying thank you to new donors promptly,
- praying over your top-twenty-five prospect list,
- reconnecting with lapsed donors,
- sending four to six newsletters per year,
- taking adequate time (I suggest 20 percent) for fundraising and donor ministry, and
- struggling through the busyness to set funding appointments.

Offer creative incentives and partnering.

Leaders can offer creative solutions. On occasion, The Navigators match money raised by ethnic-minority staff during ninety-day campaigns. Monthly gifts are matched for twelve months. Funding increases significantly.

Provide organizational grants.

InterVarsity Christian Fellowship (IV) and The Navigators have made great strides in ethnic-minority ministry by charging 1 percent of all staff's income (IV) or 1 percent of all donations (Navigators) to help minority staff. Donna Wilson, former field-training director of IV, says there have been no complaints from staff because of the historical commitment of IV toward developing multiethnic ministry. Some have said, "Why can't we do more?"

Donna emphasized, "Decision-making on distribution of funds rests with the minority-ethnic leaders and should not be controlled by Anglo leadership. This takes trust!" Though not a silver bullet, organizational grants are a huge encouragement.

Champion staff of color.

Anglo staff and friends can champion staff of color. A frequently quoted cliché is the adage, "Give a man a fish and he eats for a day. Teach him how to fish and he eats for a lifetime." John Perkins, the legendary civil-rights leader from Mendenhall, Mississippi, scoffs at the cliché. I personally heard him thunder out a third line: "Give him access to the river!"

Anglos must invite staff of color to come to the river. For example, I set up a meeting with an inner-city African American gospel-worker to meet with a giving partner of mine in the suburbs. I hosted the meeting, and my giving partners loved meeting the gospel-worker and his wife. They gladly pledged monthly support—for a higher amount than they supported me!

How about asking your Anglo staff to connect two of their donors with a gospel-worker of color? That little bit of action will produce great results and bonding in your organization.

The Role of the African American Church in Fundraising

The following insight comes from Rich Berry, former director of The Navigators' African American ministry.

I am an African American missionary. I have raised money for more than thirty-five years and have learned that the individualized approach of going to businessmen has very limited effectiveness among African Americans. There is a better way.

The African American church presents a great opportunity for raising money. I find it unthinkable that in the twenty-first century, anyone trying to raise money in the black community would not engage the church. Having pastored an African American church for twelve years, I know that the church is the principal entity in the community for social and spiritual change. It is the strongest, oldest, most revered, and most economically stable institution in the African American community. With this in mind, it would follow that the African American church should become a vital part of fundraising if African Americans are to grow deep in discipleship. It makes practical sense; it makes theological sense.

To receive financial support from an African American church, one must have a relationship with that church. Would a church give to an aspiring missionary without having a relationship with him or her? Possibly, but not likely. Instead, the missionary should serve the church on an ongoing basis (could be annual or a couple times a year), perhaps teaching a seminar or an engagement with the Sunday school. This approach would help to build a relationship with the church so that one is known, loved, and prayed for.

The African American church presents a challenge for the way most evangelical groups raise money. Going to businesspeople is quick and requires one person or family to make a decision. Relating to a church is more complicated and takes more time. In the long run the missionary will not only have the prayers of one donor but the prayers of a congregation.

My appeal to faith missionaries is to do the homework that raising money requires. Employ the principle that missiologists apply to ministry in foreign fields. Shape fundraising strategies to reflect the needs and values of the people being reached. Only when this principle is applied will there be a long-range solution to the problem of ethnic funding.

· · ·

This issue of funding for nonwhite, non-evangelical gospel-workers has the potential to divide us. But it need not! I know it sounds "white," but there is plenty of money available to do God's perfect will. However, the idea that each gospel-worker can find his or her own funding without the help of the body is unbiblical. We must work together and we can work together. Which of the suggestions above can you put into practice immediately? Let's stop talking and start acting!

Biblical Financial Management for Gospel-Workers

I have yet to meet a gospel-worker who does not have strong opinions about money. The challenge is to let the Bible—rather than common sense or our cultural or family traditions, good as they may be—guide our strong opinions. But changing our views about money becomes an emotional roadblock fast.

If anyone needs to understand money, it is gospel-workers like you and me. We are inviting people to give their hard-earned money to the Kingdom! They trust us with "their" money. Our commonsense cultural views of money are not adequate.

We cannot assume that those to whom we appeal for funding understand the biblical view of money or giving. They have strong opinions too. As gospel-workers, we are in a good position to teach them. We ought to be good models of biblical financial management and able to teach—but are we?

You might not like everything you read in chapters 23 and 24! But it is crucial not only to your fundraising but also to your discipleship as a believer in Christ. Fasten your seat belt!

23

MONEY: KINGDOM VIEW OR CULTURAL VIEW?

Six Benchmarks Reveal Your Financial Values

YOUR STRUGGLE WITH FUNDRAISING may have less to do with fundraising and more to do with your view of money. If fundraising feels like drudgery, you have a serious problem. Author Henri Nouwen said it this way:

> If we come back from asking someone for money and we feel exhausted and somehow tainted by unspiritual activity, there is something wrong. We must not let ourselves be tricked into thinking that fundraising is only a secular activity. As a form of ministry, fundraising is as spiritual as giving a sermon, entering a time of prayer, visiting the sick, or feeding the hungry.[1]

The place to begin is with our personal view of money. Martin Luther is often quoted as saying: "There are three conversions: the conversion of the head, the heart, and the wallet." I do not intend to come across as accusatory, but we gospel-workers must pay closer heed to developing a biblical view of money.

```
┌──────────────────────────────────┐
│      BIBLICAL FUNDRAISING         │
├──────────────────────────────────┤
│     BIBLICAL VIEW OF MONEY        │
└──────────────────────────────────┘
```

Biblical fundraising sits atop a biblical view of money. From interactions with gospel-workers of many cultures, I find that most have strong opinions about fundraising and about money. But many of their opinions originate from their parents, unquestioned evangelical traditions, or their own common sense. They do not bring a biblical view of money to their opinions. Here are a few symptoms displayed by mission-workers who have a cultural or commonsense view of money rather than a biblical view:

- Downplaying the fact that they need money. Rather than grappling with the difficulties of fundraising, they postpone or abdicate their fundraising responsibilities to passively "trust God."
- Allowing the lack of money to dictate their ministry planning. Their ministry vision is never larger than last year's budget.
- Clinging to a scarcity mentality bordering on miserliness. They must make do with less because they think God's pie has only eight slices.
- Worrying continually about finances. They are not sure God will provide tomorrow or in the future.
- Perpetually in debt and having no savings. They have not learned the basics of managing money.

Where to start? With the Bible, of course. Here are six benchmarks for determining if you have a biblical view of money. If you find yourself reacting negatively, don't ignore your feelings. Change might be in process.

1. Do I live as if God owns it all or just 10 percent?

I was teaching in Asia about biblical stewardship and asked, "How much should Christians give?" Immediately a hand shot up from an older Asian, who proudly reminded the group, "The tithe (10 percent) is the Lord's!"

Everyone nodded in agreement. But I countered, "And 90 percent belongs to you?"

Silence. The audience was stunned.

We are so shot through with the teaching of tithing that we act as if God cares only for *His* 10 percent; the rest is ours to do with as we please. But Haggai 2:8 says, "'The silver is Mine and the gold is Mine,' declares the LORD of hosts.'"

The 90/10 doctrine that comes from assumptions about tithing opens the door to unbiblical thinking on a grand scale. If a Christian couple together earn $120,000 per year and give 10 percent, they are free to spend $108,000 (120,000 minus 12,000 = 108,000). God has already been paid; they "eke out a living" on the balance.

This worldview gives you permission to be greedy. If you can afford to buy the latest computer tablet year by year (after you have given God His 10 percent), does that mean it is okay? More practically, should you buy a complicated Starbucks European coffee blend every morning just because you can?

If God owns it all, then *all* financial decisions are spiritual decisions. The 90 percent is just as much God's as the 10 percent. He deserves a voice in *all* our financial decisions. Just as we pray about how we should give, so we must pray about what we should save and spend. If God owns it all, as Haggai 2:8 reminds us, then "secular money decisions" must also be brought to the Lord, for they, too, are holy.

Kingdom people are caretakers—not owners. In one of Jesus' parables, a landowner instructs his servants (you and me) to care for His land and make it profitable. When He (Jesus) returns, He will review with us how faithfully we managed *His* property (Matthew 25:14-30). In 1 Corinthians 4:7 Paul asks, "What do you have that you did not receive?" Do you bring *all* your financial decisions before the Lord, or only your giving decisions? There's nothing necessarily wrong with going to Starbucks, but even a small decision like that can be brought before the Lord. You are spending His money, not yours. (More on money management in chapter 24.)

2. Am I a deeply thankful person?

If everything we have is ultimately a gift from God—entrusted to us as His stewards—then gratitude should ooze out of our character. But popular culture says differently. On the television show *The Simpsons*, Bart Simpson is asked to say a prayer before mealtime with his family. Bart bows his head and prays, "Dear God, we paid for all this stuff ourselves, so thanks for nothing."

True, Bart's parents earned the money to buy the food, but Bart verbalized the narcissistic worldview that God need not be thanked.

Unfortunately, gospel-workers can be thankless too—though in more subtle ways. As The Navigators US development director for thirteen years, I received complaints from donors who said they rarely received thanks from missionaries they supported. In my seminars I ask, "How many newsletters do you send each year?" Many mission-workers hang their heads and admit they mail only one or two per year. Why so few? "Lack of time. I am so busy!" But is that the real problem? If you are too busy to thank those who undergird your mission, then busyness is not your problem. An ungrateful heart is your problem!

Hebrews 12:28 reveals the expected lifestyle of Christians: "Therefore, since we receive a kingdom which cannot be shaken, *let us show gratitude*, by which we may offer to God an acceptable service with reverence and awe" (emphasis added). A famous old poem by Maltbie Babcock points to the Source:

Back of the loaf is the snowy flour,
And back of the flour the mill;
And back of the mill is the wheat and the shower,
And the sun and the Father's will.

Author Os Guinness says it well: "Let all your *thinks* be *thanks*."[2] When was the last time your giving partners heard a genuine thanks from you?

3. Am I surrendering to materialism?

You did not go into missions to become rich. You could have made more money in medicine or business (or in my case, professional baseball). But being in ministry does not mean we are immune to materialism.

Many believers today suffer from "affluenza." They don't fix a broken household item—they just buy a new one. They don't even turn off the lights when they leave an empty room. I suspect that some gospel-workers use "keeping up with technology" as a rationale for feeding their materialistic desires for electronic gadgets.

Though he was the most generous man on earth, Jesus was also frugal. After feeding five thousand people he said, "Gather up the extra fragments so that nothing will be lost" (John 6:12). So where are you on the frugality-affluenza spectrum?

FRUGALITY–AFFLUENZA SPECTRUM

| Tendency to hoard, miserly | Miserly, but trying to be generous | Frugal and generous | Rarely think about frugality | Affluenza, no controls |

Jesus gave a haunting warning in Luke 12:15: "Beware, and be on your guard against *every form of greed*; for not *even* when one has an abundance does his life consist of his possessions" (emphasis added). The phrase "every form of greed" suggests that greed comes in individually wrapped temptation packages. You might not be tempted by new cars, but maybe electronic gadgets are your downfall. It is easy to criticize others for a form of materialism to which we are not tempted.

Greed is similar to coveting. It is not limited to material things. Believers can also be greedy for fame, power, the attention of attractive women, or the fawning of handsome men. Once we give ourselves permission to covet, even in small things, we are in a free fall toward idolatry. In Ephesians 5:5 Paul links covetousness to idolatry: "No immoral or impure person or *covetous* man, who is an *idolater*, has an inheritance in the kingdom of Christ and God" (emphasis added).

Coveting leads to idolatry—replacing God as Lord of our lives. That is why Jesus told the rich young ruler to "sell your possessions and give to the poor, and you will have treasure in heaven" (Matthew 19:21). Jesus didn't challenge Levi or Peter to sell their possessions. Why this man? Obviously, wealth was his idol. Generosity was the only way he could break the power of idolatry.

What "form of greed" seeks you out like a laser beam? Are you saying no?

4. Do I secretly long to be rich?

Fabled American millionaire John D. Rockefeller was reportedly asked, "How much money is enough money?" He replied, "Just a little bit more."

Have you discovered this hidden phrase in 1 Timothy 6:9? "But those *who want to get rich* fall into temptation and a snare" (emphasis added). Being rich is not the problem. *Wanting to be rich* is the problem. Paul was not addressing wealthy pagan people. He was writing to Christians! He says in verse 10, "For the love of money is a root of all sorts of evil, and some by longing for it have wandered away from the faith and pierced themselves with many griefs."

A nonbeliever doesn't have a faith to wander from! And believers don't bolt suddenly, but inch by inch they *wander* from a vital relationship with Christ and the church. Such is the power of loving money.

Is money the problem? No, the *love of money* is the problem! At least pagan people admit they want to be rich, whereas Christians will not. And though we can spot money-lust in others, are we willing to admit that wanting to be rich tempts us, too?

Unfortunately, money-lust among religious leaders is not new. The religious leaders of Jesus' day, the Pharisees, tithed meticulously and even wore phylacteries (little boxes containing Old Testament Scriptures) on their foreheads. But they had a reputation: "Now the Pharisees, who were *lovers of money* . . ." (Luke 16:14, emphasis added).

As a medium of exchange, money is neutral, even good; but if you have not been converted from wanting to be rich, then you will move toward money like a flying insect to a bright light—only to be burned when you get too close.

Does everyone need to experience this "money conversion?" Yes. If Jesus is Lord of all, then certainly He is Lord of the resources He has placed in my hands to manage. Your experience need not be a dramatic angel-feathers-falling-from-heaven conversion, but surrender nonetheless. It's not a new problem. As Charles Spurgeon preached on Thursday evening, August 27, 1868, "With some [Christians] the last part of their nature that ever gets sanctified is their pockets!"[3]

But how much is enough? I once asked a successful business friend in his fifties, "How much will you need in an investment corpus at age sixty-seven so you can retire?"

His answer: "There will never be enough! Millions won't be enough! We are spenders."

His reply reveals he had not yet sorted out his life dreams, and so he had no basis to answer. As a steward, your goal is not simply to become wealthy but to develop adequate funding to accomplish the life dreams God has placed upon you. Until those dreams are identified (and written down), you are chasing an undefined "something," and you will always be short.

How much is enough? Rather than assume that you should accumulate, accumulate, accumulate, ask: What will it cost to fund my God-given life dreams?

Try this *scary* exercise. In my thirties I took a plain sheet of paper and made two columns with twenty or so blank lines (see below):

My God-inspired life dreams	
What I want to do before I die	**Cost?**
_____	$_____
_____	$_____
_____	$_____

Then I jotted down the things I wanted to do before I died—my "bucket list" (before that term was popular). And I didn't edit. Some items were big; some were little; some were selfish; some were unmeasurable; some cost little; some cost much. Then I reflected on the list and let it stare back at me. That's when I realized I needed an overall money mission or a guiding statement to give a basis for my dream list—an alternative to merely wanting to become rich.

My finance mission became: *To seek only enough of this world's physical treasure to enable me to accomplish the purposes for which Christ called me.*

The last thing I did was to estimate what each dream would cost. I review my list several times per year and add to or subtract from it as life situations change. I am encouraged as some dreams are being accomplished and others refined.

How about you? Have you written down your financial goals—the price tags of your life dreams? Did I say "written down?" Yes, on paper or on your computer screen. Listen to Tony Brooks from the Leadership Training Workshop:

> What most people do not realise is that the power of goal setting lies in *writing goals down.* Committing goals to paper and reviewing them regularly gives you a 95% higher chance of achieving your desired outcomes. Studies have shown that only three to five percent of people in the world have written goals.[4]

Take the courage to put your specific dreams down on paper. Study them; pray over them! God will reveal those that are proper and those that are improper. Don't feel guilty about what your God-given life dreams will cost. There is enough money to do what God is calling you to. For example:

- Get your kids through college or job training without debt.
- Build a liquid emergency fund equal to two months' salary.
- Save for a vehicle rather than borrowing.
- Save for a family vacation to Mauritius.
- Put down 30 percent to buy a house.

Do you get the idea? Why not take a few minutes today to put your life goals on paper?

Let's go back to 1 Timothy 6:9. Wanting to be fully funded does not mean you "want to be rich." Whether your budget is big or small, raise 100 percent plus (as I suggested earlier) 10 percent to see you through temporary shortfalls. Don't let a simple thing like money squelch your God-inspired dreams.

Do you secretly long to be rich? If you hope to escape it, you must first admit it.

5. Do I worry about money?

Gospel-workers are not chronic worriers, but many are *very concerned* about finances. When does *very concerned* migrate into full-fledged *worry*?

Have you noticed that Jesus' teaching about worry in Matthew 6 comes immediately after his teaching about money? Matthew 6:24 summarizes Jesus' comments on money: "You cannot serve God and wealth." Then in Matthew 6:25 Jesus goes on to say, "For this reason I say to you, do not be worried about your life, as to what you will eat or what you will drink."

Here's the problem: If you are *not* faithfully doing fundraising, it will be almost impossible to stop worrying (or being *very concerned*) about money. The issue is not worry but disobedience. If you know what to do (in fundraising or any other topic) but don't do it, the Bible calls that sin (James 4:17). Start working on your funding, and your worry will decrease.

If God has given us life and promised to provide the necessities of life, why do we worry over finances? William Barclay, British Bible commentator, said that "there may be greater sins than worry, but very certainly there is no more disabling sin."[5]

6. Do I have a generous spirit?

We want others to be generous, but are we? At times, I find in myself and other gospel-workers a subtle kind of stinginess. Are we afraid God might not provide again as He has in the past?

- A campus ministry leader canceled a weekend planning retreat because his three staff couldn't afford it. Yet he had $20,000 "reserve" in his ministry account. When I suggested he pay for his staff (maybe $1,000 total), he said it "never crossed my mind" to use *his* account to help his staff.
- A missionary couple received a scholarship to pay their conference fee of $2,000. Yet they had $30,000 in their ministry reserve account. When I challenged the missionary, he said he needed the reserve for a trip to Asia. How much? Maybe $4,000 tops. Sadly, others more deserving of scholarships were denied because of this couple's fear.
- Once I tried to raise support for a mission-worker who said he was in hard times. So I phoned a few of his lapsed-donor friends to ask them to restart support. They seemed surprised. I found out later that my friend had a huge reserve in his ministry account. Why did he plead poverty?

What is at the bottom of such behavior? A fear that God will not provide! Hang on to what you've got! When it's gone, it's gone!

In our early days in ministry when we were below budget, my financial guideline was to "spend as little as possible." Accordingly, I resented giving tips at restaurants, I resented paying monthly bills, and I complained about high prices. I even dreaded vacations because I resented spending money on "frivolous things" such as my kids going down the giant slide at the state fair. "We can't afford it," I pleaded. But in reality, I had a miserly spirit.

By contrast, Alma was generous. When we hosted fellow staff and students, she made sure there was enough food for seconds. Students loved coming to our house—but not because of my Bible study speeches!

Even as we approached 100 percent of funding, I still resented spending money. I don't even know why. A breakthrough came when we set up a household budget using the envelope system (cash—see the next chapter). The envelopes gave us permission to spend up to budgeted amounts rather than spending "as little as possible."

Slowly by slowly, I stopped resenting fun outings. Slowly by slowly, I stopped whining about paying bills. Slowly by slowly, I started giving better tips at restaurants.

Looking back on it now, I see that my super-frugal miserly outlook was a cover-up for the lie that God cannot provide unless it is on sale or free! But the old miserly tendency is still a temptation.

Frugality becomes miserliness when we inwardly believe, "This is all there is" or "This is as good as it gets." I didn't have a generous spirit because I didn't believe God was generous. A miserly attitude signals a belief that God Himself is miserly.

Conclusions.

Can you say yes to these six markers of a biblical view of money?

- I pray over *all* financial decisions because "my money" is not mine.
- I express daily thankfulness to the Lord.
- I know what "form" of coveting tempts me and reject it.
- I do not desire to be rich but only to have what is needed to meet God-ordained life-dreams.
- I refuse to let worry about money occupy my thoughts.
- I cultivate a generous spirit, daily displacing a miserly spirit.

Would Martin Luther say your wallet has been converted?

24

MONEY MANAGEMENT

Four Money Words You Must Know Well

RAISING FINANCES IS ONLY half your financial responsibility—the other side of the coin is finance management. Sadly, gospel-workers are often inept and sometimes scurrilous in handling money.

A friend in Omaha was a salesman for a thriving office-equipment company. As a believer, he got the "religious accounts." Why? "The other salesmen won't take them," he said. "Our church and ministry customers don't pay their bills on time. And when we charge a late fee, they subtract that from the total even though we've carried them 60, 90, or 120 days. It's a horrible testimony to the sales guys I'm trying to win to Christ."

I once asked the accounts receivable director at NavPress to identify their toughest customers to collect from. He quickly replied, "Missionaries!" But worse are stories of Christian leaders living extravagant, jet-set lives with only puppet boards watching them. Or money given for a specific project that is spent on day-to-day operating expenses.

Most of us in gospel-work have not been officially trained in money management. That is why we must know the following money words well. Let our training begin now!

Word 1: Borrowing.

Staying out of debt is a good idea—until Sears has a sale on table saws or your kids' school fees are due. I used to think missionaries would not be tempted to borrow, but they, too, are prone to accumulate debt—even in developing countries where many live meager paycheck to meager paycheck. Missionaries have the added temptation that "God will surely bring it in next month."

For some missionaries, borrowing from family or through credit cards has become a way of life. One missionary friend had the courage to say what I suspect many believe: "[Borrowing] became *God's provision* to get through tough times." Months later, he was deeper in debt.

The average credit card debt in America now stands at $16,061 per household—serious enough—and the average student loan debt as of the third quarter of 2016 is $49,042.[1] When young college grads join the mission force, they must add huge debt repayment expense to their budgets. Some are in such financial bondage that gospel service is not even considered.

Some countries, such as Japan, do not struggle as much with debt. Gospel-workers from developing countries have much lower debts than Americans, but many are in debt to family. A Filipino gospel-worker told me humorously, "We Filipinos borrow even when we don't need the money—just in case!"

Despite what your culture says about borrowing, do you know what the Scriptures teach? Two verses comment specifically. Here they are:

- Proverbs 22:7: "The rich rules over the poor, and the borrower becomes the lender's slave." If you owe someone money, he or she *rules* over you. You are not free as long as you owe money.
- Psalm 37:21: "The *wicked* borrows and does not pay back, but the righteous is gracious and gives" (emphasis added). Although it may not be a sin to borrow, it certainly is a sin not to pay back. If your brother won't repay you, show him this verse—share gently with him that he is "wicked"!

Here is an additional danger: Borrowing strains relationships. Think of someone who owes you money—even a small amount. As the debt remains unpaid, your relationship with that person becomes awkward. The debt becomes the elephant in the room. Because we don't want to strain our relationships with friends and family, Alma and I do not loan money. But we gladly *give* money without expectation of payback. We tell them it's a gift.

What about home mortgage debt? In most countries a home is an appreciating asset; you will probably not lose money over time—probably! Still, you are wise to eliminate even this debt as soon as possible.

Another trap is borrowing from parents. Parents might even say, "Don't worry about paying us back. We are in no hurry to get the money." But it is still a loan; it still brings a subtle pressure to the relationship. In my experience, wives feel the subtle pressure first. Husbands, do not ignore your wife's uneasiness about carrying loans from parents or family. Even in good family relationships, it can feel like control. Pay it off quickly. More is at stake than money.

Is there a contradiction in Luke 6:35: "Love your enemies, and do good, and *lend*, expecting nothing in return" (emphasis added; see also Matthew 5:42)? The word translated "lend" is *didomi*—"to give"—and it is used in a variety of ways. Starting in Luke 6:27, Jesus teaches about relationships—love your enemies, do good to them, give to them, bless them, turn the other cheek. Both the context and the verse itself teach that we should *expect nothing in return*. Overwhelm your enemies by your generosity. Jesus is not encouraging money lending.

In summary, the Scriptures do not condemn debt as sin, but they warn against its danger. It (1) adds financial pressure, (2) gives you another master, and (3) strains relationships.

The chart below reveals the power of debt vs. savings. Let's say you overspend by $80 per month—$960 a year. At a credit card interest rate of 18 percent, the total owed after one year is $1,133. After five years, you have borrowed $4,800 (5 × $960), but $8,104 is the amount you must pay back.

Now let's say that you want to pay off the $8,104 in the coming five years. You pay not $80 each month but $150. The total interest paid for the privilege of overspending by $80 a month is $7,494. That is known as working for your money!

OVERSPENDING

Here's what overspending your income by $80 a month will add to your debt total in five years at 18 percent annual interest.

Year	Debt Addition	Interest	Total Debt
1	$960	$173	$1,133
2	960	377	2,470
3	960	617	4,047
4	960	901	5,908
5	960	1,236	8,104

DEBT REPAYMENT

Here's what it will cost you to repay that debt in the next five years at $203.17 each month.

Year	Annual Payment	Debt Paydown	Total Debt
6	$2,438	$1,350	$6,912
7	2,438	1,142	5,616
8	2,438	894	4,072
9	2,438	582	2,216
10	2,438	222	—
Interest First Five Years		$3,304	
Interest Last Five Years		$4,190	
Total Interest		$7,494	

Now contrast debt with savings in the next chart. Instead of overspending by $80 per month, let's say you save $83 per month ($1,000 per year), earning 6 percent interest. After five years you'd have $5,975, and after fifteen years you would have accumulated $24,672!

Now you can withdraw not $1,000 but $2,000 per year for twenty years, and you'd still have $1,142 left over! That's making your money work for you!

You invested $15,000 of your money in fifteen years. Because of interest, you withdrew at $2,000 per year during the next twenty years ($40,000) and you still had $1,142 left.

SAVINGS: AN ILLUSTRATION

$1,000 saved annually at 6 percent interest compounded annually for fifteen years:

Year	Addition	Interest Earned	Ending Balance
1	$1,000	$60	$1,060
2	1,000	123	2,183
3	1,000	191	3,374
4	1,000	262	4,636
5	1,000	383	5,975
6	1,000	418	7,393
7	1,000	503	8,897
8	1,000	593	10,491
9	1,000	689	12,180
10	1,000	790	13,971
11	1,000	898	15,869
12	1,000	1,012	17,882
13	1,000	1,132	20,015
14	1,000	1,260	22,276
15	1,000	1,396	24,672

At the end of fifteen years, you could start to withdraw $2,000 annually:

16	2,000	1,360	24,032
17	2,000	1,321	23,354
18	2,000	1,281	22,636
19	2,000	1,238	21,874
20	2,000	1,192	21,066
21	2,000	1,144	20,210
22	2,000	1,092	19,303
23	2,000	1,038	18,341
24	2,000	980	17,321
25	2,000	919	16,241
26	2,000	854	15,095

At the end of eleven years of $2,000 withdrawals, you still have more on deposit than you invested originally.

27	2,000	785	13,881
28	2,000	712	12,594
29	2,000	635	11,230
30	2,000	553	9,783
31	2,000	467	8,250
32	2,000	375	6,625
33	2,000	277	4,903
34	2,000	174	3,077
35	2,000	64	1,142

If you are in debt, how did it happen? What underlying thought process gave you permission to buy something you could not immediately pay for? If you borrowed because your fundraising is lagging, ask yourself why it is lagging. Your Visa card is not an answer to prayer! Unless you address these questions, you will be in financial bondage your entire life.

But it is not too late. What actions can you take to eliminate debt—even family loans—*within a year*? I'm serious—a year! Here are a few tips:

- Get rid of multiple credit cards immediately—keep only one for convenience, and pay it off monthly. If you cannot control credit card use, you should not have one. Don't store extra cards in a desk drawer—store them in a 350-degree oven!
- Live on a budget and aggressively pay down your debt every month.
- Have a sale. Use the proceeds to pay down debt.
- Before you buy, ask yourself and the Lord, "Do I need this?" Luxury or necessity?

- Avoid shopping malls and online catalogues. Cut off the temptation before it begins!
- Sell your second car.
- Stop eating out.

Getting out of debt requires huge discipline! American finance guru Dave Ramsey advises daily on his radio show, "Live like no one else [now] so you can live like no one else [later]." To get out of debt, you and your spouse will not go on date nights. You will eat ramen soup daily. Play board games instead of going to Chuck E. Cheese's! Millennials will no longer post photos of expensive dinners on Instagram!

The pain is worth it! I saved a letter from a gospel-worker who said, "I am coming up to the three-year mark of *not* living on a credit card. . . . I am basking in the grace of God and greater financial liberty." May we all experience his testimony!

Word 2: Saving.

Missionaries would love to build savings accounts or investments, but many feel guilty doing it. It's okay for their donors to invest, but not them. It is a sign of "going down to Egypt," trusting man instead of God. Hmmm.

As with borrowing, only a few Bible verses strongly teach saving, but saving is assumed throughout the Bible. Here are three instructive passages:

- "There is precious treasure and oil in the dwelling of the wise; but a foolish man swallows it up" (Proverbs 21:20). Note the contrast: A wise person *accumulates* rather than immediately *swallowing it up*. Accumulation is sometimes viewed as a sin or politically incorrect. The problem is not accumulation itself but the motives of the person doing the accumulating. Interestingly, if your donors do not accumulate, they cannot give to your year-end cash project.
- "Go to the ant, O sluggard, observe her ways and be wise, which, having no chief, officer or ruler, prepares her food in the summer and gathers her provision in the harvest" (Proverbs 6:6-8). Even with tiny brains, ants anticipate that they need stores for days when food cannot be found. Birds such as woodpeckers store seeds in the bark of trees. Saving is hardwired into the DNA of ants and birds—what about us?
- "Thus Joseph stored up grain in great abundance like the sand of the sea. . . . The people of all the earth came to Egypt to buy grain" (Genesis 41:49, 57).

Joseph wasn't hoarding grain. His accumulation had a godly purpose—to help those in need when hard times came.

But does saving contradict Matthew 6:19-21? "Do not store up *for yourselves* treasures on earth" (emphasis added). And what about Luke 12:16-21, where Jesus calls a wealthy man a fool because he built bigger barns to store his crops. "So is the man who stores up treasure *for himself*, and is not rich toward God" (emphasis added). Note the emphasized words: "for yourselves" and "for himself." The person who accumulates *for himself*, so that he won't have to trust God, has an idol. Similarly, if you do not have godly purposes for your savings, you are merely hoarding.

How to save

In our early years Alma and I fell into the trap of trying to save what was left at the end of the month. But nothing was ever left—even though we determined not to overspend! At the newspaper I got paid every Friday. But we were broke by the following Monday afternoon! Then we'd hold our breath until Friday's paycheck.

So we switched from "save what is left" to the old adage PYF, "pay yourself first." I deposited our paycheck in our bank on Friday—except for $25. (That was big money in those days.) Next, I transferred the $25 to a savings account. And even though we had $25 less to spend the next week, we didn't die! My self-esteem soared!

After a year of this weekly discipline, we had saved enough to pay for our move to Iowa to join the staff of The Navigators. PYF worked!

Alma and I have since adjusted our strategy to PTLF/PYS—pay the Lord first, pay yourself second. Try it! Instead of depositing your entire paycheck, hold out 5 to 10 percent and immediately deposit it in a savings account—someplace where it is not easily accessible.

Now a question: Just as Joseph had a godly purpose for saving grain, what are your godly purposes for saving? The answer "Just in case I need it" borders on hoarding. "Need it" for what? How about saving for

- emergencies like repairing your car or water heater,
- your next vehicle (the guy who sold you your current car said it had eternal life—he was wrong),
- your kids' education,
- old age or when you can no longer work full-time,
- buying a home, or
- caring for aging parents?

As I mentioned in the previous chapter, write down your godly financial purposes—these are simply your life dreams. Let them stare back at you. Meditate on them. You will not be able to accomplish these desires without accumulation. One month's paycheck will not buy a new car!

How much accumulation? Accumulate enough to accomplish the dreams—personal, family, and ministry—that God has given you.

Warning: Alma and I made the mistake of combining our savings into one big emergency fund. But soon kids' college money was used for car tires. Not wise. Have different bank accounts or mutual fund accounts for different godly purposes.

Where do you start on an investment/saving strategy? The diagram on the next page is helpful.

- *Step one: Get out of consumer debt or family debt.* This is your highest financial priority! Unbelievably, some "experts" advise not paying down debt so that you can use that money to invest in higher-paying opportunities. But debt is dangerous! It gives you another boss. Even though your interest rate may be low, get out of debt! It is impossible to experience financial freedom paying interest year after year.
- *Step two: Establish a liquid emergency fund.* Set aside two to three months of living expenses in an easily accessible—but not too accessible—emergency fund. (Do not stuff it in your mattress!) Use it for car repairs, assisting extended family, medical emergencies, and so on.
- *Step three: Short-term saving.* Auto replacement, appliance purchase, family vacation, university fees, starting a business, and so on.
- *Step four: Long-term saving.* House down payment, college funds, old-age care, dreams, bonus items, and the like.

Work on step one first to get out of debt, but start a small emergency fund at the same time. After you are out of debt and have an emergency fund, then work on steps three and four, with more money going to step three. Keep all four accounts separate. For an amazing review of the power of saving, go to scottmorton.net. If you are in your twenties, you must see this chart!

How does Matthew 6:33—"But seek first His kingdom and His righteousness, and all these things will be added to you"—fit into the idea of saving and trusting God? As a college student and six-week-old believer, I was eating lunch with guys from the Bible study. A fourth-year student whom I greatly respected had been approached to buy insurance, but he said, "I'll never have a savings account or an insurance policy because it is contrary to Scripture." Then he quoted Matthew 6:33. His simplistic application seemed suspect, but who was I to disagree?

A few years later, I picked up the hobby of bird-watching. I observed that birds spend most of their waking hours—some researchers say 60 percent—searching for food. When you see birds fluttering in weed patches, they aren't just hanging out—they are in a life-or-death search for something to eat!

Matthew 6:26 says that even though birds do not sow or reap, "your heavenly Father feeds them. Are you not worth much more than they?" Okay, birds don't buy insurance policies, but some gospel-workers wrongly think that "seeking first the Kingdom" means they need not be active in funding their ministry.

God provides—but the birds must search. He provides for us, too, but we must do our part—just like the birds.

Word 3: Budget.

The "B" word. Is budgeting merely a Western concept? I cannot find *budget* in the Bible, but the principle of budgeting is certainly there. Jesus' parable of the wise and foolish virgins in Matthew 25:1-13 gives two key words that make budgeting succeed.

PRIORITIES IN FINANCIAL MANAGEMENT

The stairstep of financial priorities in establishing financial goals:

#4 LONG-TERM SAVING

House down payment, college fund, old age, bonus, dreams

#3 SHORT-TERM SAVING

Auto, appliances, vacation

#2 ESTABLISH A LIQUID EMERGENCY FUND

Two months' living expenses for unanticipated emergencies

#1 GET OUT OF CONSUMER DEBT AND STOP PAYING INTEREST

Credit cards, auto loans, home equity loans, etc.

Tip: Focus on getting out of debt and establishing a liquid emergency fund first.

In Jesus' day, wedding parties were not hurried affairs. Guests slowly meandered to the groom's house for the celebration. Next (usually at night), the groom and his party finally arrived at the bride's house. Each wedding guest was expected to carry a torch. In the parable in Matthew 25, ten virgins were invited to a wedding party; five took extra oil for their lamps, but five did not. When the bridegroom arrived late at night, the five foolish virgins had no oil, so they asked the wise virgins for some of their oil. But the wise virgins said no. Then, while the foolish virgins were going to buy oil from the merchants, the "door was shut" (verse 10).

What is the point of the parable? Be prepared for the Lord's return, even if it is later than you planned. Can this teaching be applied to daily life also? Absolutely. Let's take a look at the foolish virgins first.

What kind of thinking would say, "We needn't take extra oil"? The problem is a wrong assumption—a baseless expectation of a favorable outcome. The foolish virgins assumed that the groom would come before their oil ran out and that they could borrow from others. They assumed future outcomes over which they had no control.

They also assumed they could get help from others if they ran out of oil. So they asked the other five virgins to loan them oil. But those five said no, and the foolish virgins were shut out.

Making wise assumptions about the future is a principle of life that is ignored at our peril. Even though our knowledge of the future is limited and our control over circumstances is limited, we must plan ahead with wise assumptions. The Bible calls the virgins who failed to prepare *moros*—foolish or stupid—from which the English word *moron* is derived. A strong word from Jesus!

As you consider your financial future (near or far):

- What are you *assuming*? Are your assumptions valid?
- What *boundaries* must you set?

First, do you assume that

- your kids will get full scholarships to university,
- a large inheritance will come from your parents,
- your donors will give even if you don't communicate with them,
- you or your family will never have a medical emergency, or
- you can borrow from friends whenever you have an emergency?

The second word is *boundaries*. The wise virgins said no—they did not share their oil. Though it might seem unmerciful, the customs of Jesus' day did not allow "wedding crashers." No lamp—no entrance. A serious teaching about the finality of His coming.

The wise virgins set a boundary because the serious issue of gaining entrance to the wedding ceremony was at stake. They said no in order not to jeopardize their destiny. A good lesson for us, too.

Applying the principle of boundaries to finances means simply deciding what you will say no to financially—that's budgeting. A household budget tells you no when you reach a boundary in spending. For example—say no graciously when

- you receive an advertisement for a cool but unnecessary extra-powerful, guaranteed, super-duper leaf blower (which you will use three times a year);
- a family member wants you to give money to a "sure-fire" investment opportunity in gold mining;
- your daughter pleads with tears for an advance on her allowance to buy a special new pair of jeans that "all the other kids are wearing"; or
- you are tempted to buy the newest upgrade of the latest electronic gadget even though you would have to borrow "just a little" to pay for it.

I believe the key to saying no in finance is prayer. "Lord, I surrender my desire for that electronic gadget to you." The wise virgins said no, and you can too.

Okay, but can you succeed at budgeting without an accounting degree? Yes. First, be clear on what budgeting is not.

As Bob's funding coach, I congratulated him for finally reaching 100 percent. But oddly, he was not enthusiastic. He was still $150 short each month and thought he needed to raise his budget again. Instead, we talked about budgeting. Bob was defensive, saying, "Betty and I have an accounting system, I can tell you exactly where our money goes—budgeting is not the problem."

I said, "Bob, are you mistaking budgeting for cost accounting—recording and understanding where each dollar has gone?" Cost accounting is fine, but it is not budgeting. Budgeting requires "gates"—something that forces you to stop spending. No gates, no budget.

So Bob and Betty set up an envelope system for budgeting. First, they deposited their paycheck in the bank to pay their mortgage, utilities, school fees, saving, and giving—any major fixed cost not paid with cash. Then they took out cash—twenties, tens, and a few fives—to cover their household expenses for the next pay period.

They laid out blank envelopes on the kitchen table and labeled them. Then they put a monthly amount on each envelope.

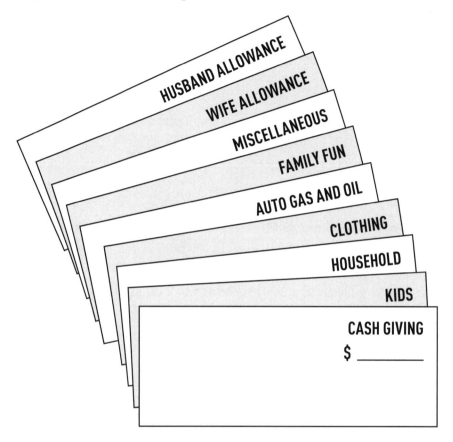

Then they inserted the agreed-upon cash in each envelope—each "dollar had a name" (a phrase often used by Dave Ramsey).

Here's the powerful secret: When an envelope is empty, you stop spending in that category! For example, when the clothing envelope is empty, you stop buying clothes until next month. Borrowing from other envelopes is not allowed.

It will take a couple of months to get the amounts right, but you now have "gates" to keep you from overspending.

Another advantage of the envelope system: You need not keep records.

Worried about having cash around the house? No problem—most of it is gone in ten days anyway! If money is left in an envelope at the end of the month, it is rolled forward to the next month. It doesn't need to be spent. But if money is left in the grocery envelope, Alma puts that in her pocket with no questions asked. A fun incentive!

What about ministry expenses? Set up additional envelopes:

- Ministry entertainment (house guests or eating out for ministry purposes)
- Ministry travel and meetings (out-of-pocket food, fuel, tolls, hotel)
- Ministry materials (Bible studies, books, worksheets) and office supplies (computer, copier, paper, ink, etc.)

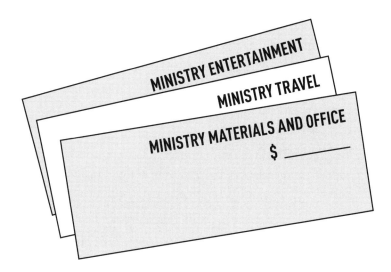

Avoid mixing ministry costs with your personal allowance, because ministry costs often usurp personal expenses.

If you are single, you might need fewer envelopes, but you, too, need a gated budget. Any budgeting system will work if it has gates—*you must honor the gates.*

Some people argue that they are naturally frugal and do not need a budget. Good for you in being frugal, but frugality doesn't reduce pressure. Here's why: The "spend as little as possible" guideline constantly nags at you to spend less! And you can always spend a little less. Missionary wives tell me of returning grocery items at the checkout because they realized they could get by without certain items. But inwardly, it produced resentment. The "spend as little as possible" guideline is intended to give freedom, but it actually produces *bondage*.

Instead, give yourself permission to spend up to the budget limit instead of being under pressure to spend as little as possible.

What about Bob and Betty? Three months after our talk, instead of being $150 short each month, they had $150 extra. The overspending was Bob picking up "this and that" for ministry purposes, such as books to give away. The envelope "gates" brought Bob's well-intentioned but undisciplined spending to a halt.

Word 4: Giving.

How's your giving?

Notice that I did not ask, "How's your tithing?" Many Christian leaders teach tithing (Hebrew *ma'aser*—10 percent) as the standard for believers to give. But is it?

You know the famous tithing verse in Malachi 3:10: "Bring the *whole* tithe into the storehouse" (emphasis added). This passage induces guilt because most Christians do not give 10 percent. But let's review the context. In Malachi 1:7-8 the Jews brought lame lambs to the altar rather than their best (the *whole* tithe) as the Law commanded. "Why not offer it to your governor?" Malachi chided. "Would he be pleased with you?" Oops! Malachi's message is still valid today: Don't sneak by with giving as little as you can—give your best to the Lord.

Another misunderstanding is the storehouse. Malachi's storehouses were granaries built in Hezekiah's day adjoining the Temple. But many Christian leaders teach that today's "storehouse" is the "church house." Accordingly, your tithe must go to your local church. If you want to support the Bible Society to distribute Bibles in India, that *cannot* come out of the local church's 10 percent. This stretches hermeneutical boundaries. Malachi would be surprised to learn that his "give your best" message now means that the storehouse is the church house!

Certainly you must support your local church—absolutely! That is where you receive teaching (Galatians 6:6). But don't use Malachi as your proof-text.

In Minneapolis a few years ago I asked a friend, "How much should a believer give?" He immediately answered, "Ten percent to the local church and offerings to other ministries—if possible." When I asked where he learned that, he said, "Isn't that what the Bible says?"

Should tithing be a goal to aim for? Yes, if you give little or nothing. Author Randy Alcorn likens tithing to the training wheels on a child's bicycle—it gets you started, but 10 percent is not the upper limit. What happens when a believer (perhaps one of your giving partners) earns $300,000 or more? We would certainly hope he has graduated beyond tithing training wheels. If he tithed $30,000, he would be forced to "eke out a living" on $270,000. That misses the spirit of biblical giving. Here is another way of thinking: What if this believer limited his personal spending in order to give more than 10 percent? Suppose he lived on $200,000 and gave $100,000—33 percent? I admit it is difficult to hold the line on expenses as we earn more and more, but we must not limit ourselves to 10 percent as an upper limit.

What does the New Testament teach about tithing?

- Paul, the strict Pharisee, tithed meticulously in his pre-Christian days, but when he taught giving to the Corinthians, the Galatians, and Timothy, he did not mention the "T-word." He did not bring Jewish law to new believers.
- Jesus mentioned tithing in Luke 11:42 and Matthew 23:23: "For you [Pharisees] pay tithe of mint and rue and every kind of garden herb, and yet disregard justice and the love of God; but these are the things you should have done without neglecting the others." Though the Pharisees tithed meticulously, they forgot love and justice. Jesus told them to not "neglect the others," implying they should still tithe and observe Old Testament laws. But His main point was the proper attitude behind tithing—not tithing itself. He was speaking to Jewish Pharisees whom He would expect to keep Jewish law anyway. *He did not ask Jews to stop being Jews.* But would He teach non-Jews who believed in Him the same thing? If Jesus expects believers today to observe the tithing law, what other specific Old Testament laws are we to obey?

  Some see this passage as an affirmation of tithing, but at best it is a weak argument for teaching tithing outside Judaism.
- In Luke 18:12 a Pharisee bragged, "I pay tithes of all that I get." Jesus said that a humble tax collector who admits his sin is preferable to a proud Pharisee who tithes. Hardly a recommendation.
- Other New Testament writers do not mention tithing.

What is the guideline for Christian giving if it is not the tithe? Luke 21:1-4 sets the standard. Jesus *saw* the rich and *saw* the widow putting gifts into the treasury. Jesus said the widow "put in more than all of them, for they all out of their surplus put into the offering; but she out of her poverty put in all that she had to live on."

Numerically, the rich men gave more, but Jesus said the woman gave more. The phrase "all that she had to live on" makes it seem she gave away all her assets—really? But since workers were paid daily, I suggest she came from her field to the Temple court of the women and gave her gift—all she had to live on *that day*—not all her assets. The notes of the NASB offer a helpful alternative reading: "the living that she had."

Either way, her giving surely affected her lifestyle. By contrast, the rich men gave out of abundance—they didn't notice it was gone. Jesus measures giving based on sacrifice, not on amount. C. S. Lewis writes in *Mere Christianity*,

I am afraid the only safe rule is to give more than we can spare. In other words, if our expenditure on comforts, luxuries, amusements, etc., is up to the standard common among those with the same income as our own, we are probably giving away too little. If our charities do not at all pinch or hamper us, I should say they are too small. There ought to be things we should like to do and cannot do because our charities expenditure excludes them.[2]

How much should you give? I suggest this: *Give in such a way that it makes a noticeable difference in your lifestyle.*

If your income as a gospel-worker is meager, should you still give? Of course, since you have a salary—even though it might vary from month to month. But 10 percent may be too much. It might be tempting to include the organizational service charge as your giving, or you may be tempted to give to your own ministry for your benefit. Sorry, but that misses the point of biblical giving. Giving even on a meager salary will help you feel dignity, since God Himself is also a giver. But it could be less than 10 percent. You are free.

But if you receive a generous salary, 10 percent is surely too little! Jesus "sees" your giving—He knows your heart. As your fellow gospel-worker living on donor income, I challenge you to give generously and sacrificially—let your giving affect your lifestyle. Just because your income goes up, does your spending also have to go up? Spending less enables you to give more!

As New Testament believers, we are not under obligation to tithe, but can't we do more under grace than what our Jewish predecessors were required to do under law?

One more thing: Why is tithing emphasized today even though it was not taught by Paul or Jesus or the early church fathers? Is it possible that for two thousand years clergy have been suspicious that laypeople will not give generously under grace without a rule? As we'll see in the next chapter, Christian leaders desiring to see the Kingdom expanded have "coaxed" God's people to give by

- enforcing detailed tithing laws,
- selling indulgences,
- renting pews, and
- publishing parishioners' giving history to "guilt" them into giving more and more.

It is risky to say, "You don't have to tithe." Will removing the tithing mantra cause Christians to be more generous? Ideally, yes! However, if we do not teach giving as a basic of discipleship, people will follow the dictates of their culture.

We are long overdue in teaching giving as part of discipleship. As a gospel-worker and a fundraiser, you have a unique opportunity to teach biblical giving in your spheres of influence. We teach the importance of the Word, prayer, fellowship with other believers, evangelism, and other "basics," but we say nothing about money—a topic Jesus spoke on constantly!

Silence sends the message that giving is not important except when you have a deficit. Also, believers will learn about giving from somewhere. If you don't teach them, they are susceptible to "health and wealth" teaching or secular culture materialism! They may assume that tithing to the local church is all the Bible teaches about giving.

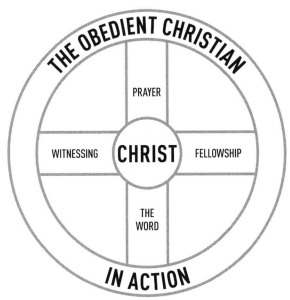

Start with the classical discipleship "wheel illustration" above. The "word" and "prayer" spokes speak to our relationship with God. The "witnessing" and "fellowship" spokes speak to our relationships with people. But what about our relationship to our possessions—that which God has put into our hands? We need to add the spoke of giving. Start to teach it in your Bible studies—not as a funding appeal but simply to disciple your people—and note the response. Try using Luke 21:1-4 as your passage for the giving spoke.

Jim Petersen, a mission pioneer to Brazil, used to say, "People need to give much more than I need to receive." That echoes Jesus' words: "It is more blessed to give than to receive" (Acts 20:35).

I was greatly touched by a Nigerian friend named Albert, who sacrificially hosted fifteen of us in his home for a fundraising seminar. At the end of our days together I asked Albert why he was so generous. He said, "If God owns me, He owns my pockets!" Nicely said.

Two additional finance management suggestions.

Know well the condition of your flock. Too many Christian workers are so spiritually minded that they downplay the pragmatic matters of life, such as saving or budgeting. Though we are spiritual beings, we live in a physical world. We must heed the proverb to "know well the condition of your flocks, and pay attention to your herds; for riches are not forever" (Proverbs 27:23-24).

You may not own a flock of sheep, but you do have assets that need close attention because "riches are not forever." By being inattentive, you could lose your "flock."

A word to husbands and wives: One of you probably has a better knack for handling the financial details than the other. Let that partner use his or her gift. But you both must know the state of your financial "flock."

In my experience it is often the wife who is the first to spot financial problems on the horizon. Husbands, listen carefully.

Avoid simple financial traps. Don't replace your vehicle every two years. Christian financial consultant Ron Blue warns repeatedly that you save money by keeping your car as long as it runs safely, even with frequent repairs. Perhaps you know the old American proverb: "Use it up, wear it out, make it do, or do without."

Don't buy a boat. (Just kidding! Or not!)

Avoid using your credit card, even if you can pay it off each month. "One of the most often cited studies is one conducted by Dun & Bradstreet, where the company found that people spend 12–18% more when using credit cards instead of cash. McDonald's reports its average ticket is $7 when people use credit cards versus $4.50 for cash."[3]

You needn't spend money to have fun. Instead of eating out, fix "Dad's Surprise" for supper. Instead of subscribing to Netflix, play Scrabble. Try creative fun nights. Our family favorite was "Paper-Sword-Pop-the-Balloon" using rolled-up newspapers as swords and tying balloons to our belts.

If you find yourself reacting negatively to this chapter, please reevaluate the source of your financial behaviors and values. Following your parents' example may be comfortable, but it may not be biblical. Following the advice of Christian friends may be more cultural than Christian. Difficult though it may be, make sure the Bible is your guide.

As Dick Towner says when he teaches his Good $ense course for the Willow Creek Association, "There's no such thing as being right with God and wrong with our money."

25
LESSONS FROM FUNDRAISING HISTORY

WE SHOULD STUDY funding history because it reveals that the Body of Christ has been historically vulnerable in the area of fundraising. As you will see from this chapter, many desperate funding tactics were used throughout Christian history to find money for ministry. Because human nature doesn't change and because the need for funding is always urgent, we are as vulnerable today as our predecessors were. I hope you find these historical tidbits helpful in avoiding today's temptations in funding.

Most of the information in this section comes from the late Luther Powell, a Presbyterian minister, who wrote *Money and the Church*. I stumbled across Powell's book in the Denver Seminary library in 1989. Finding that it was out of print, I tracked down Powell's widow, who graciously sent me a few of "Luther's old books in the basement."

What follows is not an exhaustive chronological history but rather five observations followed by three possible applications for today. But first a warning: Some of what you're about to read may contradict your stewardship convictions. You may not like it! But thanks for telling us the truth, Luther Powell!

Observation 1: Tithing was not emphasized in the early church.

In the previous chapter I suggested that the New Testament does not advocate tithing as the rule for believers in their giving. So I will not repeat myself but merely mention a few facts for perspective here. It is not surprising that immediately after the days of the apostles, the early church fathers did not emphasize tithing for nearly three hundred years. Listen to Irenaeus of Gaul (AD 120–202), who studied under Polycarp, a disciple of the apostle John: "And instead of the law enjoining the giving of tithes, [He told us] to share all our possessions with the poor; and not to love our neighbors only, but even our enemies."[1]

Cyprian (AD 200–258), Bishop of Carthage and a prolific writer, gave away a portion of his possessions to the poor after his conversion at age thirty-five. Powell says he taught the practice of almsgiving from the Old Testament, but Cyprian "completely ignores the wealth of Old Testament material on tithing." Powell summarizes: "Reference was made to the law of the tithe, but with few exceptions it was added that giving for the Christian was no longer dependent upon this taskmaster."[2]

Because tithing is so ingrained in our thinking today, we may be uncomfortable with these three hundred years of history. But the lack of teaching about the tithe among the early church fathers is important because it sharply contrasts with many who strongly emphasize tithing today—two thousand years removed from the direct influence of those closest to Christ. We must ask why.

Observation 2: Tithing migrated into religious and civil law.

As the church grew, more money was needed. And though it will be tempting to criticize the abuses you are about to read, we must remember that many good-hearted believers were trying to advance the work of the church as best they could. Let us not be too judgmental.

Powell summarizes, "As we proceed beyond the 4th century we find a growing emphasis on tithing until it becomes, first, a law of the church, and, finally, a law of the civil courts."[3] Ambrose of Milan (AD 340–397) starts down this slippery slope:

God has reserved the tenth part to Himself, and therefore it is not lawful for a man to retain what God has reserved for Himself. To Thee He has given nine parts, for Himself He has reserved the tenth part, and if thou shalt not give to God the tenth part, God will take from thee the nine parts.[4]

Do you see the subtle movement from a Jewish cultural law to a law for the church? And do you notice the implied threat for not giving the tithe? Even the beloved Augustine (AD 354–430) said the tithes "are due as a debt."[5]

In AD 585, the Second Council of Mascon went still further:

> Wherefore we do appoint and decree, that the ancient custom be revived
> among the faithful, and that all the people bring in their Tithes to
> those who attend the Divine offices of the Church. If any one shall be
> contumacious [rebellious] to these our most wholesome orders, let him be
> forever separated from the communion of the Church.[6]

In just 585 years after Christ, believers now had to tithe or face excommunication!

Fast-forward 1,100 years to England. The Protestants did no better. Tithing laws became standard and exceedingly complicated. For example, a farmer was not required to tithe on food he or his family consumed, but if it was used to feed livestock, a tithe had to be paid: "If a Man gather green pease to spend in his house . . . no Tithes shall be paid for the same; but if he gather them to sell or to feed Hogs, there Tithes shall be paid for them."[7]

Parishioners were annoyed, then angered, by these rules. A farmer who caught fish from a lake in a different parish from his home had to pay tithes to both parishes. Frustrated dairymaids brought their pail of tithe-milk to the church. Not finding the parson, they poured it on the floor in front of the altar. Farmers purposely bound their sheaves of grain so badly that they fell apart when the parsons came to collect. Church servants who were sent to collect the tithe were assaulted or their horses stolen so they could not take the produce to the church.

Many believers were fined or imprisoned because of their insufficient tithing. William Francis Luton of Bedfordshire was imprisoned nineteen months for failing to tithe a four-pence silver piece. Some were even martyred for suggesting that compulsory tithing was contrary to God's will. The Anabaptists and the Mennonites were among those who claimed tithing was against New Testament teaching.

So exasperated were parishioners around Great Britain that over the years they made up new lyrics to the tune of the beloved hymn "Old Hundred" ("Praise God from Whom All Blessings Flow"):

God save us from these raiding priests,
Who seize our crops and steal our beasts,
Who pray, Give us our daily bread,
And take it for themselves instead.[8]

Ahhh-men! Powell writes that many clergymen quit the church rather than collect the tithes.

And what about America? My grade-school history books said many colonists came "for religious reasons." But many of the religious reasons were that they couldn't stomach the invasive tithing laws in Europe.

Did the American colonists make a fresh start and make giving voluntary? No, because the perplexing issue of how to support the churches still had to be decided. The colonists thought "church rates" (tithing laws) were okay but that they had been abused in Europe. Though the "voluntary principle" was affirmed, the colonists soon reverted to taxation similar to what they had left in England. As early as August 23, 1630, the state of Massachusetts decreed that ministers should be maintained "at the public charge."

Sadly, compulsory tithing had merely moved across the Atlantic. Even patriot Patrick Henry proposed in the Virginia House of Burgesses in 1784 that a law be passed "for the support of the Christian religion." James Madison led the charge against it.[9]

Observation 3: Under pressure to fund a growing movement, Christian leaders violated their integrity.

Today it's easy to identify errors of a thousand years ago, but we must understand the tremendous financial pressure these leaders endured. Here are a few examples of integrity lapses.

Right of procuration: Visitation expenses but no visitation

Defined as a "moderate cost of food and lodging due to the bishop who visited a church," procurations were established to encourage bishops to visit distant churches. By the fourteenth century they had become fixed money payments.[10] But even when the bishops did not visit the churches, the payment was still expected, and gradually the payments went to Rome rather than to local bishops. Since they were not getting their expenses covered, the bishops visited less, contributing to the downfall of the spirituality of the local churches. One reformer called procurations the "greatest wound of the church."

The pallium

Originally a robe of honor, the pallium was required for priests to perform official services. But they or their congregations had to purchase the pallium at high prices. As years went by, the robes became smaller, but the purchase price stayed high. It finally became a patch of cloth with an insignia.

Appealing to fear and guilt

Parishioners gave in order to save their souls (and the souls of their friends and family) from hell. Giving appeared to be necessary to receive salvation for yourself and others. Listen to successful fundraiser John Tetzel of Germany, who knew the importance of emotion in fundraising:

> Indulgences are the most precious and the most noble of God's gifts. Come and I will give you letters, all properly sealed, by which even the sins that you intend to commit may be pardoned. . . .
>
> Priest! Noble! Merchant! Wife! Youth! Maiden! Do you not hear your parents and your other friends who are dead, and who cry from the bottom of the abyss: We are suffering horrible torments! A trifling alms would deliver us; you can give it, and you will not![11]

Tetzel's manipulative fundraising drove Martin Luther to post his ninety-five theses on the door of the Wittenberg Church on October 31, 1517. But in later years, even Martin Luther succumbed to railing against his own parishioners. Though Luther's words might be justified if the parishioners were selfish givers, they also could be viewed as a guilt-inducing diatribe:

> I understand that this is the week for the church collection, and many of you do not want to give a thing. You ungrateful people should be ashamed of yourselves. You Wittenbergers have been relieved of schools and hospitals, which have been taken over by the common chest, and now you want to know why you are asked to give four pennies.[12]

Subscription lists

Subscription lists showed the amounts parishioners had pledged to give. These lists were not kept secret. Pastors circulated the lists, provoking guilt and a keep-up-with-the-Joneses mentality.

Pew rent

From the days of George Washington until the early 1900s, renting or selling pews was a primary means of funding Protestant churches in America. Church committees agonized over setting pew prices; the more expensive ones were near the front, with a freebie or two in the back for walk-ins or the poor. Families sat in "their pew" for years, sometimes with a plaque announcing the owner.

But by the late 1800s the practice was dying out. Young D. L. Moody from Chicago, who would become a famous evangelist, disdained the pew rent practice and made a habit of filling the free pews in the back with rowdy young boys to whom he was ministering. The February 8, 1919, edition of *The Literary Digest* featured a story that Trinity Church in New York would be offering "free pews" as an expression to Almighty God for victory in World War I. The "sittings" would be free to all: first come, first served. The article told the story of naval war hero Bob Evans, who, though not a member, went to a prominent New York church and sat in a pew at random.

> The wealthy pew owner arrived not long after with his numerous family and cast disapproving looks on the intruder—unaware that the pews were free on this Sunday. He scribbled an indignant note to hero Evans saying, "I pay $4,000 for this pew." Quick with his pencil, Evans scrawled, "You pay too d*** much!"[13]

Pew rent died slowly, but it did finally die. But today Christ Church in Philadelphia on Market Street advertises, "Sit in the George Washington Pew!" Pew rent seems strange to us today, but it was a serious issue in early America.

Observation 4: Poor pay for preachers proved counterproductive.

Francis Asbury, the leader of Methodism on the American frontier, was heard to pray, "Lord, keep our preachers poor." One of Asbury's cohorts commented humorously, "Such a prayer was quite unnecessary!"[14]

Asbury thought low pay produced more dedicated preachers. He didn't want them to "locate"—settle in one town—but to continue itinerant preaching across the frontier. Asbury opined, "Lovers of earthly riches will not long remain traveling preachers."[15]

Asbury's preachers provide us today with a wonderful example of enduring hardship (and low pay) for the sake of the gospel. But many of his preachers did "locate," especially after a few years on the frontier. Did they quit because of low pay? There may have been several reasons, but we would be naive to think poor funding wasn't one of them.

Observation 5: Focusing on small givers is not enough.

Asbury's great heart for the poor made him appreciate those who sacrificially gave small amounts to the Methodist cause. He loved "mite-giving," in memory of the generous woman in Luke 21:1-4 who gave her two "mites" (KJV) to the Temple.

Asbury was a tireless fundraiser, going door to door asking for widow's-mite gifts (valued at about one dollar) for his poor preachers. One of his last requests "was for Mr. Bond to read the 'mite subscription' list as he lay dying."[16]

Despite his success in procuring mite gifts, Asbury's traveling preachers received less than the minimum salaries recommended by the Methodist boards. Small gifts weren't enough.

Applications for Today

Okay, there you have it—five observations from fundraising history. Now, what can we learn?

Application 1: Wrong standard for giving

Today many Christian leaders aggressively teach tithing as the primary standard for giving. But the church fathers had it right—the tithe is *not* the New Testament standard. Challenging people to give 10 percent is justified by many pastors because most believers don't give nearly that amount. Fair enough, but should we burden New Testament people with a standard intended for Old Testament Israel?

Some say that giving 10 percent is symbolic of our 100 percent commitment to the Lord and that something about the "one out of ten" idea is special. Maybe, but it's a stretch.

What about Malachi 3:10? "Bring the whole tithe into the storehouse." That is a wonderful passage, but as mentioned in the previous chapter, it is not the standard for New Testament giving. If you want people to tithe, fine, but don't use Malachi as your proof text. For more analysis of the tithe, see chapter 23.

Application 2: A spirit of demandingness

Fundraising history shows that for 1,700 years or so, clergy have been suspicious that laypeople will not give enough. Out of a genuine desire (most of the time) to see the Kingdom expanded, leaders coaxed, manipulated, or commanded God's people to give by enacting tithing laws, threatening the faithful with hell, imposing guilt on them, renting them pews, and publishing church members' giving commitments to motivate them to keep up with the Christian Joneses.

It seemed to them that if parishioners were left to their own devices, with grace alone as their guide, they would not give nearly enough to support the work of God. So they came up with schemes and "doctrine" to help the faithful decide how much was enough. Of course, I am generalizing. And there were pockets of resistance to these abuses. Nonetheless, are we also prone to these manipulations? Consider some of today's appeals:

- One evangelist sent a letter containing two vials filled with dirt taken from the very ground upon which he knelt when he prayed for the recipient last weekend. "Send one back with your gift."
- What about the common "please pray for our finances" note on the bottom of missionary newsletters? I read one just a few hours ago. Usually it is a disguised appeal for funds.
- The message abounds on Stewardship Sunday and in direct mail appeals: "If you really want to be blessed, tithe!"
- Or on late night religious programming: "Don't let these children die from disease. You can help them for the cost of what you feed your dog each week."

Application 3: Poverty equals effectiveness?

Francis Asbury was right that "lovers of earthly riches" are in danger. But does wanting to be up to budget imply we love riches? It could. Some Christian workers are undoubtedly lovers of riches, and their aggressive fundraising efforts disguise their materialistic hearts. To a lover of riches, even a book like this will be construed as license to go after money. But leaving motives aside, let's ask ourselves: Are we ministers and missionaries more effective when we are poor?

In my first assignment, Alma and I saw many conversions and changed lives—and we were severely underfunded! Did staying poor keep us productive? I don't think so. How long could we have held out with low funding? Not as long as Asbury's preachers!

Interestingly, during those "poverty years," I also started taking steps of faith to invite others to join our financial team. The exercise of fundraising faith was just as heartfelt and stretching as my evangelism and discipling faith.

Though I commend Asbury for his tireless work at both preaching and fundraising, wouldn't he have been more effective if he had gone after larger gifts for his "poor preachers"? Was he working hard? Yes, but was he working smart?

Today, unless you are on a short-term mission, you will not reach full funding with only mite gifts. You must also have major-donor gifts.

Furthermore, missionaries who scrape by on low funding year after year also experience financial pressure that erodes their confidence—and sometimes their marriages. Never having enough is emotionally and physically draining!

In my experience, many poor people are consumed mentally and emotionally with where the next meal is coming from. And so are underfunded missionaries. It's exciting for a few weeks, but soon they are worn out.

· · ·

In conclusion, which lesson stands out to you? Are you teaching a wrong standard for giving? As fundraisers, we must not make the mistake of putting rules on our giving partners. Biblical giving is voluntary; coercing believers toward generosity demeans them.

Or are you being demanding without realizing it? What words are you saying when you ask? What attitudes do you have toward your giving partners? We must avoid judging someone because they are not giving as generously as we think they could.

Or are you trying to be effective on a poverty mentality? Giving is an honor. Don't ask too little.

I encourage you to be careful of falling into the traps that have plagued full-time workers and ministers for 1,700 years. What will a twenty-first-century Luther Powell write about us?

26
STORIES FROM OTHERS

WILL THE PRINCIPLES, values, and techniques I've presented work *for you*? Can *you* be fully funded?

You will not succeed if you view what I've said as a formula to guarantee success. But to encourage you (and at the risk of shameless self-promotion), I leave you with two stories. The first comes from a skeptical missionary:

I joined the mission thinking, *Eighty percent of budget is OK. The ministry is far more important than fundraising.*

Then one year our regional director brought in a biblical fundraising seminar. Attendance was mandatory. I was skeptical because our mission usually gave lip service to fundraising.

Nevertheless, I put in many hours doing the required homework . . . the most work I'd ever done on fundraising. Then I developed a plan different from the halfhearted, hit-or-miss approach I had been using.

With my wife's support and God's help, we diligently worked out our plan. I prayed a lot as well, and God came through in amazing ways.

Remarkably, we raised $1,400 per month in just three weeks! We now had a strategy and biblical convictions, and I was actually doing fundraising instead of just worrying about it. My wife rejoiced. This year we finished at 102 percent, and I now spend part of my time helping other missionaries raise their finances. If I hadn't applied these guidelines, I'm not sure I would be in missions today. I now have hope, skills, and accountability that I didn't have before.

The second story comes from a Canadian missionary.

The biblical study on how God funds His work has been the most important ingredient of my fundraising training. Through Bible study, reflection, and . . . dialogue with other missionaries, my convictions began to form. I believe it is crucial for missionaries to have their convictions grounded in the Scriptures if they are to raise personal support for the long haul.

One of the astonishing things I discovered is that the Bible has few examples of the "tell-nobody-but-God" method of funding. I respect those who hold to this method, but I don't see this as the norm in Scripture.

I've come to realize that it is a tremendous privilege to be fully supported by friends, family, and churches for the work God has called my wife and me to.

We have been fully funded for five years. We have savings and no debt. We know that the key to fundraising for us is face-to-face appointments. We also know our fears and how to trust God with them. And we don't question our calling as we used to when we were below budget. Also, since we know we can be fully funded, we can believe God for fellow missionaries to be fully funded as well. I feel like I've gotten to know God better, and I truly feel like I have been caring better for my wife and children.

· · ·

Wow! You made it through to the end. Well done. What's next? It's time to finalize your funding plan, but first stop and take a deep breath. Before creating your plan, ask God to speak to you deeply about your fundraising attitudes and views on money. Take a few minutes to browse through the chapters one by one, slowly and reflectively. Highlight those Scriptures and ideas that speak to you in your unique situation. My prayer is that you will experience a deeper walk with God as you do your part in raising support, and that as God does His part, He will bless you beyond all you could ask or think.

Next, if you haven't done it already, go to scottmorton.net and download the "International Fundraising Bible Study." Take time to study well what the Bible says about funding; it will save time and bring you joy and peace in the funding process. As you do this study, the Lord will give you His ideas about your funding strategy and whom to invite to join you. I suggest twenty hours of study.

Third, dive into creating your funding plan. Download and print the worksheets you need from scottmorton.net. Here they are:

- Top 25 Worksheet (who needs to hear your story?)
- Up Till Now Report (to record the results of your appeals)
- Financial Appeal Action Plan (to record your fundraising plan)
- Phone Call to Set an Appointment Worksheets
- Creating a Personal Budget
- Creating Your Personal Giving Plan

And now I leave you with a story I heard just today, and a final word. A young short-term gospel-worker had one month before her deadline to depart for her ministry assignment in Europe. She was faithfully carrying out her fundraising strategy but had $3,000 in cash still to raise. She went for a run one morning, as she did frequently, and she intended to go about three miles. But for whatever reason she kept going. After six miles she'd had enough and realized she was desperately thirsty. She "just happened" to be near a friend's mother's house, so she texted her friend to ask, "Would your mom mind if I stopped for a drink of water?" Fine.

The mother came out to visit, and they started talking about the gospel-worker's upcoming ministry adventure in Europe. The mother asked how much she still needed to raise.

"Three thousand dollars," she replied.

The mother said, "Let me get my checkbook."

This gospel-worker just now called me as she was walking back from her six-mile run holding a check for $3,000. She will never forget this day of God interceding miraculously.

Not all your funding encounters will be this spectacular, but if God has called you for ministry, He will act on your behalf—He already is. Count on it!

Now a final word: *persistence.*

- After dancer Fred Astaire's first screen test, a 1933 memo from the MGM testing director said, "Can't act. Slightly bald. Can dance a little." Astaire kept that memo over the fireplace in his Beverly Hills home.
- An expert said of famous football coach Vince Lombardi, "He possesses minimal football knowledge. Lacks motivation."
- Louisa May Alcott, the author of *Little Women*, was advised by her family to find work as a servant or seamstress.
- Ludwig van Beethoven handled the violin awkwardly and preferred playing his own compositions instead of improving his technique. His teacher called him hopeless.
- Walt Disney was fired by a newspaper for lacking ideas. He also went bankrupt several times before he built Disneyland.[1]

If Fred Astaire, Vince Lombardi, Louisa May Alcott, Ludwig van Beethoven, and Walt Disney didn't give up, neither should you. Talk this over with the One who has called you to mission service. At His throne, you'll find "grace to help in time of need" (Hebrews 4:16). Thanks be to God!

Introduction to the Online Appendix

WITH THIS BOOK comes an online appendix. Go to scottmorton.net/resources to find the Bible study I've mentioned roughly 283 times, as well as absolutely essential worksheets and other materials. Click on "Fund Your Ministry Appendix" to download the worksheets. I recommend printing them out, especially the Top 25 worksheet.

This online appendix is copyrighted, but I am giving you permission to photocopy those PDF pages you need for your personal use. No forwarding, no marketing, no problem.

The appendix at scottmorton.net includes the following:

- "International Fundraising Bible Study"
- Financial Stress Test for Missionaries
- Monthly Budget Worksheet
- Brainstorming for Partners Worksheets
- Top 25 Potential Partners Worksheet
- Financial Appeal Action Plan
- Up Till Now Report (a worksheet to record your funding progress)
- The Mystery of "Calling" (a Bible study to help you find your place in the Kingdom)
- Creating Your Personal Giving Plan (a Bible study)
- How to Become Poor from Proverbs (a Bible study)
- Sample Letter for a Short Term Mission-Worker

At scottmorton.net you can also find short videos and articles on additional fundraising topics from gospel-workers around the world.

Notes

CHAPTER 2: OBSTACLES

1. Booker T. Washington, *An Autobiography: The Story of My Life and Work* (CreateSpace, 2016), chap. 4.

CHAPTER 3: QUESTIONS OF CONSCIENCE

1. Fred G. Warne, *George Müller: The Modern Apostle of Faith*, 8th ed. (New York: Fleming H. Revell, 1914), 5.
2. Ruth Moon, comp., "Are American Evangelicals Stingy?", *Christianity Today*, January 31, 2011, http://www.christianitytoday.com/ct/2011/february/areevangelicalsstingy.html.
3. Elizabeth O'Connor shares this story from an unknown source in her book *Letters to Scattered Pilgrims* (New York: Harper & Row, 1978).
4. The story of Charles Spurgeon challenging a church's inadequate stipend is from Steven J. Cole, "Lesson 17: Paying Your Pastor(s) (1 Timothy 5:17-18)," Bible.org, accessed December 6, 2016, at https://bible .org/seriespage/lesson-17-paying-your-pastors-1-timothy-517-18.

CHAPTER 4: TEN CRUCIAL ATTITUDES YOU MUST NOT NEGLECT

1. George Mueller, quoted in Arthur T. Pierson, *George Mueller of Bristol: And His Witness to a Prayer-Hearing God* (Old Tappan, NJ: Revell, 1899), appendix N.
2. Henri Nouwen, *A Spirituality of Fundraising* (Nashville: Upper Room Books, 2011), 14, 21.
3. Ibid., 16–17, 21.
4. Bill Hybels, *Leadership Axioms: Powerful Leadership Proverbs* (Grand Rapids, MI: Zondervan, 2008), 22.
5. David Myers and Thomas Ludwig, "Let's Cut the Poortalk," *Saturday Review*, October 28, 1978, www .davidmyers.org/davidmyers/assets/CutPoortalk.pdf.
6. *Peanuts*, September 16, 1985, accessed December 8, 2016, at http://peanuts.wikia.com/wiki/September _1985_comic_strips.

CHAPTER 5: SIX BAD ASSUMPTIONS

1. National Philanthropic Trust, "Charitable Giving Statistics," accessed December 8, 2016, at www.nptrust .org/philanthropic-resources/charitable-giving-statistics/.

CHAPTER 6: THREE BENCHMARKS FOR AN EFFECTIVE STRATEGY

1. Sharon W. Corsiglia, "When It Comes to Selling, Girl Scout Markita Andrews Is a Real Cookie Monster," *People*, March 22, 1982, http://people.com/archive/when-it-comes-to-selling-girl-scout-markita-andrews -is-a-real-cookie-monster-vol-17-no-11/.

CHAPTER 7: SOCIAL MEDIA AND EMAIL IN FUNDRAISING

1. Nancy Schwartz, "Does Your Email Fundraising Measure Up?" May 27, 2016, https://www .networkforgood.com/nonprofitblog/does-your-email-fundraising-measure-up/.
2. Johnny Cash, "Flesh and Blood," *I Walk the Line*, Columbia Records, 1970.

CHAPTER 15: DONOR MINISTRY

1. Michael LeBoeuf, *How to Win Customers and Keep Them for Life*, rev. ed. (New York: Berkley, 2000), xv.
2. Tom Peters, "Attentiveness Is Greatest Gift Customers Can Get," *Chicago Tribune*, December 12, 1994, http://articles.chicagotribune.com/1994-12-12/business/9412120031_1_attentiveness-vegetarian -topsy-turvy-times.
3. Jocelyn Noveck, "Power of the Pen in an E-mail Age," *Los Angeles Times*, March 3, 2006, http://articles.latimes.com/2006/mar/03/entertainment/et-letters3.
4. Maddie Crum, "Sorry Ebooks. These 9 Studies Show Why Print Is Better," *Huffington Post*, February 27, 2015, http://www.huffingtonpost.com/2015/02/27/print-ebooks-studies_n_6762674.html.

CHAPTER 16: WRITE NEWSLETTERS PEOPLE LOVE TO READ

1. Alvera Mickelsen, *How to Write Missionary Letters*, 9th ed. (Carol Stream, IL: Media Associates International, 2007), np.
2. See Dave McCasland, *How to Write Effective Newsletters* (Colorado Springs: The Navigators, 1994).
3. Thomas Jefferson, letter to John Minor, August 30, 1814, https://founders.archives.gov/documents /Jefferson/03-07-02-0455, accessed January 9, 2017.
4. George Orwell, "Politics and the English Language," from *Shooting an Elephant and Other Essays* (New York: Penguin Classics).
5. McCasland, *How to Write Effective Newsletters*.
6. Sandy Weyeneth, *Writing Exceptional Missionary Newsletters* (Pasadena, CA: William Carey Library, 2013).

CHAPTER 21: ESPECIALLY FOR SINGLE WOMEN MISSIONARIES AND THEIR SUPERVISORS

1. " 'The Queen of Okoyong': The Legacy of Mary Slessor," BBC News, January 2, 2015, http://www.bbc .com/news/uk-scotland-tayside-central-30577100.
2. David Barrett, Todd M. Johnson, and Peter Crossing, "Missiometrics 2007: Creating Your Own Analysis of Global Data," *International Bulletin of Missionary Research* 31, no. 1 (2007): 25–32.

CHAPTER 22: ESPECIALLY FOR GOSPEL-WORKERS OF COLOR AND THEIR SUPERVISORS

1. Eric Robinson, "How Support Raising Keeps Parachurch Ministries White," *Minister Different*, February 18, 2014, http://ministerdifferent.com/support-raising-white/.
2. Samuel Perry, Dallas Theological Seminary graduate and Ph.D. candidate in sociology at the University of Chicago: "Diversity, Donations, and Disadvantage: The Implications of Personal Fundraising for Racial Diversity in Evangelical Outreach Ministries," *Review of Religious Research* 53, no. 4 (January 2012): 397-418.

CHAPTER 23: MONEY: KINGDOM VIEW OR CULTURAL VIEW?

1. Nouwen, *A Spirituality of Fundraising*, 21.
2. Os Guinness, *The Call* (Nashville: W Publishing, 1998), 193. Emphasis added.
3. Charles Spurgeon, "A Cheerful Giver Is Beloved of God," sermon delivered August 27, 1868, at Metropolitan Tabernacle, Newington, UK, accessed January 12, 2017, http://www.spurgeongems .org/vols13-15/chs835.pdf.
4. Tony Brooks, "The Power of Writing Down Your Goals," The Leadership Training Workshop, April 30, 2012, http://theleadershiptrainingworkshop.com/2012/04/the-power-of-writing-down-your-goals/. Emphasis in original.
5. William Barclay, *The Gospel of Matthew*, Daily Bible Study Series (Philadelphia: Westminster Press, 1958), 258.

CHAPTER 24: MONEY MANAGEMENT

1. Erin El Issa, "2016 American Household Credit Card Debt Study," NerdWallet (blog), accessed January 12, 2017, https://www.nerdwallet.com/blog/average-credit-card-debt-household/.

2. C. S. Lewis, *Mere Christianity* (San Francisco: HarperOne, 2015), 86.

3. Lindsay Konsko, "Credit Cards Make You Spend More: Studies," *NerdWallet*, July 8, 2014, https://www.nerdwallet.com/blog/credit-cards/credit-cards-make-you-spend-more/.

CHAPTER 25: LESSONS FROM FUNDRAISING HISTORY

1. Luther P. Powell, *Money and the Church* (New York: Association Press, 1962), 21.

2. Ibid., 23.

3. Ibid., 26.

4. Ibid., 27.

5. Ibid., 27–28.

6. Ibid., 30.

7. Simon Degge, *The Parsons Counsellor* (London: Richard and Edward Atkins, Esquires, 1677), 448.

8. "Revolt of British Farmers against the Tithe," *The Literary Digest*, September 23, 1933.

9. Powell, *Money and the Church*, 118.

10. Margaret Deanesly, *A History of the Medieval Church 590-1400*, 9th ed. (New York: Routledge, 1969), 171.

11. Powell, *Money and the Church*, 59.

12. Roland Bainton, *Here I Stand: A Life of Martin Luther* (Nashville: Abingdon, 1950), 351–52.

13. *The Literary Digest* 60, no. 6 (February 8, 1919): 354–60.

14. Powell, *Money and the Church*, 101.

15. Ibid., 102.

16. Ibid.

CHAPTER 26: STORIES FROM OTHERS

1. Jack Canfield and Mark V. Hansen, *Chicken Soup for the Soul: 101 Stories to Open the Heart and Rekindle the Spirit* (Deerfield Beach, FL: Health Communications, 1992).